Rethinking World Politics

Series Editor: **Professor Michael Cox**, *London School of Economics*

In an age of increased academic specialization where more and more books about smaller and smaller topics are becoming the norm, this major new series is designed to provide a forum and stimulus for leading scholars to address big issues in world politics in an accessible but original manner. A key aim is to transcend the intellectual and disciplinary boundaries which have so often served to limit rather than enhance our understanding of the modern world. In the best tradition of engaged scholarship, it aims to provide clear new perspectives to help make sense of a world in flux.

Each book addresses a major issue or event that has had a formative influence on the twentieth-century or the twenty-first-century world which is now emerging. Each makes its own distinctive contribution as well as providing an original but accessible guide to competing lines of interpretation.

Taken as a whole, the series will rethink contemporary international politics in ways that are lively, informed and – above all – provocative.

Rethinking Asia's Economic Miracle

The Political Economy of War, Prosperity and Crisis

Richard Stubbs

First published 2005 by
PALGRAVE MACMILLAN
Houndmills, Basingstoke, Hampshire RG21 6XS and
175 Fifth Avenue, New York, N.Y. 10010
Companies and representatives throughout the world

PALGRAVE MACMILLAN is the global academic imprint of the Palgrave
Macmillan division of St. Martin's Press, LLC and of Palgrave Macmillan Ltd.
Macmillan® is a registered trademark in the United States, United Kingdom
and other countries. Palgrave is a registered trademark in the European
Union and other countries.

ISBN-13: 978–0–333–96460–6 hardback
ISBN-10: 0–333–96460–8 hardback
ISBN-13: 978–0–333–96461–3 paperback
ISBN-10: 0–333–96461–6 paperback

This book is printed on paper suitable for recycling and made from fully
managed and sustained forest sources.

A catalogue record for this book is available from the British Library.

A catalog record for this book is available from the Library of Congress.

10   9   8   7   6   5   4   3   2   1
14 13 12 11 10 09 08 07 06 05

Printed and bound in China

To Grace

Contents

List of Tables and Figures

Tables

Figures

Preface

This book has a long history. In 1972 I went to Malaysia to undertake research for my doctoral thesis on the Malayan Emergency. While working in the National Archives and the Rubber Research Institute Library I discovered how significant the Korean War-induced commodity boom had been for Malaya/Malaysia's subsequent political and economic development. At the same time as I travelled through the region I experienced first hand the impact that America's prosecution of the Vietnam War had on the societies and economies of Singapore, Thailand and Malaysia. However, it was not until the late 1980s, after a move to Toronto, that I began to compare the experiences of the three Southeast Asian countries to the post-Second World War histories of the non-communist countries of Northeast Asia. I was fortunate to be invited by Michael Donnelly and Paul Evans to participate in a series of informal workshops under the auspices of the University of Toronto and York University's Joint Centre for Asia Pacific Studies on the political economy of the emerging Asia-Pacific region. The lively discussions at these workshops forced me to bring some order to my views on how the region had developed during the Cold War years. Since then, as I have undertaken further research in various parts of East and Southeast Asia and taught courses on the political economy of the region, I have slowly drawn the different threads of the analysis together. However, it was not until a research leave in 2003–4 that I had the opportunity, free from administrative responsibilities, to put my arguments on paper.

The long gestation period of this book has meant that I have acquired a great many debts. I am grateful to the Social Science and Humanities Research Council of Canada and McMaster University's Arts Research Board, both of which have funded my research as well as my participation in conferences where I was able to present some of the ideas developed in this study. I would also like to thank the following institutions and their staff for their help in tracking down and providing sources: the Australian National University Library, the Chulalongkorn University Library (Thailand), the Institute of Defence and Strategic Studies Library (Singapore), the Institute of

Southeast Asian Studies Library (Singapore), McMaster University Library (Canada), National Archives of Malaysia, the Public Record Office (UK), the Royal Institute of International Affairs Press Clippings Library (UK), University of Hawaii Library, University of Hong Kong Library, the University of Malaya Library, the University of Toronto Library. In addition, Susan Dejesus, Sarah Eaton, Peter Frise, Nicole Gallant, Lim Kuan Sui, Nicole Marques, Jennifer Mustapha, Austina Reed, Stephanie Serra, Klarka Zeman and Juliet Zhang have provided valuable research assistance.

A great many people have offered advice, information or encouragement along the way. In particular I would like to thank Amitav Acharya, Mark Beeson, Mitchell Bernard, Roland Bleiker, Shaun Breslin, Phil Deans, Wendy Dobson, Michael Donnelly, Paul Evans, Peter Ferdinand, Natasha Hamilton-Hart, Eric Helleiner, Richard Higgott, Yoshi Kawasaki, Andrew McDowell, Sorpong Peou, John Ravenhill, Etel Solingen, Geoffrey Underhill and Joe Wong. McMaster University's Political Science Department is a most congenial place in which to work. As always the staff, Gerald Bierling, Manuela Dozzi, Mara Giannotti, Lori Ewing and Stephanie Lisak, have at various times helped out in any number of ways and I am forever in their debt. My colleagues, especially Marshall Beier, Tom Lewis, Robert O'Brien and Tony Porter, were always most supportive. I wish to acknowledge the work of Keith Povey, who shepherded the manuscript through the production process. I owe a special thanks to my publisher at Palgrave Macmillan, Steven Kennedy, for pushing me to write the book and providing helpful comments on various drafts. In addition, I am particularly grateful to Michael Donnelly, Mick Cox, Sarah Eaton, Austina Reed, Grace Skogstad and an anonymous reviewer for Palgrave Macmillan for reading all or parts of the manuscript and passing along constructive comments that proved particularly valuable.

My family deserve a special mention. David and Matthew helped unearth sources and sort out troubled computers. On occasion they were also willing to discuss the way in which wars make states and economies. My greatest debt, however, is to my wife, Grace. I have already thanked her for reading various drafts of the manuscript. In addition, she tutored me on the key aspects of institutionalism and did her best to ensure that my overall argument was clear and logical. On our many walks through the ravines and byways of Toronto she also listened, cajoled and offered advice and encouragement as

I moved from chapter to chapter. I am convinced that without her wise counsel and support this book would not have been written. It is to her that the book is dedicated.

While I have received an enormous amount of help from many quarters, not everyone will agree with the argument that I have made. It is clearly important, therefore, that I emphasize that I alone am responsible for any errors in fact or judgement that may be found in the following pages.

RICHARD STUBBS
Hamilton/Toronto

Map of East and Southeast Asia

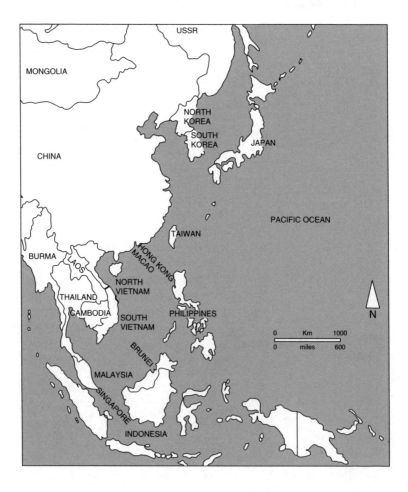

1

Introduction

For half a century following Japan's invasion of Pearl Harbor in 1941, two sets of events dominated life in East and Southeast Asia. First, the region was home to the most dynamic and successful set of economies in the world. Out of the chaos and confusion of the Second World War and its aftermath, the economies of Japan, South Korea, Taiwan, Hong Kong, Singapore, Malaysia and Thailand all rose to become major players in the global economy. The transformation was extraordinary. For example, in the turbulent years of the early 1950s, the per capita incomes of South Korea, Taiwan and Thailand were only a quarter of that of Chile, a third that of Peru, and well behind the per capita incomes of a number of Britain's African colonies such as those that later became Nigeria and Ghana (Johnson 1987: 136; Maddison 2003). By the turn of the century, South Korea and Taiwan had per capita incomes fifty per cent higher than that of Chile, which is considered by many to be the one major economic success in South America. Similarly, in 2000 Malaysia and Thailand, despite the Asian economic crisis of 1997–8, had per capita incomes that were twice that of Peru and more than six times higher than that of Nigeria or Ghana (Maddison 2003). Indeed, the seven successful East and Southeast Asian economies industrialized to such an extent and produced such remarkable annual growth rates over a sustained period of time that they have been widely characterized as 'miracle' economies (*Economist* Editorial 1989; Gereffi and Wyman 1990; Johnson 1982; World Bank 1993).

Second, the region was embroiled in a series of wars. Starting with the Second World War and continuing on through the Chinese civil

1

war, the Korean War, the Vietnam War and the series of local guerrilla wars that broke out across the region during the forty years after 1945, the states of East and Southeast Asia endured a number of major military encounters. Most importantly, there was the all-embracing and overarching Cold War which drove the Korean War and the Vietnam War and which repeatedly threatened to explode into open conflict in places such as the Taiwan Strait. The Cold War required that even those East and Southeast Asian states that were not directly engaged in one of the major wars needed to be constantly preparing for the possibility of fighting either the internal or external threat of armed communism. Indeed, what was referred to as 'The Asia Rimland' – the chain of states from Japan on to South Korea, Taiwan, Thailand and down to Malaysia and Singapore that encircled the Soviet Union, Communist China, North Korea, North Vietnam, Cambodia and Laos – constituted the frontline fortresses in the attempt by the United States and its allies to contain any possible communist advance (Russett 1966).

Is there, then, a connection between these two sets of events? Was it mere happenstance, a chance occurrence, that the most successful economies in the half century after the Second World War were all to be found in a region of the world consumed by confrontation and conflict? Can a link between the two sets of events perhaps explain the fact that, as a World Bank (1993: 2) study of East and Southeast Asia's prosperity points out, 'If growth were randomly distributed, there is roughly one chance in ten thousand that success would have been so regionally concentrated'? The possibility of a link between the Cold War and the rapid economic growth that East and Southeast Asia experienced also raises questions about the role of the United States and how exactly its influence shaped the rapid industrialization of the region. Similarly, if the Cold War and East and Southeast Asia's remarkable economic growth were more than simply parallel sets of events, how did the military stand-off between America's allies and the communist-dominated countries of the region affect the industrializing process that occurred in the 'miracle' economies? Indeed, what impact did the various 'hot' wars and the all-pervasive Cold War have on the form of capitalism that emerged in the highly successful economies of the region? And just as importantly, why did some of the economies of East and Southeast Asia prosper as a result of the Cold War while others stagnated?

Moreover, if the Cold War was so important in promoting economic growth in East and Southeast Asia what were the consequences of it being gradually phased out during the 1980s? Did the effects of the forty years or so of the Cold War linger on or were they quickly superseded by the growing pressures exerted by the US on the governments of the region to open up their economies and by the forces of globalization that appeared to be demanding changes in economic policy? To what extent were the long-term effects of the Cold War on the political, economic and social life of the 'miracle' economies factors in the Asian economic crisis that enveloped the region in the late 1990s and did they have any role to play in the subsequent revival of the region's economic fortunes? And finally, did the Cold War and its political and economic legacy influence the emergence of an increasing sense of regionalism among the countries of East and Southeast Asia during the late 1990s and the early years of the twenty-first century? It is to these questions that this book is addressed.

Competing Explanations

Since the 1970s a variety of explanations have been put forward to account for the success of the Asian 'miracle' economies. Generally these explanations fall into five broad categories each of which emphasizes a particular facet of the spectacular economic growth of the seven successful Asian economies. The neoclassical economic and statist explanations are the ones that have attracted the most attention and about which most has been written. However, the cultural, Japan-centred, and American hegemony explanations also need to be examined as they too have their proponents. Some of these explanations overlap in part with others, while for some scholars a combination of these various explanations is most helpful in ana-lysing the reasons for the success of the Asian economies (e.g. Clark and Chan 1992; Cumings 1984a; So and Chiu 1995).

Neoclassical Economic Explanations

The neoclassical economic explanations emphasize that the market and the price mechanism are the most effective ways to organize domestic economic relations. Neoclassical economists maintain that unfettered markets are more effective in promoting economic development than governments, which are incapable of making fully informed decisions. To be successful, it is argued, economies should be outward-looking so as to engage the international economy, and market-conforming. Governments should play only a very limited and clearly prescribed role in terms of providing public goods, such as the provision of national defence, the maintenance of the rule of law, and the guaranteeing of property rights. For the neoclassical economists the key is to 'get the prices right'. Relative prices in a well-functioning market ensure that resources are allocated to industrial sectors and companies which operate efficiently and which enjoy a comparative advantage. In practical terms the key policies are thought to be the dismantling of barriers to trade, such as tariffs and quotas, and allowing the market to determine exchange rates, interest rates, the price of labour and the inputs for industry.

During the 1970s, following on from some initial work done by I.M.D. Little, T. Scitovsky and M. Scott (1970), neoclassical economists began to analyse the East Asian economic success story in ever greater detail. Much of the early analyses were undertaken in country studies commissioned by the US-based National Bureau of Economic Research under the direction of J.N. Bhagwati and A.O. Krueger (e.g. Bhagwati 1978; Krueger 1978). By the end of the 1970s and into the early 1980s, neoclassical economists were publishing a steady stream of analyses which used the success of countries like Japan, South Korea and Taiwan to press their case for greater adherence to market-oriented development policies and, more generally, for the rapid liberalization of developing economies (e.g. Balassa 1981; Balassa and Associates 1982; Hughes 1980; Little 1982; Patrick and Rosovsky 1976). In these studies the private sector and especially the export manufacturing industries were argued to be the key to rapid economic growth. Variations on this basic interpretation of the economic success of Asia's high-performing economies have continued to be favoured by most Western-trained economists ever since. Indeed, in analysing the Asian economic crisis those who follow the neoclassical economic line of argument emphasize the extent to which increasing government interference and government-sponsored 'cronyism' undermined the efficient operation of the market (*The Economist* 1998; Greenspan 1998; McLeod and Garnaut 1998). Proponents of the neoclassical economic explanation pointed out that, by ignoring economic principles and following policies that sought to distort the markets governing exchange rates and interest rates, the governments of Thailand, Malaysia and South Korea were bound to create trouble for their economies.

Analyses by neoclassical economists of the market-oriented model of development, then, highlight a number of important features of the Asian economic success story. These include: capital formation – the development of physical and human capital or resources within an economy – and the efficient allocation of resources; the remarkable savings rates of the successful economies; stable and effective exchange rates; the ability to attract foreign investment; the promotion of the export of manufactured goods; the supply of a well-educated and skilled labour force; the effective use of new technologies; and the need for a competent, stable and non-interventionist government. Of course, different analysts emphasize different aspects of the overall approach. For example, Paul Krugman (1994: 70), building on the work of Alwyn Young (1994) and Jong-Il Kim and Lawrence Lau (1994), has emphasized the economy-wide impact of 'an astonishing mobilization of resources', especially the 'extraordinary growth in inputs like labor and capital', as the determinants of economic success in East and Southeast Asia rather than productivity growth which has been the prevailing view among economists up to that point. Krugman's argument has been challenged by a number of analysts (e.g. Haggard and Kim 1997; Rodrik 1998; Stiglitz 2001). The opposing, orthodox, view singles out the importance of new technologies and their incorporation into industrial sectors through learning, entrepreneurship and innovation as keys to the productivity growth within the 'miracle' economies (Nelson and Pack 1999).

Despite the important contributions made by the neoclassical economists to our understanding of the success of Asia's 'miracle' economies, two major criticisms can be identified. First, apart from some early analyses (e.g. Cole 1980; Jacoby 1966) neoclassical economists were determinedly ahistorical in their theoretical approach. As a consequence most economists were generally oblivious of the need to account for the origins of the resources — such as capital, technology and an educated workforce — that allowed governments to implement what were depicted as the market-conforming policies of the economically successful Asian governments or to develop their export-oriented strategies. Similarly, they were equally uninterested in explaining where the resources came from for the development of the economic infrastructure or for the high savings rates that they argued were significant in stimulating rapid economic growth. For example, in his discussion of total factor productivity (TFP), Krugman (1994: 70) notes the vital 'role of rapidly growing inputs' in the development of the newly industrializing countries of Asia but fails to ask how the large quantities of capital and trained labour came to be available in the first place.

Second, and by far the most strongly voiced criticism, was that the neoclassical explanation grossly underestimated the extent to which the state intervened in the seven successful economies to direct economic development. For example, the switch from import-substitution industrialization to an export-oriented industrialization strategy can only be understood in terms of the political dynamics of the societies involved (Haggard 1990). In addition, the state was central to economic planning and the overall orchestration of the economy (e.g. Johnson 1982; 1987), and played a critical role in the development of particular industries (e.g. Amsden 1989; Chang 1994; Wade 1990). For many analysts, then, the neoclassical explanation, which attempted to generalize across all the successful Asian economies, totally misread the importance of the guiding hand of the state.

Statist Explanations

As might be expected from their criticisms of the neoclassical explanation for the success of Asia's 'miracle' economies, the statists emphasized the pervasive role of the state in driving economic policy. In particular, they argued that strong states not only decided on the overall economic strategy to be adopted but also intervened to plan and execute most aspects of economic policy from the allocation of capital to the emasculation of labour. Indeed, central to the state's role in developing the economy was the generation of an industrial policy which set out the overall goals of the economy and the means for attaining them. The state, and its various agencies, then, made sure that the industrial policy, which included creating a competitive advantage for chosen industries and even companies, was followed. The statists, therefore, see a strong state as crucial in promoting high levels of economic growth, productivity and international competitiveness.

The statist position was first set out in detail by Chalmers Johnson in his 1982 book, *MITI and the Japanese Miracle*. He posited the concept of the capitalist 'developmental state', which, while committed to private property and the market, intervened in the economy by way of a small group of elite bureaucrats in order to guide and promote economic development. In a series of books, journal articles and book chapters during the 1980s, others took up this line of argument using South Korea, Taiwan and Singapore as their case studies (Deyo 1987; Gold 1986; Haggard and Moon 1983; Koo 1984; Lim 1983; Rodan 1989; Whang 1987).

This 'counter revolution' of the statists (Islam 1994: 92) reached something of a climax with the publication in quick succession of three major studies. In 1989 Alice Amsden published a detailed analysis of South Korea's 'late industrialization'. She argued, provocatively and somewhat at odds with Johnson's market-conforming approach, that one of the keys to South Korea's economic success was that not only had 'Korea not gotten relative prices right, it ha[d] deliberately gotten them "wrong"' (Amsden 1989: 139). Amsden emphasized the extent to which it was the state rather than the market that directed capital into particular industrial sectors and selected groups of companies, while at the same time it imposed strict performance criteria to ensure that resources were used efficiently. Most notably, she highlighted the role of government in promoting technological adaptation as a means by which late-industrializing economies might catch up with their more industrialized competitors. A year later Robert Wade published an exhaustive analysis of Taiwan's extraordinary rate of economic growth (Wade 1990). Among other points, Wade noted the importance of capital accumulation and the high levels of investment in particular industries which resulted from government manipulation of the credit system and which gave a few key industries and companies a comparative advantage when they moved into the very competitive international marketplace. Wade also argued that in economies like the one in Taiwan, market failure was likely on a number of fronts and that the state, therefore, needed to step in and 'govern the market'. In the same year Stephan Haggard (1990) produced an analysis that examined the internal political dynamics that allowed Hong Kong, Singapore, South Korea and Taiwan to move from an import-substitution strategy to an export-oriented industrializing strategy and then combined elements of the market with strong state guidance to implement their industrial policies. With the appearance of these landmark books by Amsden, Haggard and Wade, the statist explanation started to rival the neoclassical economic explanation as the main contender in the battle to account for the success of Asia's 'miracle' economies. Other studies in the statist vein quickly followed (e.g. Woo 1991; see also the discussions in Onis 1991 and Woo-Cumings 1999).

During the next decade or so the debate between the statists and the neoclassical economists was fuelled by a widely read World Bank research report, *The East Asian Miracle: Economic Growth and Public Policy* (1993), and then by the Asian economic crisis. The World Bank's policy research report addressed the question, 'What caused East Asia's success?' It concluded that 'In large measure the HPAE [High Performing Asian Economies] achieved high growth by getting the basics right' (World Bank 1993: 5, 347–52) This conclusion, of course, supported the neoclassical economists' orthodoxy that was the basis for the World Bank's official policy. But the report (1993: 5) also noted that, 'In most of these economies, in one form or another, the government intervened – systematically and through multiple channels – to foster development, and in some cases the development of specific industries.' This observation gave ammunition to the statists. The report's attempted compromise between the neoclassical and statist positions was termed the 'market friendly approach'. However, this approach, as laid out in the report, tended to lean more to the neoclassical position, while the data in the body of the report provided ample evidence for the proponents of the statist position (Amsden 1994; Kwon 1994; Lall 1994; World Bank 1993: 85–6). As a result of this ambivalence, the World Bank report, rather than giving either side a clear-cut advantage in the debate, only provoked further exchanges. Similarly, the Asian economic crisis served to reinforce entrenched positions. The neoclassical economists argued that the crisis was caused by the increasingly corrupt Asian governments that moved away from the principle of market-led prices in such areas as interest rates and exchange rates and provided too many guarantees for dubious bank loans By contrast, the statists saw the problem in terms of the unregulated movement of global capital – widely termed 'hot money' – and the diminishing power of the state to manage the domestic financial sector (e.g. Wade 1990; 2004).

Just as the neoclassical economic explanation has strengths and weaknesses, so too does the statist explanation. The strength of the statist approach lies in its acknowledgement of the role of the government and the many detailed empirical studies which document the state's contribution to promoting sustained, rapid economic growth. Significantly, Johnson's (1992) 'developmental state' concept, while being questioned in a number of ways, stimulated considerable discussion about the merits of state intervention. As a result, analysts were forced to examine the nature and extent of the state's role in East and Southeast Asia's economic success (Haggard 2004; Wade 2004; Woo-Cumings 1999).

The statist explanation also invites three criticisms. First, there is no consensus as to what kind of state intervention is required to promote rapid economic growth. For example, should state intervention be market-conforming or market-distorting? Not all states intervened in the same way or to the same extent but each was, nonetheless, able to promote rapid economic growth. Clearly the state was much more interventionist and directive in South Korea and Singapore than it was in Hong Kong. Second, and a point most often made by analysts representing the neoclassical economic school of thought, as the global and domestic economies became more complex the state was often unable to intervene in an effective manner. It had neither the capacity nor was it able to generate the needed information to monitor and actively direct a quickly evolving and rapidly expanding domestic economy in an equally rapidly globalizing world. Indeed, what was seen as the developmental state's strengths – its promotion of particular industries and even companies and the well-entrenched relations linking government to the business sector – were viewed as liabilities over time. The argument is that they led to cronyism and the inefficient allocation of resources. Third, while some analysts do note the importance of tracing how the relatively strong states of the seven successful Asian economies emerged (e.g. Cumings 1984a; Johnson 1982; Woo 1991), there is no systematic analysis of their origins. Why should the seven successful Asian economies be so different from so many other countries of the Third World where, as Joel Migdal (1988) has correctly pointed out, the norm was for 'strong societies and weak states'? Certainly, the role that war played in mobilizing resources to allow for the development of a strong interventionist state is not widely analysed.

Cultural Explanations

In attempting to show why all the successful Asian economies came from the same part of the world some analysts put forward an explanation based on culture and its impact on political and economic institutions and development. The case essentially rests on the advantages conferred on a society by the Confucian culture (e.g. Hicks and Redding 1983; Redding 1990; Tu 1996). The point made is that Confucianism emphasizes such crucial factors as obligations and loyalty to the family as the basic social unit, obedience to legitimate authority, the high value placed on education, duty, hard work and self-discipline. All of these characteristics of Confucianism (sometimes combined with elements of Buddhism) are said to play a major role in the rapid and sustained economic development of the region's 'miracle' economies.

From the early 1970s onwards, as the success of first Japan and then the four newly industrializing economies (NIEs) – South Korea, Hong Kong, Taiwan and Singapore – became evident, analysts attempted to assess the extent to which culture and especially Confucian culture was a contributing factor (e.g. Hofheinz and Calder 1982; Kahn 1970; Morishima 1982; Tai 1989). Lucian Pye (1985), for example, argues that power and authority in East Asia were rooted in regional cultures and that strong governments were a product of the acceptance of authority as well as the need for harmony and unity. Tu Wei-Ming (1996: 8) notes that while there are considerable variations in the structure and function of the family in Chinese, Japanese and Korean societies, 'the family's supreme role in capital formation, power politics, social stability, and moral education is comparable in all East Asian communities'. He goes on to argue that the 'classic Confucian vision that "only when families are regulated are states governed" (stated in the opening passage of the *Great Learning*) is still taken absolutely seriously in East Asian political culture' and that 'the metaphor of the family is widely present in all forms of social organization' (Tu 1996: 8).

For other commentators, the various East Asian cultures are crucial to understanding everyday economic relations and business practices. Such commentators emphasize in particular how Confucian culture has contributed to the creation of the kinship-based business networks that characterize Chinese economies, as well as distinctive Chinese management practices. They also point, more generally, to the importance of social obligations, rather then legal contracts, in business relations (W.K.K. Chan 1982; Redding 1991). Similar arguments have been made about the impact of Japanese culture on Japan's management practices (Dore 1997; Eisenstadt 1966). Other analysts, while acknowledging that many differences among the main regional cultures have consequences for the conduct of economic relations, have nonetheless stressed the network capitalism that is common to Chinese, Korean and Japanese approaches to business activities (Castells 1996).

As with the other explanations of the success of Asia's 'miracle' economies, the cultural explanation has both strengths and weaknesses. Crucially these explanations underscore the point that the political and economic institutions that emerged to develop and implement economic policy were generally compatible with the cultures of the various societies of the region's successful economies. Indeed, had the political and economic institutions not been consistent with the prevailing culture, they would likely not have survived very long. Certainly, as these institutions evolved they were, in part at least, shaped by the culture of each of the societies they served.

Yet it is clearly very difficult to make a case that cultural factors alone account for Asia's remarkable economic growth. Criticisms of the cultural explanations of Asia's economic success fall into two main categories. First, if Confucianism is so significant a factor in the region's success, why did Confucian societies prior to the Second World War not achieve the remarkable economic growth attained by the same Confucian societies after the War. This lack of a historical perspective is underlined by Weber's conclusion that in the past Confucian values had played an important role in the backwardness of Chinese society (Weber 1968; on Korea see also Cha 2003). Some commentators have attempted to get around this problem by arguing that Confucianism has been transformed into a new, more economically supportive version (Tu 1996; see also the discussion in Berger 2004: 179–83). However, this argument has been greeted with scepticism primarily because it seems to distort Confucianism and ignore the other factors that may explain the region's success (Cha 2003; Gomez and Hsiao 2001). Second, scholars have argued that there are too many differences among the various Confucian cultures of East and Southeast Asia for there to be one set of cultural factors which explains all of the region's economic successes (Biggart and Hamilton 1997; Hefner 1998). An extension of this argument is that, if Confucianism is so critical to economic development, then why have Thailand and Malaysia been able to replicate some measure of the success achieved by Japan, South Korea, Taiwan, Hong Kong and Singapore? While both had economically prominent Chinese communities, Thailand has been heavily influenced by Therevada

Buddhism, which is a different form of Buddhism from that popular in China and Japan. And, most significantly, Malaysian society is predominantly Muslim.

Japan-Centred Explanations

Another set of explanations, which seeks to account for the fact that all the successful economies were in the same region, focuses on the role of Japan. There are two distinctive strands to these analyses. The first strand emphasizes the importance of the Japanese colonial experience for the rapid economic development experienced by South Korea and Taiwan from the 1960s onwards (Cumings 1984a; Kohli 1994; Kohli 1997). The argument is that although Japanese colonial occupation of South Korea and Taiwan was harsh and repressive, it was during this period that the foundations for the later economic success were laid. A strong, centralized, bureaucratic state; increased agricultural productivity; the development of an indus-trial sector which included heavy industry as well as the processing of agricultural products; and a clearly defined class structure were all said to be the result of Japan's colonial policies during the period from around 1900 to 1945. As Atul Kohli evocatively puts it, 'the grooves that Japanese colonialism carved on the Korean soil cut deep' and from the early 1960s onwards South Korea 'can be argued to have fallen back into the grooves of an earlier origin and traversed along them well into the 1980s' (Kohli 1994: 1271).

The second strand to the Japan-centred set of explanations emphasizes that Japan should be viewed as both the engine of growth for East and Southeast Asia and the model for the successful development of its regional neighbours (Fukuda 1988; Hatch and Yamamura 1996; Lim 2003; Petri 1993). From the late 1960s onwards Japan started to pour substantial amounts of aid first into South Korea and then, beginning in the 1970s, into Southeast Asia. During the 1970s Japanese foreign direct investment also began to flow into South Korea, Taiwan, Hong Kong and later in increasing amounts into Singapore, Malaysia and Thailand. Japanese capital became the major factor in driving Asia's 'miracle' economies forward. In addition, South Korea and Taiwan saw themselves as moving down a similar path to development that had been followed by Japan and, therefore, sought to adopt some of the policies that had ena-bled Japan to achieve rapid and sustained economic growth. Some

Southeast Asian governments, notably the Malaysian government, also attempted to emulate the Japanese economic model with the hope of replicating Japan's success (Mahathir and Ishihara 1995: 130–2).

The strength of these arguments lies in highlighting the important role played by Japan in East and Southeast Asia. Clearly, history matters and Japan has been a significant player in the region for over a century. Even if Japan reshaped places like Korea and Taiwan through brutal and repressive means, the positive aspects of its colonial legacy for later economic development have to be acknowledged. Importantly, then, the development trajectory that was established by the Japanese should to be taken into consideration when evaluating the post-Second World War success of South Korea and Taiwan. Moreover, from the 1970s onwards the dynamism of the Japanese economy was successfully exported to a number of its regional neighbours and Japan served as a major engine of growth. Certainly the timely influx of Japanese capital into Asia's 'miracle' economies was a significant factor in their sustained economic development.

Yet the Japan-centred explanations for the success of the Asian economies also have their limitations. Crucially, while Japanese colonial rule in South Korea and Taiwan left a significant legacy, Japan had virtually nothing to do with the British colonies of Hong Kong, Singapore, Malaysia or the formally uncolonized Thailand, all of which also achieved 'miracle' status. Indeed, the Japanese occupation of the Malayan peninsula, Singapore and Hong Kong during the Second World War left nothing but a trail of death and destruction. Moreover, by the time the Japanese started to pour substantial aid and investment into the successful Asian economies in the late 1970s, their economies were already reasonably well established as were their overall development trajectories. Hence, as with the other explanations, the Japan-centred approaches fail to provide a satisfactory answer as to why all the seven Asian 'miracle' economies did so well.

American-Hegemony Explanations

American hegemony, variously defined, has been integral to a number of explanations of the success of the Asian economies. In particular, Marxists, neo-Marxists and others on the left took up this theme as it became clear that the economic success of the 'miracle' economies undermined the claims of dependency theorists (Higgott 1983). For World-System theorists, who highlight the emergence of a capitalist world economy dominated by core–peripheral relations and governed by the drive for the accumulation of capital, American hegemony was seen in terms of its dominant military power and its role as the major centre of capital accumulation in the world (Wallerstein 1995). As a result of the geography of the Cold War, Japan, South Korea and Taiwan were significant beneficiaries of American assistance as the US sought to retain its dominant position. For geopolitical reasons, then, East Asia gained from the exercise of US hegemony in a way that no other area of the world did (Arrighi 1996; So and Chiu 1995; Wallerstein 1997). In a somewhat similar vein the role of American hegemony is also emphasized by Gramscians, such as Robert Cox (1987), who see a US-led world order to which elites in peripheral states sign on so as to gain military support and access to capital and trading opportunities. Moreover, the establishment of American hegemony from the late 1950s onwards was seen as providing the framework for the development of transnational production with East Asia as the front line as the US government encouraged American manufacturers to relocate to the region (Bernard 1989; 1994). These arguments have been taken up and expanded by a number of analysts who underscore the significance of the exercise of US hegemony to the development of specific East Asian economies as well as to the region and the world at large (Berger 2004; Cumings 1999a; 1999b; Gills, 1993; 2000; Hersh 1993).

The American-hegemony explanation has a number of strengths. First, as with the Japan-centred explanations, it stresses the importance of taking an historical approach to the development of the successful Asian economies. For example, Barry K. Gills (2000) points to three key moments when the US intervened in East Asia: when Japan was defeated during the Second World War; when South Korea and Taiwan were built up during the late 1950s and early 1960s; and when an attempt was made to dismantle the post-Second World War East Asian capitalism during the years after the end of the Cold War. Bruce Cumings (1984a; 1999b) also notes that the pervasive influence of the US in the region dates back to the immediate post-Second World War period and that the US has continued to play a key role in the region's economies right through to the Asian crisis of 1997. Second, this set of explanations highlights America's role in injecting capital into the region during the 1950s and 1960s through various types of aid, foreign direct investment (FDI) and increased trade. And, third, these explanations help to underline America's commitment to maintaining the security of the region. This interest in security helped to sustain a reasonable level of stability for those societies outside the theatres of war and ensured that friendly governments were kept in power no matter how authoritarian they were.

Yet the American-hegemony explanation also has its weaknesses. First, most of the analyses which employ an American-hegemony explanation concentrate on the economic success of Japan, South Korea and Taiwan (e.g. So and Chiu 1995). There are remarkably few analyses of the impact of American hegemony on the wider region and on the economic success of Hong Kong, Singapore, Malaysia or Thailand. Second, most of the accounts of Asia's economic success that emphasize American hegemony take a broad-brush approach. It is not always clear exactly how US influence in the region was translated into rapid and sustained economic growth for all the successful economies. Certainly, there is no convincing explanation as to why Hong Kong, Singapore and Malaysia, which had no direct US economic support, were able to prosper while the Philippines, which housed both a major US air force base and a major US naval base, became an economic basket case. Third, although analysts who use an American-hegemony approach allude to the importance of geopolitics, few examine the consequences for economic development of the various wars in the region. For example, with one or two notable exceptions (e.g. Havens 1987), there are no full-scale analyses of the economic impact of the Vietnam War on the economies of East and Southeast Asia. Finally, the American-hegemony explanation for the rise of the 'miracle' economies discounts both the spur to regional development provided by the linkages between the various overseas Chinese communities and the strong role played by Japanese aid and investment from the 1970s onwards. Undoubtedly, Japanese aid and FDI were major factors in the continued, strong economic performance of Singapore, Malaysia and Thailand up to the Asian crisis of 1997–8.

Rethinking the Explanations for Asia's Economic Success

The strengths of the five categories of explanations outlined above suggest a number of ways in which a fuller, more satisfactory account of Asia's economic success may be achieved. First, history and geography matter. Without an historical perspective it is impossible to appreciate all the factors that have gone into the making of the Asian economic success story. Moreover, the location of the successful Asian economies in relationship to the region's wars is clearly crucial as some proponents of the American-hegemony explanation suggest. Second, the five sets of explanations of East and Southeast Asia's economic successes use different levels of analysis. Three of the categories of explanation – neoclassical economic, statist and cultural – tend to operate at the level of the state or society. The Japan-centred explanation offers a regional perspective while the set of explanations which concentrate on the exercise of American hegemony entail an international perspective. The clear need is for a way to allow each level of analysis to make a contribution to a full assessment of the factors contributing to the success of 'miracle' economies. Finally, it is crucial that any explanation of how economic success was achieved in the seven 'miracle' economies takes into account the decision-making processes developed, and the economic and administrative policies followed, in each case.

This book argues that the key to the analysis of East and Southeast Asia's economic success is war and the geopolitics of the region. The argument that runs through this study is that the fighting of wars, the preparation for war, and America's use of the seven East and Southeast Asian societies – Japan, South Korea, Taiwan, Hong Kong, Singapore, Malaysia and Thailand – as part of a crescent of containment in its battle against communism had a profound, and on balance very positive, effect on their economies. The various 'hot' wars, including the Second World War, the Korean War and the Vietnam War, as well as the Cold War, drew Japan and, most importantly, the US into East and Southeast Asia. These wars created the circumstances which prompted the US to invest substantial resources in specific countries which then spilt over into key parts of the region. The 'hot' wars and the all-embracing Cold War also had a huge impact on the development of the political organizations and institutions as well as the economic policies of the various societies of the region. And just as significantly, the historical sequence in which the wars took place was also critical.

The wars of East and Southeast Asia and the geopolitical context did not have a uniform impact on all the economies of the region. At the end of the Second World War all of the seven societies had different cultures, societal organizations, political traditions and economic institutions. Moreover, the two major 'hot' wars, the Korean War and the Vietnam War, occurred in different parts of East and Southeast Asia, at different times, and drew the US into the region in different ways. The consequence was that each of the seven economies was influenced differently by each war. Yet, it will be argued that the imperatives of the Cold War, and especially the necessity of preparing for war and responding to the sequence of geopolitical events that swept through the region, drove the development of the economic and political institutions of each of the seven countries in very similar directions. As a result of these relatively common experiences — and although there were still major differences among them — by the early 1990s the political and economic institutions of the 'miracle economies' were much more alike than they were in the immediate aftermath of the Second World War. So, broadly, were their economies. It will also be argued that despite the Cold War being phased out in parts of East and Southeast Asia from the early 1980s onwards, as the conflicts and tensions subsided, many of the administrative and economic policies that were spawned by the 'hot' wars and especially the Cold War remained in place. They were embedded in the political, administrative, economic and social institutional practices of each of the affected countries. As a result these embedded policies had a major role in the events leading up to the Asian crisis and in the recovery that followed. Moreover, the legacy of the Cold War was also a factor in other key developments. It shaped the rapid economic rise of China and the growing regionalism to be found in East and Southeast Asia during the 1990s and the early years of the new century.

The discussion of the extraordinary economic growth of the 'miracle' economies also sheds light on economic development more generally. It underscores the need for an injection of substantial amounts of capital over a sustained period and equally for the development of an institutional state that has the capacity to produce a coherent, credible economic plan and, just as importantly, to be able to implement it. In the case of the seven successful Asian economies the key catalyst was the sequence of wars that engulfed the region. Of course, in advancing this argument the analysis does not seek to downplay the horrors of war. The fighting that consumed major parts of East and Southeast Asia in the many wars that broke out across the region killed or maimed millions of people. They left many millions more homeless, their families broken and their communities devastated. Rather the point is that war and the fear of war that pervaded the seven Asian 'miracle' economies created an imperative that saw resources mobilized and political and economic institutions developed in such a way as to encourage a form of rapid economic growth that no other economies experienced. It is possible that for other developing countries the deployment of large amounts of capital and the development of an effective institutional state capacity will be generated in ways other than through war. However, despite the widespread trauma and destruction that accompanied it, this analysis will argue that the key to the phenomenal success of Asia's 'miracle' economies in the second half of the twentieth century was the sequence of wars that overtook the region.

The Overall Approach

The Effects of War

'War shapes lives' is the inscription engraved on one of the aluminium outside walls of the Daniel Libeskind-designed Imperial War Museum North in Salford, England. This statement emphasizes the central role that war has played in the lives of countless individuals and in the ebb and flow of societies. Certainly, there can be little doubt that war and the evolution of societies, states and economies have historically been inextricably intertwined. From the Sixth century BC Greek philosopher Heraclitus of Ephesus, who stated that, 'War is the father of all and the king of all'(Porter 1994: 1, 2) to the modern-day political theorist, Jean Bethke Elshtain, who argues that, 'War creates *the* people' and that, 'War produces power, individual and collective' (Elshtain 1987: 167, emphasis in the original), there is general agreement among scholars that war is a profound agent of political, social and economic change (Porter 1994: 3; Stein and Russet 1980: 399).

Wars, or organized collective violence on a broad scale, come in many forms and sizes. In examining its impact, war should be broadly conceived so that it includes the widespread devastation and global reach of the Second World War as well as the limited and confined actions of many insurgency and terrorist campaigns. In addition, as studies of warfare in Europe have shown (Tilly 1975; Tilly 1992), it is not just the fighting of a war and its repercussions but also the threat of war and the consequent mobilization in preparation for a possible conflict, that influence the social, political and economic developments within a society. Whatever the scope and scale of a war, it invariably has a major effect on the individuals and institutions it touches.

The effects of both the threat of war and the fighting of a war on the social, political and economic life of a society are many and varied. However, building on the work done by Bruce D. Porter (1994: 11–19) and incorporating points made by a number of other analysts (Bean 1973; Bond 1983; Crouzet 1964; Deane 1975; Tilly 1992; Wheeler 1975), it is possible to divide the consequences of the preparation for, and the prosecution of, a war into three broad categories. First, are the destructive and disintegrative effects of war. These effects include widespread loss of life, forced migration, and social and political dislocation as well as the greatly diminished capacity of the institutional state and even its total destruction. Also included in this category are severe shortages of essential commodities such as food and fuel; the destruction of the economic infrastructure and productive capacity; and the undermining and, in the worst cases, the breakdown of the economy and the collapse of the debt-ridden state. Even if war itself does not lead to the total destruction of a society, some combination of these effects may lead to a revolution or the outbreak of civil war that can prolong the downward spiral of social, economic and political disintegration.

Second, are the formative and developmental effects of preparing for and fighting a war. An external threat can be used to rally domestic support and unify a society. Territorial gains can be consolidated and new resources acquired. Government and power can be centralized, state bureaucracies enlarged and rationalized and the revenue base broadened and deepened. New war-fighting technologies can be developed, under-employed people mobilized and given jobs, and capital put to productive use. Moreover, there can be growth in those sectors of the economy given the opportunity to be innovative, or given priority by governments and not destroyed by fighting. Significantly, many of these formative effects tend to have long-term consequences. For example, taxes which have been raised and bureaucracies which have been expanded may be reduced after wars but they never seem to return to their previous pre-war levels.

Third, are the reformative and redistributive effects of the threat of war and the prosecution of a war. The conscription and the full mobilization of a society serve to socialize, integrate and increase the educational and skill levels of large portions of the population. Opportunities are created for a popular leader to introduce reforms which might not otherwise gain support. Government intervention in the economy and society in order to promote economic development as well as social cohesion and compliance can become a habit. Spending on the war effort can redistribute domestic wealth, while the redistribution of wealth regionally and internationally can take place as a result of the dispersal of economic and military aid to allies as well as through the emergence of new markets and changes in trading patterns caused by a war.

The location of a war is crucial to the effects it has on a particular society. Hence, although any country engaged either directly or indirectly in a war may feel both its negative and positive effects, generally, those states on whose territory wars are fought are most likely to suffer the disintegrative effects of war. Those states that are on the periphery of the theatre of war but allied in one form or another to one of the protagonists are most likely to experience the formative, reformative and redistributive effects of war. Similarly, the way in which a civil or guerrilla war is fought — for example, whether the military or the civil side of the state is in charge of the counter-insurgency campaign — will determine whether the fighting has primarily a disintegrative or formative impact on the state and society (Rich and Stubbs 1997) Any society can experience a mix of the disintegrative, formative and reformative effects of war and the threat of war, either as one major war unfolds or, as was the case in East and Southeast Asia from the Second World War onwards, as a sequence of wars engulfs a region. Finally, when there is simply the threat of war, or during the early stages of a war, the formative effects predominate; however, as a war wears on and the fighting takes its toll, the disintegrative effects are likely to come to the fore.

Which East and Southeast Asian Economies?

To some extent all the states and economies of East and Southeast Asia were affected by the Cold War and by at least one of the series of wars that broke out throughout the region. However, only a certain number achieved relatively high economic growth rates and per capita incomes during the period from the outbreak of the Cold War in Asia in 1950 to its close in 1989. The purpose of this study is to show that the economic development of what have been identified here as the seven successful economies — Japan, South Korea, Taiwan, Hong Kong, Singapore, Malaysia and Thailand — cannot be fully understood without an appreciation of the role played by the series of wars, especially the Cold War, and the more general geopolitical context that engulfed the region. But why choose these particular states? Japan is an obvious candidate in that it rose rapidly from the rubble of the Second World War to become the second largest economy in the world. Chowdhury and Islam (1993: 2) note that, 'Japan can be regarded as the first of the post-war NIEs.' Its rates of growth for the 1950s and 1960s, especially in the manufacturing sector, were nothing short of phenomenal, and by the early 1990s its per capita income rivalled that of the US.

South Korea, Taiwan, Hong Kong and Singapore were clearly the most successful economies in the region after Japan. Collectively they were given the label, 'New Industrializing Country' (NIC), or 'Newly Industrializing Economy' (NIE) to accommodate the Chinese government's insistence that neither Hong Kong nor Taiwan were countries but, nominally at least, parts of China. Although a number of definitions have been posited (e.g. Chowdhury and Islam 1993: 2–10; OECD 1979 and Tan 1992: 1–4), there is no official definition of an NIC or an NIE. However, economies that fit this category are usually viewed, in terms of the global economy, as occupying the transitional stage between the less developed countries of the developing world and the advanced industrial countries of the North. The main characteristics of the NIEs are generally thought to be high growth rates that have been sustained for a long period of time, levels of per capita income that put the country squarely in the mid-level range among world economies, and a manufacturing sector that provides a substantial portion of the GNP and contributes to a high proportion of the country's total exports. South Korea, Taiwan, Hong Kong and Singapore clearly fit this profile.

Malaysia and Thailand began to be considered as the next NIEs, or near-NIEs, by the late 1980s (Balakrishnan 1989; Charoenloet 1991; *Economist* Editorial 1989; Hamilton 1987; Holloway 1991; Jansen 1991). Starting in 1960 both experienced relatively high levels of economic growth. By 1990 Malaysia had achieved a per capita income of US$2,300 and Thailand a per capita income of US$1,400 which put them squarely in the mid-level range among world economies (Asia Development Bank 1992: 289). And both were increasingly reliant on the manufacturing sector as the key part of their export-oriented industrializing strategy. Indeed, by the late 1980s manufacturing contributed to a substantial portion of each country's GNP with a relatively high percentage of workers engaged in the industrial manufacturing sector. Increasingly, analysts considered the two countries as having highly competitive, industrializing economies that could be viewed as following fairly closely in the footsteps of the four East Asian NIEs (Tan 1992: 154–66). The focus of the analysis in the following pages will be on the seven East Asian industrialized or industrializing economies of Japan, South Korea, Taiwan, Hong Kong, Singapore, Malaysia and Thailand.

Table 1.1   Average annual GDP growth rates, 1950–96

	1950s	1960s	1970s	1980s	1990s
Japan	8.6	10.5	4.4	4.0	2.1
Hong Kong	9.5	9.9	9.4	6.9	5.2
Taiwan	8.4	9.9	9.3	8.2	6.7
South Korea	6.0	8.3	7.7	9.4	7.2
Singapore	5.4	10.0	9.1	7.4	8.9
Malaysia	4.1	6.6	7.7	5.4	8.7
Thailand	6.4	8.2	6.9	7.6	8.1
Indonesia	3.8	4.2	7.8	6.1	7.6
Philippines	7.1	4.9	5.9	1.0	2.3

Sources: Data from International Bank for Reconstruction and Development (IBRD) 1971; World Bank, various years; World Bank 2001; Republic of China, various years.

This selection of countries leaves out the Philippines and Indonesia. From having the highest standard of living in East and Southeast Asia after Japan in the mid-1950s, the Philippines had, by the end of the 1980s, become the economic straggler of the Association of Southeast Asia Nations (ASEAN). Throughout the 1960s and 1970s the GDP growth rate of the Philippines lagged well behind that of Singapore, Malaysia and Thailand. And between 1980 and 1992 real per capita income actually declined (Hutchcroft 1998: 1). Through the late 1980s and into the 1990s the per capita GNP of the Philippines was only half that of Thailand (Asia Development Bank 1992: 289). As a consequence of its erratic and sluggish economic growth the

Philippines has rarely been put forward as a possible member of the Asian NIEs. It, therefore, provides an interesting case of a state that was part of the US battle against Asian communism but which did not develop in the same way as the seven industrializing economies. Indeed, the Philippines is in many ways the regional exception that proves a number of rules.

Indonesia is not included in the seven industrializing economies that are the focus of this study for two main reasons. First, Indonesia's low per capita income does not put it in the category of an NIE or even a near-NIE. Only in 1996 did Indonesia very briefly exceed the $1,100 per capita income benchmark established in 1979 for NIEs by the Organisation for Economic Cooperation and Development (OECD) (Balassa 1980; OECD 1979). Indeed, Indonesia has consistently had a per capita income that is less than half that of Thailand. Second, although Indonesia experienced reasonable levels of growth during the 1970s and parts of the 1980s, much of this was the result of increased production of oil and liquified natural gas and the general rise in energy prices (Robison 2001: 111). In the 1990s Indonesia did start rapidly to expand its manufacturing sector. However, its economy was still heavily reliant on the extraction and export of raw materials. Interestingly, the World Bank included Indonesia along with the seven industrializing East Asian economies as one of the eight high-performing Asian economies (HPAEs) in its 1993 policy research report, *The East Asian Miracle* (World Bank 1993). It did so essentially for political reasons. The aim was to bolster the resolve of the Indonesian government to move away from its traditional import-substitution approach and adopt the open economy policies advocated by the US as well as the influential Washington-based international economic agencies, the IMF and the World Bank. The main criteria for inclusion in the World Bank's list of HPAEs were simply high growth rates from 1960 to 1985 and a relatively equal income distribution (World Bank 1993: 2–4). Little emphasis was placed on the level of per capita income or on the extent of industrialization. The World Bank's criteria do not make Indonesia eligible for inclusion in the list of successful industrializing economies analysed in this study.

There are two additional reasons for excluding the Philippines and Indonesia from the group of countries labelled here as 'miracle' Asian economies. First, during the 1990s the OECD placed Hong Kong, Korea, Malaysia, Singapore, Taiwan and Thailand in a separate category it designated 'Dynamic Asian Economies' (DAEs). Neither Indonesia nor the Philippines were thought to be sufficiently advanced economically to be included by the OECD in this category (OECD various dates). Secondly, neither Indonesia nor the Philippines rises to the level of an NIE in terms of 'governing capacity' (Hamilton-Hart 2002: 5–9, 183) or the 'quality of institutions' (Knack and Keefer 1995 and Easterly and Levine 1996, quoted in Rodrik 1998: 90). Indeed, Rodrik (1998: 90) notes that, when it comes to the ranking of their governing institutions, the Philippines is only slightly above Bangladesh, and Indonesia is at about the same level as Burma, Congo and Ghana.

The question of whether or not to include Indonesia or the Philippines in the list of industrializing Asian economies highlights the problem of comparing the economies of Northeast Asia with those of Southeast Asia. Many analysts (e.g. Abbott 2003: 34; Booth 2002; MacIntyre 1994a: 6) agree with Doner and Hawes (1995: 175) who examine the Northeast Asian NIEs and Southeast Asia's ASEAN-Four (Indonesia, Malaysia, the Philippines and Thailand) and conclude that while 'the two regions share a pattern of relative success in industrialization and export diversification, the reasons for this success are different both within the two regions and, even more so, across the two regions'. However, as Stephan Haggard has noted in a review of business–government relations in the two regions, when assessing the economic success of key Southeast Asian states, 'the contrast with the Northeast Asian NICs should not be overdrawn' (Haggard 1994: 286, and also 281–2). The problem is that the political and economic development trajectories of Indonesia and especially the Philippines are far enough removed from those of South Korea and Taiwan that any analysis that includes them, along with Malaysia and Thailand (e.g. Doner 1991), diverts attention from the important similarities between the growth of the three most successful Southeast Asian governments and economies – Singapore, Malaysia and Thailand – and the four Northeast Asian governments and econo-mies – Japan, South Korea, Taiwan and Hong Kong. This study will highlight these similarities.

And, finally, how should China be evaluated? Clearly, the destruction of the Kuomintang regime took place within the context of the war with Japan and the Second World War. Similarly, the consolidation of the new Communist regime from 1949 onwards took place against the backdrop of the Korean War, the stand-off with Taiwan, the Vietnam War and the overarching Cold War. And while China's remarkable economic growth has taken place most obviously from the early 1990s onwards and there are many differences between its success and the success of the seven 'miracle' economies, its achievements need to be placed in the context of the historical sequence of geopolitical events that swept through the region. As with the other success stories of East and Southeast Asia, no analysis of China's economic rise is complete without an assessment of the role played by the region's 'hot' wars and the ever-present Cold War.

The Effects on What?

The purpose of this book is to show the link between the Cold War and the various 'hot' wars that engulfed East and Southeast Asia, on the one hand, and the economic success of seven East and Southeast Asian economies, on the other. In other words, the emphasis is on how the regional and international system influenced the development of the domestic political economy (cf. Gourevitch 1978). The argument is that economic success was the product of the virtuous interplay of a number of social, political and economic institutions and that these institutions were shaped in good part by the regional and international geopolitical environment. Institutions are defined here as the regularized procedures, practices and norms that structure relations between individuals in and across the economy, polity and society (see Hall 1986: 19; Hall and Taylor 1996: 38). Institutions, can, therefore, range from more formal structures such as legislative organizations or government bureaucracies to the relatively informal relations that characterize some government–business links or the networks of individual politicians (Ikenberry 1988: 226–9; Orrù 1997: 304–6).

   Economic activity is the product of various institutions. Buying and selling in the marketplace and the organization of production are significantly shaped by the institutional structure of the national economy within which these activities take place (Zysman 1996: 177). As Peter Hall argues, 'markets are themselves institutions' and 'the market setting in which entrepreneurs and workers operate is a complex of interrelated institutions whose character is historically determined' (Hall 1986: 35). As scholars such as Karl Polanyi (1944) and Alexander Gerschenkron (1962) and more recently Geoffrey Underhill (1998: 19) and Eric Helleiner (1994) have argued, it is political interaction and ultimately state institutions that are particularly influential in fashioning the economic institutions of a society.

For example, it is state ministries and agencies that are primarily responsible for the creation and transformation of national markets through the rules and regulations that they put in place and enforce. Hence, the national markets for capital and labour and for goods produced by local firms are all heavily influenced by political interaction and by the policy choices of state institutions. Similarly, other aspects of economic activity, such as agricultural production, industrial strategies, and the provision of needed economic and social infrastructure, are all significantly and directly affected by state policies.

Given the crucial role it plays, it is important to lay out a working definition of the state. There are any number to chose from. Indeed, the term is often used differently in international relations and in comparative politics (Brown 1997: 67–84; Halliday 1987; Hobson 2000: 1–14; Migdal 2001: 1–13; Skocpol 1985). However, for the purposes of this analysis an essentially institutional or Weberian approach will be taken (cf. Skocpol 1979: 29). The state encompasses the set of civil and coercive institutions which are more or less coordinated by an authoritative executive which seeks to exert exclusive, legitimate control, ultimately by force if necessary, over a given population and territory. Formal civil institutions include ministries or departments, agencies and adjudicative organizations that manage the economy and regulate the society. Formal coercive institutions include the police, para-military and military organizations of the government that are meant to provide security from external and internal threats to the population and to the general integrity of the state. Obviously, the two clusters of institutions can have an impact on each other. For example, a well-managed and growing economy can provide the resources for building up the military arm of the state. At the same time, an effectively deployed police force can help provide the domestic stability that is required for strong economic growth.

The effectiveness of state institutions in carrying out their functions varies considerably. Indeed, as a number of scholars have pointed out, a state's effectiveness, or its capacity to carry out policies in accord with set goals and in a relatively consistent and rule-abiding way, may vary across policy areas (Hamilton-Hart 2002: 7–9; Skocpol 1985: 17–18). Generally, however, state capacity may be thought of as being dependent on well-developed, coherent, administrative structures housing trained personnel that can both plan and implement policies (Rueschemeyer and Evans 1985). But also a state's policies, in order to be relatively successful, must mesh positively with the policy environment. Moreover, state capacity does not always require direct intervention. It may mean the state giving the power to a particular industry or set of firms to forge ahead with a special project (Weiss 1998: 37–9). This possibility raises the issue of state autonomy from social forces.

As Hall (1986: 17) has argued, 'The capacities of a state to implement a program tend to depend as much on the configuration of society as of the state.' Certainly, the relationship between state and society is crucial to any understanding of how a state operates and has long been one of the central features of the social science literature. The extent to which state institutions are captured or influenced by particular social groups or classes within the society has preoccupied analysts from Karl Marx, who famously argued that, 'The executive of the modern state is but a committee for managing the common affairs of the whole bourgeoise' (Marx and Engels 1950, quoted in Miliband 1969: 5), to Robert Dahl (1961), C. Wright Mills (1956), and Bob Jessop (1982). Others, operating out of both Marxist and pluralist traditions have viewed the state as essentially autonomous: that is acting in its own interests relatively free of the influences that can be exerted by dominant interests in a society (e.g. Block 1977; Nordlinger 1981).

However, from the perspective of this study, the most interesting approach has been advanced by Peter Evans (1995). His notion of 'embedded autonomy' captures the seeming contradiction of a state that has considerable capacity to act independently of societal interests, including the interests of the dominant economic sections of society, while at the same time having links into the business community that allow it to steer the economy in a particular direction. Evans points out that neither autonomy nor embeddedness are, by themselves, a guarantee of anything. Autonomy can be put to many uses including the predatory exploitation of a society while embeddedness can simply mean the capture of the state by business interests (Evans 1992: 163–5). He suggests that the two come together in a positive way when autonomy is 'embedded in a concrete set of social ties which bind the state to society and provide institutional channels for the continual negotiation and renegotiation of goals and policies' (Evans 1992: 164).

Importantly, then, a state may be considered 'strong' or 'weak' in terms of its relative autonomy from societal influences and its capacity to effectively manage its economy and regulate its society in accord with clearly established and legitimate goals. However, as Joel Migdal has noted, 'Strong states have been a rarity' (Migdal 1988: 269). Certainly, they have been the exception outside North America and Europe. Migdal argues that in most of Africa, Asia and Latin America two global trends disrupted traditional patterns of social organization and created the 'strong societies and weak states' that characterize much of the developing world. He identifies one global trend as the expansion of the European market economy to many parts of the world and its ability to penetrate all levels of society. This process undermined old forms of social control and led to the rise of local strongmen who had links to foreign entrepreneurs but relatively few commitments to any centralized authority (Migdal 1988: 52–96). For Migdal the other global trend was the way in which colonial rulers tended to reinforce the propagation of the European market economy. 'Through specific policy decisions, colonizing rulers made crucial economic and political resources available to some but not to others in the local societies' (Migdal 1988: 105). Local strongmen thrived under these conditions and central authorities tended to be weakened. Migdal's persuasive argument raises a crucial question: how is it that while most newly independent developing countries had weak states and strong societies, the seven successful economies of East Asia, as most analysts agree, had strong states and weak societies?

In answering this question it is worthwhile beginning with the framework that Migdal himself employs and combining it with some aspects of the theoretical insights of Charles Tilly and Chalmers Johnson. Migdal (1988: 4, 269–75) outlines a set of requirements for the rise of strong states that have the capacity to penetrate society, regulate social relationships, extract resources, and appropriate or use resources in determined ways. At the start of the process, he notes (1998: 269), is 'the importance of massive societal dislocation, which severely weakens social control'. This dislocation he contends, is a necessary but not a sufficient condition for the emergency of a strong state. Migdal then suggests four other necessary factors to create strong states 'once the existing patterns of social control have been broken'. The first factor is 'a world historical moment in which exogenous political forces favour concentrated social control' (1988: 271–2). The second factor is 'the existence of a serious military threat from outside or from other communal groups inside the country' (1988: 273). The third factor posited by Migdal (1988: 274) is 'the existence of a social grouping with people sufficiently independent of existing bases of social control and skilful enough to execute the grand designs of state leaders'. The fourth and final factor is that 'skilful top leadership must be present to take advantage of the conditions to build a strong state' (Migdal 1988: 275). Interestingly, Robert Wade (1990: 337–42) has used Migdal's conditions to analyse the 'hard states' of Taiwan, South Korea and Japan but he does not go beyond this trio to see if Migdal's factors may also be applied to the other successful societies of East and Southeast Asia. This study argues that they can.

The work of both Charles Tilly and Chalmers Johnson on state development can help round out this set of conditions for the emergence of a strong state. Tilly, in expanding on his aphorism that 'war makes states' (1985: 170), emphasizes that over the many centuries of European state development the interaction of coercion and capital in state making is crucial (Tilly 1992). In particular, the origins of the resources used by the state in preparing for war or actually conducting war, and how they are mobilized, have an impact on the state's development. Indeed, it is clear from Tilly's analysis that strong states cannot emerge unless sufficient resources, be they in the form of money, skilled manpower, or organizational and technical knowledge, are available. For his part Johnson complements the last two conditions laid out by Migdal by emphasizing the need for, among other factors, 'the existence of a small, inexpensive, but elite bureaucracy staffed by the best managerial talent available' (Johnson 1982: 315); and 'a political system in which the bureaucracy is given sufficient scope to take the initiative and operate effectively' (1982: 315).

The strong state is, of course, crucial to the concept of the developmental state, which was first set out by Johnson (1982) and which has been explored by other analysts of East and Southeast Asia's political economy (see especially the collection edited by Woo-Cumings 1999, as well as, for example, Beeson 2004; Castells 1992; Deans 2000; Onis 1991). The developmental state, in its ideal form, is generally portrayed as being rooted in a nationalist project to ensure the survival of a society in the face of a major threat. Characteristically, it has a well-trained, elite state bureaucracy, with a lead or pilot agency, that is given sufficient scope to intervene in the economy to promote economic development. 'Developmental intervention' takes place on the basis of rational, pragmatic planning and is predicated on policy instruments that include the timely allocation of resources, incentives, strictly enforced performance criteria, and persuasion as ways of shaping the market. The developmental state is also associated with a blurring of the public–private divide, investment in education and a reasonably equitable distribution of wealth.

'Developmental intervention' took place in four areas of the economy (Li 2002: 82). These areas were physical economic infrastructure, including utilities; human infrastructure, including education; fiscal and budgetary policy; and industrial policy, including managing the domestic market. Each of these areas linked into the others and these linkages were crucial in promoting the overall growth of the economy. The degree to which the developmental state intervenes in each area obviously differed from society to society. Equally, over time the extent of state intervention may also vary in the same sector of the economy.

The approach taken in this study is very much an historical one. It looks at the development of the institutional states of the seven successful Asian economies, the economic policies they developed, and the economies themselves over an extended period of time (cf. McDonald 1996). Unlike many of the studies of the successful East Asian economies, the idea is not to take a snapshot of the economy and analyse the combination of factors that drives its success (or failure in the case of the Asian crisis of 1997–8) at that moment in time. Rather the purpose of this study is to analyse the unfolding of events over a number of decades – to shift from 'snapshots to moving pictures' as Pierson puts it (2000b: 72) – in order to demonstrate how specific historical events contributed to the way in which the state and the economy developed. Indeed, the analysis broadly follows an 'institutionalist' and more specifically an 'historical institutionalist' line of argument (Hall and Taylor 1996; Steinmo, Thelen and Longstreth 1992; Thelen 1999). Building on the working definition of an institution set out earlier, the purpose, then, is to identify how 'the regularized procedures, practices and norms that structure relations between individuals across the economy, polity and society' develop over time. The value of historical institutionalism is that it 'explicitly focuses on intermediate variables in order to integrate an understanding of general patterns of political history with an explanation of the contingent nature of political and economic development' (Thelen and Steinmo 1992: 28). Particularly helpful for the purposes of this analysis are a number of the core features of institutionalism and especially historical institutionalism.

First is the notion of path dependency. As William J. Sewell Jr's (1996: 262–3) widely used definition puts it, that 'what has happened at an earlier point in time will affect the possible outcomes of a sequence of events occurring at a later point in time'. More specifically, going down one path at a fork in the road means that future options, for example in terms of the creation of institutions and the adoption of specific policies, are restricted (Hall and Taylor 1996: 41; Krasner 1988: 83; Pierson 2000a). Once a particular set of institutions has been established, then patterns of institutional interactions emerge which can be a major constraint on future choices about institutional development and policy options. New institutions become more difficult to create if they are in competition with existing ones and existing institutions become more difficult to change or modify the longer they survive. In addition, as state institutions become entrenched so do many of the policies they promote. But, of course, institutions have to be created in the first place and, despite often becoming a part of the landscape, they do not always go on for ever. This raises the issue of the circumstances in which institutions are created, recreated and eventually give way to new or much-reformed institutions.

Second, historical institutionalism develops the idea of a critical juncture or watershed in the life of a society. G. John Ikenberry makes the point that '"Critical junctures" or episodic events refer to unanticipated and exogenous events that drive institution-building' and goes on to note that war is a significant 'catalyst of change from this perspective' (1988: 233). Critical junctures are usually precipitated by a crisis and produce a particular set of consequences (Collier and Collier 1991: 29–34). It is important to note that there may be a voluntary aspect to the set of consequences produced by a crisis in that choices may be made about how to deal with the problems that are created. New institutions may be established, old ones reformed and new policies adopted. But equally, it is possible that a crisis is of such a character and magnitude – a crisis prompted by the destructive effects of war, for example – that its consequences, or legacy, leaves a society with little choice as to how to respond. When a crisis does allow choices with regard to domestic policy, the response will depend on a number of factors. These include the character of the pre-crisis institutions; the nature of the crisis, for example the type of war to be prepared for or fought; the resources, including human and monetary, available to create new institutions; and cultural factors that may help to shape reformed and new institutions. Of course, the magnitude of a crisis and, therefore, the effects of the corresponding critical juncture, may vary. Some crises may engulf the whole of a society while others may have a significant impact on only a major policy area.

As Collier and Collier observe (1991: 31), there is no automatic outcome to a crisis but rather a particular set of consequences may be 'perpetuated through ongoing institutional and political processes'. This observation raises a third important aspect of historical institutionalism: the notion of feedback. Of course, feedback can be negative and the institutional arrangement or 'legacy' unstable and short-lived. However, as Stephen Krasner (1988:83) points out, a key to historical institutionalism is that, 'path dependent patterns are characterised by self reinforcing positive feedback'. This feedback can come in different forms. For example, it may be simply that particular policy goals are achieved. This result produces what some have called output or performance legitimacy (Scharpf 1999; Stubbs 2001) and a decidedly positive feedback for those institutions and policies responsible. Or, it may be that the institutional arrangement reinforces the power distribution within a society and, hence, receives vital support from the dominant elite groups. Equally, it is possible that positive feedback is generated because institutional structures and institutional actions conform to cultural needs and expectations. Whatever the reason, the result is that self-reinforcing or positive feedback creates a situation in which institutions and other actors adapt to the existing arrangement in ways that push them further down the path that has been chosen and further away from paths not chosen (Thelen 1999: fn27).

The three concepts of path dependency, critical juncture and feedback point to a fourth: the timing and sequence of events. As a number of comparative institutionalists indicate, it is not just what happens at any point in time that matters but *when* something happens. Equally significant is the order in which events take place (Ikenberry 1988: 225; Pierson 2000b; Tilly 1992: 14). Obviously, the order in which a series of crises affects a society may be crucial. For example, the sequence in which the destructive, formative or reformative effects of war are felt is clearly important. Similarly, the order in which different types of events, such as economic recessions, wars, or the gaining of independence, are experienced may have an impact on the development of a society's political, social and economic institutions. Equally, the timing of the way in which a series of international events intersect with the relatively independent unfolding of events within a society can be significant. It should also be noted that a relatively minor crisis may have more impact on institutions and policies that have been in place for a relatively short period of time while a more significant crisis may have less impact on a more mature set of institutions and well-entrenched policies. Certainly, the timing and order in which events take place can have a major impact on the particular path that a society takes through history.

Finally, while cultural factors alone cannot satisfactorily explain events, they should not be discarded altogether. Institutionalist scholars of various stripes have emphasized that culture can have an important role to play in the emergence, development and policies of institutions (Hall 1989; Katzenstein 1996; March and Olsen 1989; North 1990; Powell and DiMaggio 1991). Indeed, one aspect of culture, norms, is an integral part of the way institutions are viewed in this study. For the purposes of this analysis culture is thought of as a slowly evolving system of learned, shared meanings which members of groups, of varying sizes, use to help them make sense of the world and guide their behaviour. Taken here to include ideas, values, beliefs and norms as aspects of the 'shared meanings', culture can have a variety of effects on the institutions and the policies they put forward. It can shape the way societies perceive crises and the problems they produce, constrain the range of solutions put forward to solve particular problems, and help to legitimize certain policy proposals while making others less acceptable to the general community (Bell 2003; Campbell 1998; Thelen 1999).

Overall, then, a sequential historical institutionalist approach can help to identify ways in which the geopolitical context, in conjunction with other factors, contributed to the success of the seven East and Southeast Asian economies. Intriguingly, a number of analysts have noted factors that could be included in an analysis of the region's prosperity; however, they take a snapshot approach and tend to see each factor in discrete terms rather than as historically linked (e.g. Little 1979). However, other analysts have pointed the way noting the importance of the sequence in which events take place. For example, Robert Wade (1992: 312) and James Riedel (1988: 38) have referred to tumblers in a combination lock falling into place, while Frederic C. Deyo (1987: 239) has written about the need to take into consideration what he terms 'linkage sequencing'.

This approach, he suggests, comes out of 'the importance of external geopolitical factors in fostering the domestic political and institutional capacity to manage external economic relations' and is centred on 'a consideration of the sequencing and interaction of particular phases of external linkage' which 'permits a fuller understanding of the external underwriting of strong developmentalist states in East Asia' (see also Appelbaum and Henderson 1992: 5–11; Vogel 1991: 91).

However, although other commentators have adopted aspects of the approach used in this study, none has sought to provide the comprehensive examination of the 'miracle' economies set out in the following pages. Indeed, this book advances our understanding of the political economy of East and Southeast Asia in three significant ways. First, it examines the political and economic developments of all seven of the Asian 'miracle' economies – Japan, South Korea, Taiwan, Hong Kong, Singapore, Malaysia and Thailand – and contrasts them with those economies of the region that were less successful, such as the Philippines and Indonesia. Second, it sets out the development of the region's key political economies from before the Second World War to the first years of the new millennium, exploring both the region's triumphs and its crises. Third, it weaves together in an unprecedented fashion an analysis of the sequence of major geopolitical events of the region over the last century and an historical institutionalist approach to the political and economic development of the key economies of East and Southeast Asia.

2
The Old Order and Its Destruction

The Second World War had a devastating impact on much of East and Southeast Asia. The scale of the destruction was immense. Many social, political and economic institutions were washed away in the onslaught brought about by the fighting. The Japanese occupation of parts of China and its army's sweep through Southeast Asia combined with the American bombing campaigns of the final year of the war to ensure that in nearly every corner of the region much of the physical infrastructure was destroyed and the social institutions severely dislocated. One eyewitness to the Japanese occupation of Singapore saw 'a whole social system crumble suddenly before an occupying army that was absolutely merciless' (Lee 1998: 74). An American journalist who entered Tokyo a few days after Douglas MacArthur accepted the surrender of the Imperial Japanese government writes of its being a 'sea of rubble' (Christopher 1983: 17). And miles away in Hong Kong, 'thousands of buildings lay derelict, engulfed by vegetation and crawling with rats' (Snow 2003: 263). Even after the war's end, chaos and destruction rippled through the region as bouts of localized violence flared up in different places. Some fighting simmered on for months as the tensions and conflicts unleashed by the Second World War played themselves out. In Korea it produced a full-scale war.

Yet analysts of the region's later economic success either downplay the importance of the Second World War, or more usually, ignore it altogether. The many, essentially ahistorical, assessments of the rise of the seven 'miracle' economies – Japan, South Korea, Taiwan, Hong Kong, Singapore, Malaysia and Thailand – undertaken by those advancing a neoclassical economic perspective obviously omit the Second World War as a factor. Similarly, analysts offering a cultural or American-hegemony explanation neglect the impact of the war on later developments. The advocates of the cultural explanation tend to emphasize the timeless nature of culture and, therefore, do not see the war as a major landmark. Those who champion an American-hegemony explanation start their analyses with the beginning of the America's intervention in the region from the end of the Second World War onwards rather than going back to the events of Second World War itself. A few statists (e.g. Johnson 1982) acknowledge the importance of the war on the nature of the state that emerged in its aftermath but generally they begin their analysis with the advent of the strong state in the 1960s.

The one set of explanations that does take a longer, historical view of the rise of the 'miracle' economies is the Japan-centred approach (e.g. Cumings 1984a; Hsiao and Hsiao 2003; Kohli 1994). Those who adopt this approach stress the extent to which Japan's economic success prior to the outbreak of the fighting in the Pacific in 1941 laid the foundations for later success not only in Japan but also in its former colonies of Korea and Taiwan. Necessarily, they downplay the importance of the Second World War years as they wish to emphasize the continuity of the institutions and practices on which the rapid economic rise of Japan and its colonies was built both prior to and after the Second World War.

In contrast this chapter underscores the importance of the events of the Second World War. First, it sets out the major elements of the old order in the seven 'miracle' economies so as to understand which aspects of each society were destroyed by the war and which survived. This historical overview also emphasizes that the seven 'miracle' economies have very different backgrounds and, therefore, any attempt to attribute Asia's strong post-Second World War economic growth to, say, Japan's colonial legacy has severe limitations. Second, it details the devastating impact of the Second World War and argues that the war and the turmoil it left in its wake demolished much of the old, conservative order. Many of the social, political and economic institutions that had buttressed the pre-war system were either swept away or were so severely weakened that they could no longer preform their previous functions. Other institutions survived but often in a much altered state. In each of the seven societies examined in this study – Japan, South Korea, Taiwan, Hong Kong, Singapore, Malaysia and Thailand – the balance between continuity with the old order and change brought about by the war was slightly different. However, in each case the old order was sufficiently weakened that pre-war institutions could not resist adaptation to the new realities that engulfed East and Southeast Asia (Vogel 1991: 86). The discontinuities caused by the Second World War and its aftermath were crucial factors in East and Southeast Asia's economic growth (Haggard, Kang and Moon 1997). Because of the destruction of the old order brought about by the War and the conflicts that followed in its wake, the Cold War environment that pervaded East and Southeast Asia from the late 1940s onwards critically shaped the transformation of the old, weakened institutions as well as the development of the new ones.

The period of the Second World War and it tumultuous aftermath, then, constitute the first critical juncture in the series of events that are analysed in this study. Specifically, the argument of this chapter is that the remnants of the old order that withstood the destructive military actions of this period and aspects of the 'new order' that were created by the fighting and its consequences combined to provide the initial building blocks in the sequence of events that eventually produced the seven 'miracle' economies. The chapter first looks at the old order or 'antecedent conditions' in Japan, South Korea and Taiwan. These societies are bound together by Japanese imperial ambitions and so are usefully analysed as a group. Similarly, the British colonies of Hong Kong, Singapore and Malaya prior to the Second World War are examined together. The old order in Thailand, the one country in Southeast Asia that was not formally colonized, will be detailed separately as will be the undermining of the old order by the 1932 'Revolution' and its turbulent repercussions. The chapter then outlines the devastation caused by the Second World War and the associated aftershocks in each of the seven societies. It concludes with a review of the key conditions that emerged out of this first phase of events that paved the way for the later phenomenal growth of the seven economies.

The Old Order

Japan and Its Colonies

From 1868, when the emperor was officially restored to the centre of power and the Meiji era began, to the height of the Second World War, Japan's first period of rapid modernization went through a number of phases. Reforms in the political, economic and social life of the country, combined with international and domestic influences to shape the different stages in the country's accelerated development. As a result of these changes, by the early 1940s Japan had acquired a colonial empire, including Korea and Taiwan, and had emerged as a major economic and military force on the world stage.

Initial reforms entailed the centralization and consolidation of government around the popular notions of 'imperial rule' and 'national unity'. Full internal control was ensured by the establishment of a central bureaucracy and the development of a well-organized conscript army with relatively modern weapons. Key elements of the system of feudal privileges were abolished and the education system began a process of modernization under a new ministry of education. Although aspects of former feudal relations and values were still pervasive in Japanese society, much of the country's social life, especially in the cities, was noticeably transformed by the Meiji Restoration.

Seeking to get out from under the influence of the Western powers and the unequal treaties inherited from the shogunate, Japan's new leaders embarked on a series of initiatives with the goal of building a 'rich country, strong army'. Among the most important of these programmes were: establishing a national land tax system which stabilized the national budget; promoting a national banking system; building up the economic infrastructure, including railroad, postal, and telegraph networks; developing factories which were later sold to private interests; and helping promising firms by leasing and selling equipment and providing loans. The emerging major private sector firms, or *zaibatsu*, were the chief beneficiaries of government support with strategic industries such as shipbuilding given special preference as the government actively pursued the goal of catching up with the Western powers. As Calder (1993: 25) has argued, these policies 'strongly established the tradition of state involvement in providing business credit and subsidies to private firms'. Japan's political and business leaders, many of whom emerged out of the former samurai class and had transformed themselves into industrial entrepreneurs, were also determined to learn from the West. Western experts were brought to Japan to provide advice on everything from modern mining techniques to medicine. And students as well as high-level official missions were sent to various Western countries to acquire the latest technology and business practices which were then quickly, and often successfully, put into effect. Major productivity gains were made not just in industrial production but also in the agricultural sector during the Meiji period (Francks 1992).

The Meiji Constitution was drawn up in 1889. It produced a parliament, or Diet, in 1890 consisting of a lower House of Representatives, chosen by a very restricted electorate, and the upper House of Peers, initially at least mostly appointed members from the ranks of the old feudal nobility. Political parties – notably the Liberal Party, the Constitutional Progressive Party and the Constitutional Imperial Party – attempted to exert as much influence as they could over the prime minister and the cabinet. However, the Diet's powers were limited, with all executive authority vested in the emperor, who was also supreme commander of both the army and an increasingly modern and powerful navy. Essentially, the government was run through the emperor by an oligarchy composed of a 'small group of samurai who had participated in the Restoration movement and had worked together to build the Meiji state' (Ike 1963: 164). The oligarchy proved reasonably effective and cohesive. As a result, while there were a number of expressions of dissent from within the ranks of the politicians and occasionally open discord among the wider public, Japanese society was relatively stable.

By the 1890s Japan was approaching the original Meiji goal of having both a flourishing economy and a strong military. Evidence for this turn of events came in the mid-1890s when Japan took on the Chinese as both sought to control the Korean peninsula. Japan's decisive victory in the fighting, brought about in the main by its smaller, but more technologically advanced and tactically sophisticated navy, was evidence of its regional ascendancy. In 1902 the Anglo-Japanese Alliance was signed and in 1904 the Japanese navy soundly defeated a Russian naval fleet and later its army captured Mukden, the capital of Manchuria. Having acquired Taiwan after the 1894–5 Sino-Japanese War, Japan formally annexed Korea in 1910 and then generally extended its influence in Manchuria.

However, by the early years of the twentieth century, time had started to take its toll on the members of the original Meiji oligarchy. Slowly, the provisions of the constitution in tandem with a series of domestic and international events enabled members of five distinct, small, elite groups to gradually take over the exercise of power from the old oligarchy. First, there was the military elite. The chiefs of staff of the army and navy were directly responsible to the emperor and were given the 'right of autonomous command'. Moreover, those at the head of the army and the navy gained increased stature with the military victories over China and Russia. Second, there was the bureaucratic elite. Like the military they were directly constitutionally responsible to the emperor. The senior bureaucrats in the central ministries were key figures in decision making and their status was further elevated by a merit system by which only the very brightest became 'officials of the emperor'. Third, there was a group of influential advisors to the emperor. As the members of the original oligarchy died, their places as advisors to the emperor were taken by senior and respected ex-bureaucrats and ex-ministers. Their influence lay in the advice they gave the emperor on such vital matters as the selection of prime ministers. Fourth, there was the economic elite. This group was mostly made up of the leaders of the dominant *zaibatsu* (business conglomerates). As the instruments of the country's increasing prosperity and the source of the funding that parties needed to fight elections, the *zaibatsu* gained in stature as the economy grew and as democratic norms were advanced. Finally, there was the political party elite based in the Diet. Party leaders gained their power from the fact that the approval of the House of Representatives was required for any increase in the government's budget. As the country developed and the budget increased so did the influence of the party leaders.

Relations among the various elites were characterized by both competition and cooperation. Each group sought to influence major decisions about the path that the Japanese society should take but they were also brought together by their common interest in the emergence of an effective government. During the 1920s the party elite gained an ascendancy as democracy became a valued goal both within Japanese society and internationally. However, as the economy stumbled towards the end of the 1920s and the world depression started to affect Japan in early 1930, the military elite became increasingly influential. The military argued that the political parties and their allies among the economic elite were to blame for the economic failures of the country and in particular for the backwardness and poverty of the rural areas. The military elite also denounced the corruption of the politicians and what it, and a broader coalition of conservative nationalists, saw as a weak foreign policy. Assassinations of politicians at home, including the murder of a prime minister, were parallelled by assertive military actions in Manchuria and later in other parts of China. Bypassing the Diet, the military came to dominate the political life of the country and to exercise significant control over an economy which was increasingly geared to supporting the expansion of Japanese influence in China. From the outbreak of war in July 1937 onwards, large numbers of troops were deployed as the Japanese army occupied northern China and the fighting eventually spread to parts of central and southern China. With the attack on the American fleet in Pearl Harbor in December 1941 and the opening of the Second World War's Pacific theatre, the military controlled all aspects of Japanese life.

The militarization of Japan was especially significant for the way in which it affected the development of the economy in the 1930s and early 1940s. A massive increase in public borrowing, which was undertaken in order to escape the depression of the early 1930s, enabled the military to direct large amounts of money into heavy industry. Production in such areas as steel, vehicles, electrical equipment, ships and the aircraft needed for Japan's imperial expansion in China rose rapidly. Old *zaibatsu* were joined by new ones as well as by a rising number of small- and medium-sized enterprises as additional industrial productive capacity developed. At the same time the government intensified its commitment to national planning and to developing an industrial strategy that was rooted in economic nationalism. The form of neomercantilism that resulted from these policies supported the country's imperial goals. Banks and other credit-granting institutions were also centralized. The government acquired considerable authority to direct capital to specific industries and even companies. A heavier reliance on planning and greater central control over the economy brought additional responsibilities for the bureaucracy, especially the Ministry of Commerce and Industry (MCI). In turn responsibility generated power as the

MCI emerged to become the 'economic general staff' for the militarized government (Johnson 1982: 154–6). In particular, the MCI
managed the government–industry cooperation that was crucial for
the economic growth that was required to attain the imperial goals.

Japan's colonial empire was critical to the remarkable economic
development it achieved in the 1930s and early 1940s. The first colonial acquisition, in 1895, was Taiwan. The government, wishing to
underline the point that it was an equal of the Western colonizing
powers, moved quickly to establish total control over the island.
Firm, often abusive, rule through the use of the police, the military
and, what Cumings (1984a: 52) refers to as 'sharp "administrative
guidance"', was instituted. Agricultural development was given
priority from the outset with particular emphasis placed on the
production of sugar and rice for export to Japan. A land survey was
completed by 1906. It led to the establishment of property rights, the
elimination of absentee landlords, and the imposition of property
tax obligations that required landowners to find ways of increasing
production. Weights, measures and currency were unified; the
island's transportation and communication infrastructure was built
up; and irrigation systems constructed. The Japanese administration
also introduced scientific methods, new technologies and modern
business practices that helped to produce a marked increase in
agricultural productivity. At the same time it slowly established
a broad-based educational structure and improved the public health
system.

During the 1920s a period of limited political liberalization in
Taiwan was followed, beginning in the early 1930s, by a greater
degree of repression and assimilation. As increasingly militarized
Japanese government ventured into Manchuria and eventually, in
1937, went to war with China. As a result, Taiwan was drawn even
more closely into the Japanese economy and its role gradually
amended to support Tokyo's expanding imperial ambitions. From
the mid-1930s onwards the Japanese began to broaden the island's
economic base beyond the two commodities of sugar and rice. Ferti-
lizer production was increased to satisfy the growing Taiwanese
market and to ensure further increases in agricultural exports, some
Japanese textile machinery was moved to Taiwan, and metal products – most notably aluminium – and industrial chemical plants were
built. Consumer goods were also imported from Japan. The
increased profits resulting from these developments went directly to

Japan. And, after the attack on Pearl Harbor, as Japan extended its reach into Southeast Asia, Taiwan was assigned the task of processing the region's raw materials and then feeding them into the imperial war machine (Gold 1986: 43–4).

For Taiwan, then, the fifty years of Japanese rule brought many significant changes which yielded mixed outcomes. On the one hand, harsh treatment was compounded by the subservient position of the Taiwanese in the social, economic and political life of the island. And on top of this, towards the end of the Japanese period of occupation, school children and a significant number of bureaucrats and workers were forced to learn Japanese and to immerse themselves in Japanese customs. On the other hand, the Japanese brought with them to Taiwan many of the policies that had modernized the Japanese economy and produced such remarkable growth rates. The rule of law and a centralized government with a strong coercive and bureaucratic capacity brought about a relatively stable social order. An extensive infrastructure, modern scientific methods, the provision of public education for boys and girls, investment capital and guaranteed markets prompted a mobilization of the island's resources and, most impressively, a steady rise in agricultural productivity. Modern commercial institutions and elements of an industrial sector were also established. And while Japanese occupied the top positions in all elements of the society, 56 per cent of bureaucrats were Taiwanese, albeit mostly at the lower levels, and Taiwanese workers were employed in Japanese industrial plants and thus gained some knowledge of modern industrial techniques. The overall result of Japan's modernization of the island was a noticeable improvement in incomes, and the population's general standard of living. Indeed, it is likely that 'in 1945 Taiwan was the most agriculturally, commercially, and industrially advanced of all the provinces of China' (Wade 1990: 74).

Japan formally annexed Korea in 1910 although it had been highly influential in the peninsula since its victory in the Russo-Japanese War of 1904–5. In some ways the form of Japanese colonial rule, its goals, and its economic policies in Korea and in Taiwan were very similar. Korea's traditionally centralized, but relatively powerless, state was replaced by a firm, often harsh, central colonial authority. Order was maintained through the army when necessary, but more usually through the use of an expanded police force and a greatly strengthened bureaucracy. Both reached down into every village and urban neighbourhood. A land survey, completed by 1918, and property laws, based on those developed in Japan during the Meiji period, paved the way for property rights and for an effective taxation system. In order to maintain discipline among the peasantry, landlords were kept in place and, as in Taiwan, the colonial administration introduced more advanced agricultural methods to increase the production of rice and ensure a steady rise in the export of milled rice to Japan. In return Korea imported increasing amounts of Japanese manufactured goods. As in Taiwan, considerable investment was also made in the peninsula's roads, railways, port facilities, power supply and other aspects of the economic infrastructure as well as in the education system, especially at the elementary level. And, during the 1920s, just as in Taiwan, a limited number of locally owned businesses developed.

Where Korea's experience differs from that of Taiwan is in the timing and way in which the Korean economy was tied into Japan's economy in the 1930s. With the annexation of Manchuria in 1931–2, Korea's location made it the obvious economic base for Japan's push into China. Cheap hydroelectricity and raw materials such as coal, iron ore, copper, magnesium and tungsten from northern Korea were used to pursue the rapid industrialization of the colony. Japanese government and later *zaibatsu* investment in war-related, heavy industrial development meant that during the 1930s Korea's growth in manufacturing production averaged well over 10 per cent per year (Kohli 1997: 1280; Woo 1991: 31). Particular emphasis was placed on chemical and steel production in the north, and machinery, machine tools, heavy vehicles, electrical machinery, aeroplane parts, and consumer goods including textiles, in the south. Indeed, Korea's industrial capacity became so critical to the Japanese imperial war effort that Cumings (1984b: 487) has suggested that it 'probably accounted for about a quarter of Japan's industrial base by 1945'. In addition, Korea was supplying over half of its rice production to Japan with cheaper grains imported to feed Koreans. By the early 1940s Japan's wartime economy had become highly dependent on Korea and Manchuria both as sources for raw materials and industrial products and as markets for manufactured goods (Borthwick 1992: 198; Macdonald 1988: 182).

Material changes in Korea were matched by some key social developments. While the landed class remained firmly entrenched, large numbers of peasants, especially from southern Korea, moved into industrial jobs around the country. The number of Koreans employed in the industrial sector rose markedly during the period of heavy industrialization (Cumings 1981: 26). These industrial workers were a substantial portion of the total population of approximately 25 million. Many others were drawn into the police force and the bureaucracy. Also by the 1940s four million, or over 15 per cent, of the Korean population lived outside the country (Borthwick 1992: 200). Some were in Manchuria as unskilled labourers or as bureaucrats or members of the police, while many were moved to Japan as labourers of various kinds. Indeed, with so many male Japanese in the military and with the Japanese government refusing to admit Japanese women either into the military or the labour force, by January 1945 Koreans, including women and children, made up 32 per cent of Japan's labour force (Cumings 1981: 28–9; Mathias 1999). Korean women were also forced to serve as prostitutes, or 'comfort women', for the Japanese army as it ranged across East and Southeast Asia (Hicks 1996; Soh 1996).

By 1942 and the beginning of the war in the Pacific, Japan had forged, through war and imperial ambition, an integrated and relatively autarkic empire which served its expansionist goals. Building on the country's experiences during the Meiji period, the Japanese government implemented in their newly acquired colonies of Taiwan and Korea similar policies to those they felt had served them well in rapidly modernizing their own economy and society. Taking responsibility for economic development, the state worked with the privately owned businesses, primarily the *zaibatsu*, to develop particular policy tools, such as central planning, directed investment, the harsh treatment of labour, and the use of modern technology, to bring about strong industrial growth. In late 1944, however, the tide of war had begun to turn against the Japanese and it was increasingly cut off from its colonies. And by 1945 the destructive aspects of war had begun to consume not only Japan but also Korea and Taiwan.

The British Colonies

Three of the seven successful East and Southeast Asian economies – Hong Kong, Singapore and Malaysia – were originally British colonies. Of these Hong Kong and Singapore were city-ports. Hong Kong was pieced together by the British starting with acquisition of the island of Hong Kong in 1842 at the end of the first Anglo-Chinese

Opium War and ending with the takeover of the New Territories on a ninety-nine-year lease in 1898. The British ruled through a governor, an executive council and a legislative council, and a relatively small bureaucracy. Operating on the principle of 'free trade', the colony was first dependent on the trading of opium from India to China, and, in return, the trading of goods such as textiles, sugar and rice from China to Britain. It also became the port from which many Chinese emigrated to overseas destinations. As British trading and commercial interests in East and Southeast Asia escalated, and especially when Japan and Korea opened up to international commerce, Hong Kong's usefulness as a strategically placed natural harbour, coaling station and safe trading port grew. Moreover, as China's trade with the rest of the world expanded, so Hong Kong's role as an entrepôt became increasingly important. Indeed, by 1900 over 40 per cent of China's foreign trade went through Hong Kong (Hui 1999:34).

Despite being overtaken by Shanghai as the primary centre for British economic interests in China, from 1900 to the invasion by the Japanese in 1941, Hong Kong remained a steadily growing and important entrepôt and trading centre for the region. During periods of turmoil in China, Hong Kong received increased waves of immigrants, the majority of whom found work in the port's thriving trading and shipping industries. Trading and shipping-related activities, including shipbuilding, were clearly at the heart of Hong Kong's economy. However, from the early part of the century until immediately prior to the advent of the Great Depression, there was also a growing, mainly Chinese-owned and -operated, manufacturing sector. Hong Kong's politics altered little during this period. Political power was centred in the hands of a small but relatively efficient British-staffed colonial bureaucracy with the Chinese society of Hong Kong strongly discouraged from any political activity. The British maintained law and order, in the face of strikes and demonstrations, through the use of a strong police force and a few thousand troops.

Singapore had a very similar history to that of Hong Kong. An outpost of the East India Company, it was acquired by Sir Stamford Raffles in 1819 because of its great strategic potential as a safe harbour. It commanded the southern end of the Strait of Malacca, a vital trading route between Europe and the Far East. Administratively Singapore was merged with Penang and Malacca in 1824 to become the Strait Settlements. In 1867 the Strait Settlements became a crown colony with the usual British colonial institutions: an executive council made up of the governor and senior colonial administrators, and a legislative council made up of senior administrators and local businessmen appointed by the governor. This form of government remained essentially unchanged from 1867 to the Japanese invasion in December 1941 (Turnbull 1989: 106 and 208). In practice the colony, which became the administrative centre of the Strait Settlements and the heart of Britain's colonial territories in Southeast Asia, was run by a small cadre of colonial bureaucrats. As with other British colonies, the administrators stayed out of the everyday affairs of the local community. Their main task was to maintain law and order, to coordinate regional administrative practices when appropriate, and ensure that the port ran reasonably efficiently.

As with Hong Kong, Singapore's economic development up to the Second World War was centred around its secure harbour, its strategic location on a major trading route and its role as an entrepôt for the region. The colony really started to come into its own in the last quarter of the nineteenth century. The opening of the Suez Canal in 1869 underscored Singapore's value as a link in the chain of commercial stations tying Britain and India to Hong Kong, Shanghai and Japan. As Britain's industrial revolution took off, Japan opened its economy to trade, and steam ships replaced the old sailing so ships, so Singapore's business expanded rapidly. In the first two decades of the twentieth century Singapore was given a further boost by the opening up of rubber plantations and the boom in the tin industry in neighbouring Malaya. Singapore's port became the transshipment point for the export and import of goods for the Malayan peninsula as well as other parts of the region and the headquarters for shipping companies and agency houses which financed the expansion of the rubber and tin industry in Malaya. In addition, Singapore became a major naval base and repair depot for British operations in the Far East. Its defences were reinforced so that it could continue to command the critical sea lanes of the Strait of Malacca. In many ways, then, Singapore's location as a strategic military and trading port drove its economic development.

While Hong Kong and Singapore were city-port colonies, Malaya, which along with Sabah, Sarawak and Singapore was in 1963 to become Malaysia, was more of a traditional British colony. During the late eighteenth century and through the nineteenth century, the British pieced together a patchwork of colonial territories on the Malay peninsula. Penang and Malacca were Strait Settlements (along with Singapore) populated largely by Chinese immigrants and their descendants. The four Federated Malay States were each nominally ruled by a legally sovereign Malay sultan but were effectively ruled by British administrators. The five Unfederated Malay States were similarly ruled by Malay sultans with advice from British administrators who did not always have a clearly defined role. While Kuala Lumpur gradually emerged as the political centre of the peninsula, Britain's philosophy of indirect rule meant that, to some extent at least, power was shared with the Malay aristocracy, especially in the Unfederated Malay States. Indeed, British officials generally believed strongly in the continued political pre-eminence of the Malays over the Chinese and Indian immigrant populations. Many were sympathetic to the maintenance of a relatively efficient, but largely decentralized, administrative structure. This *ad hoc*, indirect approach to governing the peninsula continued up until the Japanese invasion in 1941.

Malaya's economic development was limited until the tin and natural rubber industries started to develop in the third quarter of the nineteenth century and the early part of the twentieth century. Tin had been mined in small quantities along the west coast of the peninsula for many centuries prior to the arrival of the British, but with the advent of the steam engine and other modern methods from 1880 onwards the tin industry in Malaya took off. Indeed, by 1904 Malaya produced half the world's tin (Turnbull 1989: 172). In the following years European miners introduced the gravel pump and dredge mining, both of which served to keep Malaya as the most efficient and largest tin producer in the world. At the same time rubber trees were being introduced into the country. Planting on British-owned estates and Asian smallholdings increased markedly during the early part of the nineteenth century so that by the early 1920s Malaya had become by far the leading producer of natural rubber in the world (Barlow 1978). Chinese migrants came to work the tin mines and Tamil Indians were brought in as labourers for the rubber plantations. To provide access to the tin mines and rubber plantations, and to move their products to market, a network of roads and railway lines were built that linked the interior of Malaya to Kuala Lumpur and to ports such as Port Klang, Penang and Singapore (Drabble 2000). By the late 1930s Malaya, with its nearly four million people, had become, in British colonial terms, a successful colonial territory, exporting rubber and tin to the world and importing British manufactured goods.

Thailand

From the 1851 accession to the throne of King Mongkut, until the coup of 1932, Thailand, or Siam as it was known prior to 1939, went through an extended period of reform and state centralization. Surrounded in the west and south by the British in Burma and Malaya, and in the east by the French in Indochina, both King Mongkut, who ruled from 1851 to 1868, and his son King Chulalongkorn, who ruled from 1868–1910, sought to mollify the two imperial powers through negotiations. At the same time, the threat from Britain and France led the Siamese rulers to massively increase the state's capacity so as to consolidate their own position and make colonial incursions less likely (Girling 1981: 45–50; Ramsey 1976). By the end of Chulalongkorn's reign, Siam had clearly defined its borders with Burma, Cambodia and Laos; developed a conscripted standing army to ensure internal security; created a centrally controlled police force and a centralized judiciary; and reached out to the West to acquire new knowledge and technology. But, the 'centrepiece of the new absolutist state was the civilian bureaucracy' which was 'the embodiment of the centralization of power' (Pasuk and Baker 1995: 235) The new bureaucracy was dominated by the members of the very large extended royal family, several of whom were sent overseas to be educated. However, as the salaried officials increased nearly seven-fold between 1890 and 1919, lower ranks were bolstered by a growing number of members from the wider society (Pasuk and Baker 1995: 236). The most important ministry was the Ministry of the Interior, which established control over even the most far-flung of provinces and essentially paved the way for the other ministries to exercise their authority throughout the country (Girling 1981: 53).

One reason why this centralization and state-building could take place during the late nineteenth and early twentieth centuries was the increase in economic productivity over the same period. King Chulalongkorn gradually abolished the feudal system of slavery and corvée, or forced labour; opened the door to increased Chinese immigration; built a new railway network linking Bangkok to most parts of the country; and reorganized and streamlined the collection of taxes. As with the Malayan economy, international developments, especially the opening of the Suez Canal and the introduction of the steamship, also helped bolster the economy by increasing demand for the country's main export commodity, rice. However, while more land was put into rice production and some advances were made in the processing of rice, relatively little was done to apply new technologies, such as the use of higher-yielding varieties or the installation of flood control and irrigation schemes on a large scale, to increase productivity in the rice-growing sector. Similarly, with Siam's three other export commodities, tin, teak and natural rubber, little was done prior to the Second World War to make use of new technologies and production methods. On top of this, the local small-scale industries suffered from the opening up of European agency houses in Bangkok at the end of the nineteenth century. They, and a growing number of Chinese merchants, quickly dominated the shipping, banking and insurance businesses and increasingly imported goods from overseas to satisfy the growing urban markets. Hence, while Siam's economy expanded during King Chulalongkorn's reign, it developed many of the same features as the British colonial economies in the region.

The 1932 'Revolution' undermined aspects of the old social order and paved the way for the rapid development of key political institutions. The 'Revolution' brought about the end of the era of absolute monarchy in Siam, markedly increased the power of the military and the bureaucracy and led ultimately to a period of greater economic nationalism. The 1932 coup was instigated by army and navy officers and bureaucrats. They reflected a growing resentment among the country's rapidly urbanizing elite towards the closed and distant nature of the country's political and military structures and especially towards the domination of the top military and government positions by members of the extended royal family. Spurred on by the worldwide depression, which hit Siam hard during the early 1930s, the coup leaders struck on 24 June 1932.

The period from 1932 to the signing of a formal alliance with the Japanese in December 1941 was politically turbulent. Different factions among the original coup leaders competed for power. Out of this manoeuvring came important developments. First, by 1935 the number of military personnel had doubled and the government spent 26 per cent of the national budget on the military (Pasuk and

Baker 1995: 256). Second, policies geared towards curtailing both colonial and Chinese immigrant influences in the economy and providing for a stronger role for the government in economic development were implemented. For example, in the late 1930s controls were imposed on Chinese immigration and Chinese businessmen were prohibited from participating in specific aspects of the economy. At the same time the government took over and increased public investment in public utilities and railways and the manufacturing of consumer goods. This new phase of economic nationalism, which was modelled in part on the Japanese Meiji period, was propelled forward by the slogan 'a Thai economy for the Thai people' and the renaming of the country 'Thailand'. Hence, by the time the Japanese arrived in December 1941, the military – bureaucracy alliance, albeit with some infighting, was firmly in control of the country and interventionist economic nationalists were highly influential in managing the economy.

The seven societies which eventually achieved 'miracle economy' status looked very different on the eve of the fighting in the Second World War's Pacific theatre. Japan possessed by far the most advanced economy. It had a strong central government and an industrial base that allowed the Japanese military to conquer much of East Asia. Yet it was highly dependent on the raw materials and markets of its colonial territories. Although they were both far behind Japan in their development trajectories, Korea and Taiwan also possessed dominant central governments and relatively modern agricultural and industrial sectors. Korea was slightly more advanced but both of these Japanese colonies relied heavily on Japanese capital, entrepreneurial and organizational skills, capital goods, and science and technology. Hong Kong and Singapore were classic entrepôts closely tied to Britain's commercial colonial empire. Each exported raw materials to Britain and other parts of the world, while acting as a transshipment point for, primarily British, manufactured goods destined for their respective hinterlands. They had also developed some shipping-related industries and commercial and financial sectors which served the entrepôt trade. Malaya was a typical British colonial possession. It had a relatively weak central administration and served British colonial interests by exporting tin and natural rubber and importing British finished goods. By contrast Thailand had sought to get out from under its semi-colonial links to Britain and France. It had already overturned aspects of the old order, developed a strong central government dominated by the bureaucracy and the military, and asserted its independence of both colonial and Chinese business influences through policies that centred on government intervention and public investment. However, many of these differences among the seven societies were about to be washed away by the destruction of war.

The Destruction of War

The end of the Second World War and the havoc and confusion that it left in its wake constitute a critical juncture in the series of events that ultimately led to the emergence of the seven Asian 'miracle' economies. Some argue that Japan was the most severely affected. Reischauer and Craig (1978: 190–1), for example, state that in 1945 Japan's 'newly won empire and ancient homeland both fell in ruins in perhaps the largest single catastrophe to overwhelm any nation in modern times'. But each of the other societies, except Thailand which had gone through a turbulent period of social dislocation in the wake of the 1932 'Revolution', was also greatly affected by the massive economic and social upheaval and extensive hardships that were generated by the Second World War and its often violent and chaotic aftermath. The result was that many elements of the old order were swept away either as a consequence of the fighting during the war or by the events it precipitated.

In Japan, the physical and human toll of the Second World War, especially during the last few months of the fighting, was immense. While American bombing raids took place in 1944, it was the elimination of much of the Japanese air force by early 1945 that allowed for increasingly effective low-level, night attacks on major Japanese cities. Saturation bombing was a common occurrence throughout the months leading up to the surrender of Japan. Most damage was done by incendiary bombs, often referred to as 'fire bombs', which set alight to the mainly wooden buildings in the major urban centres and created 'fire storms' that levelled large areas. And in August 1945 Hiroshima and Nagasaki were almost totally demolished by the first and only atomic bombs to be used in war. By the end of the war, more than 1.74 million soldiers, sailors and airmen as well as nearly 1 million civilians had been killed, almost 8 million people were homeless, and 40 per cent of Japan's urban areas had been destroyed

(Allinson 1997: 45–8; Chapman 1991: 5; Christopher 1983: 17–18; Dower 1999: 45–8; French 2003). The devastation of the final year of the war and Tokyo's surrender, then, clearly 'presented a true rupture with the past for Japan both domestically and internationally' (Hein 1993: 102).

In many ways the immediate post-war years of the American occupation only added to the destruction and misery experienced by Japan's 72 million people including the 5.1 million who returned to their homeland from around Asia in the first eighteen months after the war (Dower 1999: 54). Hunger was endemic. Rations provided only about a third to a half of what was generally thought to be required for a reasonably healthy existence (Allinson 1997: 48–52; Chapman 1991: 6). As a result of the hunger and the lack of basic amenities, such as running water and sewage disposal, in some towns and cities disease was difficult to control. And jobs were scarce. Key parts of the economic infrastructure, such as the railways and the power supply, had been destroyed. A large number of factories were similarly laid waste during the last few months of the war adding to the rolls of the unemployed. Many of the remaining factories that were still operational were later stripped of their equipment in order to provide reparations for those countries who laid claims against the Japanese for their wartime activities. The demobilization of the armed forces by General Douglas MacArthur, the Supreme Commander of the Allied Powers (SCAP), added to those seeking jobs. On the other side of the ledger, the closing down of all military-related industries drastically reduced the number of jobs available. Moreover, with Japan shorn of its colonies, Japanese industry lacked the raw materials to get many of the remaining factories up and running again. At the end of 1945 of the 72 million people in Japan over 13 million, or around 45 per cent of the economically active population, were estimated to be jobless (Chapman 1991: 8; Mitchell 1982: 44, 89).

The end of the Second World War also brought major social changes in Japan. The old leadership was disgraced and dismissed. The emperor was allowed to stay in office but with his political powers taken away he essentially became a symbolic figurehead. Seven of the top leaders, including the Prime Minister General Tojo, were hanged and others given long prison sentences. Top military officials, senior bureaucrats and business leaders were prohibited by SCAP from continuing in office or going back into business. At the same time *zaibatsu* holding companies were dissolved and the capital of *zaibatsu* families taxed with the aim of eliminating their wealth. And paramilitary and ultranationalist organizations that had been at the centre of pre-war Japanese politics were disbanded. Land-reform measures, introduced by SCAP, forced absentee landlords and those owning roughly over 2.5 acres to sell to the government, which in turn sold the land to former tenants (Tsuru 1993: 20–2). The old landed class was essentially destroyed, while the mass of small-scale farmers prospered in the post-war period of food short-ages and quickly developed into a large, conservative and influential segment of society.

Overall, then, Japanese society was radically altered by the events of the last few months of the Second World War and the first few years of the American Occupation. Much of the country lay in ashes and the general population was devastated by the fighting and its consequences. For the most part, the old conservative order was brushed aside. The military elite and the group of advisors to the emperor lost all power and only those politicians not associated with the militarization of Japan during the late 1930s and early 1940s survived to restore the Diet's role in the country's political life. The economic leaders who survived had to operate in new and innovative ways. And even in the bureaucracy, the institution that came through the war and the American Occupation relatively unscathed, officials had to adapt old habits and organizational structures to new circumstances.

With the surrender of Japan on 15 September 1945, the United States and the Soviet Union quickly agreed to divide responsibility for administering Korea. Each moved to rebuild its part of Korea in very different ways. North of the 38th parallel the Soviet administration was developed around local peoples' committees. In the zone south of the 38th parallel the Americans, unprepared for their responsibilities, established the US Army military government in Korea. Fearing that the people's committees and other local organizations that sprang up were agents of communism, it resurrected the old Japanese-colonial administrative structure, rehired a number of the conservative and moderate Korean bureaucrats, and brought back many of the Japanese-trained police. In 1948 the Americans held elections amid accusations of bribery and other forms of corruption and established the Republic of Korea (ROK). In the north, the Soviets also held elections and founded the Democratic

People's Republic of Korea. The occupying forces on both sides of the 38th parallel were withdrawn, leaving two competing camps, created in their occupiers' images, to face each other. In South Korea the new ROK government, under Syngman Rhee, proved to be not only highly corrupt but also incompetent. It simply compounded the problems that had emerged under the American occupation forces.

Neither the American military administration nor the ROK government were capable of fully containing the social ferment and economic chaos that gripped the peninsula in the wake of the end of the war and the collapse of Japanese colonialism. As Alice Amsden (1989: 35) has noted, the 'end result of Japanese colonialism in Korea was a society that was unable to support itself and totally at odds. Peasant opposed landlord, and those who resisted Japanese colonialism opposed those who collaborated.' The deep divisions between the peasants and uprooted labourers on the one hand, and the landlords and small conservative Korean elite created by the Japanese on the other hand, were only exacerbated by the economic problems that the new political division prompted. With the country divided, trade with Manchuria and Japan abruptly coming to a halt and the loss of Japanese management and entrepreneurial skills, the economies of both parts of Korea were in serious trouble. The southern zone was cut off from the raw materials and industrial capacity of the northern zone which in turn lacked the money, skills and markets to quickly revive its own economy. As a consequence large numbers of workers returned from the mines, power plants and industrial factories of the north to their homes in the south only to find the situation just as bad as in the towns and cities they had fled. Social unrest was endemic and on such a scale as to produce a 'cauldron' of peasant rebellion, labour strife, guerrilla warfare and open fighting along the 38th parallel. As a result of this tumult, between the end of the Second World War and the beginning of the Korean War, approximately 100,000 Koreans lost their lives to fighting and economic hardship (Cumings 1981: xxi, xxv; Merrill 1983: 136).

The Korean War, which broke out in late June 1950, ultimately left the peninsula totally devastated. Initially, the North Korean army swept down the peninsula with the army of the South holding on precariously to a small area around Pusan. In the few months that the North occupied the region, landlords lost their traditional power base in the country as much of their land was confiscated and redistributed to tenants. The fighting also produced a good deal of destruction. The Americans, under the UN flag, then launched a counter-attack which forced the North to retreat all the way up to the Yalu River. Large portions of the major urban centres and many rural villages were destroyed as the American air force bombed strategic areas of the peninsula and the UN forces fought their way northwards. The Chinese then entered the battle and forced the front line back to close to the original 38th parallel dividing line. During this phase of the war the fighting was intense and ravaged much of North Korea. It also created more problems for the South in that about 2 million refugees fled the fighting, flooding the already chaotic and economically destitute southern towns and cities with another round of refugees. Altogether about 4 million Koreans, Chinese and UN forces lost their lives during the Korean War (Macdonald 1988: 52). In South Korea it was estimated that more than 1.3 million had been killed, wounded, missing, or were prisoners of war. The overall economic damage was conservatively estimated at one year's gross domestic product (Lowe 1997: 254; Macdonald 1988: 52; Rees 1964: 460–1). The Korean peninsula lay in ruins.

In Taiwan the process by which the island's society and economy became unravelled was rather different, but the results were nearly as devastating. During the Second World War general neglect and American bombing in the later stages of the fighting 'reduced much of the island's industrial plant and infrastructure to rubble' (Gold 1991: 26). The end of the Second World War only compounded the problems faced by the Taiwanese. Obviously with Japan's surrender all the Japanese administrators, businessmen and workers left, taking with them their organizational, technical and managerial skills. Then, in accordance with the Cairo Declaration of 1943 and the Potsdam Declaration of July 1945, Taiwan was handed over to the Nationalist, or Kuomintang (KMT), government in China. The result was 'a period of rapid underdevelopment' (Gold 1986: 49). Substantial portions of Taiwan's stock of raw materials, especially rice and sugar, and its remaining industrial plant were shipped to the mainland not only to bolster the KMT cause in the civil war but also for private gain. At the same time the new government proved to be corrupt, incompetent and incapable of maintaining minimum standards of law and order.

The post-Second World War chaos in Taiwan came to a head at the end of February 1947. Sparked by the beating of a woman selling black market cigarettes and the shooting of a bystander, large crowds of Taiwanese turned on their mainlander oppressors. A period of violence ensued during which several Taiwanese-run local administrations were established. In early May the Nationalists sent over from the mainland more than 10,000 troops who restored the Nationalist government to power across the island. By the end of May nearly 20,000 Taiwanese had been killed, many from Taiwan's social and intellectual elite (Gold 1986: 50–2). And the economic problems mounted. In particular, inflation, spurred on in part by the transfer of capital from the war-torn mainland, took hold to such a degree that wholesale prices in Taipei increased by 3,500 per cent in 1949 (Ho 1978: 104). By early 1950, then, much of the economy was foundering.

Compounding the island's economic woes, the slow trickle of mainlanders taking refuge on Taiwan had become, by late 1948, a flood. Once it became obvious that the KMT was about to lose the war against the Chinese Communist Party on the mainland, their leader, Chiang Kai-shek, sent his son, Chiang Ching-kuo, to Taiwan to prepare for the inevitable retreat. In his attempt to stabilize the island, Chiang Ching-kuo instigated another brutal wave of repression against local and mainland opponents. Those who were not executed were locked away. He also set about developing an extensive security framework, which was designed to ensure the continued supremacy of the KMT, and rounded out his efforts by declaring martial law in December 1949. By early 1950, the exodus of nearly 2 million mainlanders made up of KMT administrators, military personnel, their families and other refugees had increased the island's population from 6 million to 8 million. In a few short years Taiwan's economy had been destroyed and its society transformed.

For the three British colonies, the combination of the havoc caused by the Japanese invasion, the hardships created by the occupation, and the chaos of the post-Second World War years left their societies severely dislocated and their economies in tatters. Japan invaded Hong Kong on 8 December 1941, the day after the attack on Pearl Harbor. 'By Christmas Eve Hong Kong was "a sea of fire"' (Snow 2003: 71). Over the next few years, hundreds of thousands were driven out of Hong Kong by the lack of basic services and the shortages of food. By the summer of 1945 there was open consumption of opium; empty houses were being stripped 'of anything that could be used as firewood including their wooden floorings, window-frames, staircases and even front doors'; and 'grass grew in the streets' (Snow 2003: 214–15, 263). As one observer has noted, at the end of the Japanese occupation the British returned to 'a run-down, war-damaged, pre-industrial society with no very evident future' (Youngson 1982: 2, cited in Burns 1991: 108). Following the return of the British, Hong Kong, rather like Taiwan, was caught up in the Chinese civil war. Refugees flooded into the colony to such an extent that a wartime population of 600,000 rapidly grew to 1.6 million by 1948. At the same time Hong Kong's economy was slow to recover. The port-city's entrepôt role was undermined by the detrimental impact that the civil war had on the mainland's economy and the relatively weak regional economy.

As they retreated down the Malayan peninsula to Singapore in the face of the Japanese invasion of December 1941, the British adopted a 'scorched earth' policy. This policy, and the battles that took place as the Japanese moved closer to Singapore, destroyed many port facilities, roads, railways and bridges, and much of the machinery in the important tin mining industry. After about eight weeks of intense fighting Singapore formally surrendered to the Japanese on 15 February 1942. During the occupation years both Singapore and Malaya suffered from neglect with many buildings and elements of the economic infrastructure falling into disrepair. Adding to these problems, from late 1943 onwards food became increasingly scarce and the general population suffered from various levels of malnutrition. Moreover, the end of the Japanese occupation and the return of the British did not bring any great respite. In both Malaya and Singapore the British Military Administration (BMA) found it impossible to maintain law and order . Particularly troubling was the racial violence which had its roots in the Japanese policy of incorporating Malays into an administration whose treatment of the Malayan Chinese community was very harsh (Cheah 1983). In addition, the British colonial administration had great difficulty providing both Malayans and Singaporeans with an adequate daily ration of rice at a fair price (Stubbs 1989b: 20–1).

The economic problems faced by Malaya and Singapore presented fertile ground for the growth of the Malayan Communist Party (MCP). Eventually, in June 1948 a state of emergency was declared. It signalled the beginning of a guerrilla war between the rural-based armed units of the MCP, many of whom were originally from Singapore, and the Malayan government (Chin 2003; Short 1975; Stubbs

1989b). The government's inept economic and social policies exacerbated the terrible conditions and generated support among the Malayan-Chinese community for the MCP guerrillas. Social tensions, especially those between the Malay and the Malayan-Chinese communities, increased and attacks on rubber plantations and tin mines made post-war economic recovery even more difficult. Indeed, by early 1950 the situation for the government looked very bleak. The costs of fighting the emergency meant that the government faced 'a serious financial crisis' and official reports indicated that communism was 'getting a more and more serious hold' (Stubbs 1989b: 83, 98). In both Malaya and Singapore social and economic chaos was clearly on the immediate horizon.

For Thailand, which had suffered its traumatic disruptions in the decade after the 1932 'Revolution', the Second World War was not the cataclysmic event it was for most of its neighbours. In accordance with the country's long-standing policy of mollifying major powers that threatened its sovereignty, the government of Phibun Songkhram signed a military alliance with Japan on 12 December 1941. The alliance gave Japanese troops a base from which to launch their attack on Malaya and Singapore. For this and other favours Thailand was awarded jurisdiction over adjacent parts of Cambodia, Laos, Burma and Malaya. However, not all Thais were in accord with the government's policy and, as Japan's hold on the region became increasingly tenuous, a Free Thai Movement emerged. The Movement was backed by the US and facilitated by Pridi Phanomyong, who was the regent at the time acting in Bangkok on behalf of the absent school-age King Ananda. The end of the war required the Thai government to undertake some careful diplomatic manoeuvring. The British demanded reparations. However, the new prime minister, Seni Pramoj, who replaced the discredited Phibun and who had been Thailand's wartime ambassador to Washington, denounced all agreements with Japan and requested that the United States intercede on its behalf to persuade the British to moderate their demands. Thailand was forced to give back the territory it had gained but was otherwise dealt with very leniently. Internally, the military was weakened and lost its influence because of its association with the Japanese. For a short period the forces of democracy, led by Pridi, gained the upper hand. However, infighting, during which those who favoured democracy were labelled by some as communists, the unexplained violent death of the king, and severe, debilitating economic problems brought on by the post-war regional economic malaise eventually led to the return of the powerful military in a coup in November 1947.

The period of the Second World War and its chaotic aftermath were clearly a watershed for what was to become East and Southeast Asia's 'miracle' economies. The physical destruction of the towns and cities, especially capitals, and of the economic infrastructure was devastating. The large numbers of people killed, injured or forced to flee their homes meant that the social fabric of the six of the seven societies were in tatters while the seventh, Thailand, was still recovering from the post-1932 coup upheavals. Certainly, much of the old, conservative social order was severely crippled by the events of this period. As a result, the social and political arena was left relatively clear for new institutions to be constructed. However, the general state of the region was so bad by the late 1940s that nearly every analysis of the time assumed that these societies were essentially condemned to perpetual poverty and would for ever be preoccupied with chronic levels of political and social instability.

Conclusion

The initial building blocks that eventually led to the creation of the seven 'miracle' economies were shaped by the events of the Second World War and its tumultuous aftermath. Most of the main social, political and economic institutions that were created in the period prior to the Second World War were either destroyed or severely weakened by the fighting during and immediately after the war. Those that did survive relatively intact, such as the bureaucracies in Japan and Thailand, gained a central role in the post-Second World War life of their societies. But many institutions did not survive the war or were so diminished by the events of the war that they became virtually irrelevant to post-war social, political and economic developments. Most significantly, the conservative social and political institutions that buttressed the old order in each of the societies under examination here, except to some degree in Thailand, were major casualties of the widespread social dislocation caused by the waves of fighting during the war and in the years immediately afterwards.

Did the relative prosperity of Japan, Korea and Taiwan during the period prior to the Second World War make their economic success in the decades following the war inevitable? Certainly, those who argue that there is a 'phoenix factor' at work, in the way that losing states in wars quickly recover the ground that their economies lost, take this position (Kugler and Arbetman 1989; Organski and Kugler 1977; Organski and Kugler 1980). However, such studies are limited to aggregate analyses of major powers and tend to have difficulty incorporating such confounding factors as the recession of the 1930s, the Marshall Plan in Europe and – as will be demonstrated in the next two chapters – US aid to East and Southeast Asia. Significantly, Wheeler (1975; 1980), who also examines the history of the impact of war on economic development, concludes that wars have very different effects on different societies. His overall argument is that war 'generally affects the industrial growth of states negatively' and that the 'greater the sacrifice of lives, the more harm was done to the state's industrial growth (Wheeler 1975: 52).

Clearly, there was nothing inevitable about the return of Japan, South Korea and Taiwan to rapid growth in the post-Second World War years. Indeed, the war rent asunder key linkages that fuelled the rapid growth in the economy of the Japanese imperial system. Raw materials were no longer shipped from Manchuria, Korea and Taiwan to Japan. Industrial production in northern Korea, which had complemented production in Japan, was brought to a halt. Korean workers in Manchuria and Japan returned home as did Japanese managers and workers. Japanese investment in Korea and Taiwan all but ceased. And Japan no longer had its empire as a protected market for its goods. Importantly, of course, neither Manchuria nor North Korea, despite having been within the Japanese imperial system, regained the kind of growth in their economies in the post-war years that they had experienced under the Japanese. In other words, being under Japanese colonial rule did not guarantee rapid economic development in the post-war decades. And as the success of Hong Kong, Singapore, Malaysia and Thailand indicate, it was not necessary to have a Japanese colonial background in order to be part of the Asian 'miracle'.

This is not to suggest that the pre-war experiences of Japan, Korea and Taiwan are unimportant. Despite the fact that most of the economic infrastructure, major buildings, social, political and economic institutions and practices were demolished by the fighting, or were so severely battered or enfeebled as to be unrecognizable, a few did survive the war and its horrendous aftermath. These surviving remnants of the pre-Second World War Japan and of Japanese colonialism, in addition to the technical and organizational knowledge and skills retained by the many who lived through the colonial period, could in theory be put to good use. However, the knowledge and skills had to be disseminated and most importantly the social, political and economic institutions that could use the knowledge and the skill sets that many in the population had gained during the pre-war years had to be put in place. As Kobayashi (1996: 325) has commented, 'it was the intrusion of the American influence in the region that allowed the early postwar regimes in South Korea and Taiwan to make effective use of [the] legacy of the Japanese colonial period'. It is to the impact of the American influence on East and Southeast Asia and the emergence of the Cold War that this study now turns.

3

Saved by the Korean War

The Korean War broke out on 25 June 1950 and had an immediate and dramatic impact on the geopolitics of East and Southeast Asia and the economic fortunes of the region. Some analysts of Asia's economic success acknowledge the importance of the Korean War to the process of creating the 'miracle' economies. In particular, those who seek to explain the success of the Asian economies in terms of the exercise of US hegemony have recognized the Korean War as marking the beginning of US involvement in the region (e.g. Cumings 1984a). Similarly, early analysts who employ the neoclassical economic explanation and some who adopt a statist perspective in accounting for the success of the seven 'miracle' economies note the significance of American economic and military aid in helping to get the economies of Japan, Taiwan and later South Korea on their feet after the devastation of the Second World War and its aftermath (eg. Cole 1980; Johnson 1982).

However, the full range of consequences of the Korean War for the region's political economies is not widely recognized. For example, US aid has invariably been examined in isolation, rather than in conjunction with other factors. As a result, the synergistic importance of US aid to the building of the institutions that formed the foundations for the later success of the economies of Japan, Taiwan and South Korea is often underplayed (e.g. Little 1979: 465–500; Reidel 1988: 25; Scott 1979: 371; Wade 1990: 82–3). Moreover, while the impact of the Korean War on Japan, South Korea and Taiwan has been explored in some detail, the war's effect on the other 'miracle' economies – Malaysia, Singapore, Thailand and

Hong Kong – has generally been ignored or underestimated. This is not just the case for those who use the cultural or Japan-centred explanations but also for the proponents of the neoclassical economic, statist and US-hegemony explanations of the Asian success story. The need, then, is for a full analysis of the effects of the Korean War on all of the 'miracle' economies, beginning with the crucial consequences of the outbreak of the fighting.

The North Korean army's capture of Seoul and its successful drive south down the peninsula forced the United States government into a clear-cut and long-term decision about its strategic commitments in East and Southeast Asia. Having pulled the last of its combat forces out of South Korea in July 1949, members of the Truman Administration and Congressional leaders engaged in a wide-ranging debate about American policy towards East and Southeast Asia in light of what was perceived to be an increasing communist threat. Discussion focused especially on whether the threat to Western Europe was greater than the threat to East Asia; how to deal with the new communist government in China; if and how to support the governments of South Korea, Taiwan and French-held Vietnam; and whether to try to reinvigorate the Japanese economy so as to create a bastion against the spread of communism in Asia (Cumings:1990: Fleming 1961: 592–7).

With the advent of the Korean War these discussions became moot. As Dean Acheson, the secretary of state at the time, noted a few years later, 'Korea came along and saved us' (Cumings 1990: 761, 918). He meant, of course, that the Korean War allowed the Truman Administration to ward off Republican criticism that it was soft on communism and to rally Congressional and wider public support for 'a rapid build-up of America's political, economic and military strength' in preparation for the confrontation with the Soviet Union that was thought to be inevitable. The Administration's plan was set out in a National Security Council document known as NSC-68 and officially became policy in April 1950. But there was some reluctance within Congress and the country to contemplate funding the NSC-68 programme. The outbreak of the Korean War united the country and produced a speedy and substantial rise in annual military spending from 'a fiercely maintained ceiling of US$15 billion' to 'nearly US$50 billion in 1953' (Horowitz 1965: 260; Levin and Sneider 1983: 38). As Acheson noted in his autobiography on his time as secretary of state, 'it is doubtful whether anything like what happened in the next few years could have been done had not the Russians been stupid enough to have instigated the attack against South Korea' (1969: 374).

But the Korean War also 'saved' six of the 'miracle' economies of the region and helped transform the seventh. In the short term, the Korean War and the onset of the Cold War meant that large amounts of military spending as well as military and economic aid were pumped into the region. This new-found revenue resuscitated the depressed economies of Japan, Taiwan and eventually South Korea. The stockpiling of what was feared might become scarce raw materials needed to conduct the Korean, and a possible European, War similarly had a major impact on the economies of Malaya, Singapore and Thailand. The Korean War also cemented in place America's long-term commitment to providing economic and military aid to what were seen as the key East and Southeast Asian fortresses of Japan, South Korea, Taiwan and Thailand, against the threat of communist expansion in the region. Furthermore, the Cold War spending by the US, as well as by the European states that feared that the Korean War was the prelude to an invasion by the Soviet Union across Western Europe, created a regional and worldwide prosperity that further helped to revive the economies so severely battered by the Second World War and its aftermath. And the outbreak of fighting on the peninsula transformed the economy of Hong Kong. The city-port saw its role as an entrepôt virtually eliminated by the entry of China into the war and the consequent cessation of trade between the new communist state and the major Western powers. Hong Kong was forced to rely on the wealthy refugees fleeing the newly installed communist government in China to get its economy up and running again.

The Korean War, then, must be considered a second critical juncture. During the crucial transition period of the Korean War, and the years immediately after the cessation of fighting in 1953, key institutions were put in place and reforms to old institutions undertaken that established a distinct trajectory for the social, political and economic life of the seven societies under review. Importantly, because of the events of the Second World War and it turbulent aftermath, most social, political and economic institutions in the seven societies had been so severely weakened that they could easily be reorganized and adapted to the new circumstances. In some cases entirely new institutions could be created. The destructive and disintegrative effects of the Second World War were followed by the formative and developmental effects of the early years of the Cold War. The sequence in which these events took place was decisive.

This chapter details the many ways in which the Korean War set the stage for the later development of the seven 'miracle' economies. It reviews the means by which the Korean War 'saved' ailing economies around East and Southeast Asia. It also examines the way in which the Korean War helped to secure in place key new, and transformed, political and economic institutions in the seven societies under study. Obviously the Korean War had different effects on each society. These effects depended on the amount of resources made available and through what channels, the nature of the existing political and economic institutions, and the role that society played in each political economy. The chapter looks first at Japan and Taiwan, both of which received massive injections of capital and other forms of aid from the US. Then, the experiences of Malaya, Singapore and Thailand in relation to the Korean War are examined. Each benefited considerably, although indirectly, from the outbreak of war in the Korean peninsula. The chapter goes on to explore the way in which the war affected the politics of South Korea and its long-term military and economic relationship to the US. Finally, the chapter reviews how the Korean War, in conjunction with the civil war in China, transformed Hong Kong from a major entrepôt to a growing export manufacturing centre.

Japan and Taiwan

For Japan the Korean War was, in Prime Minister Yoshida's words, 'a gift of the gods' or as others have put it a 'very welcome "divine wind"' (Bowen 1984: 2; Dower 1979: 315; Samuels 1994: 133: Tsuru 1993: 72). Certainly, when the Korean War broke out the Japanese economy was in a desperately weakened state. From the end of the Second World War to the start of the Korean War it had sputtered along bogged down by bouts of inflation, high levels of unemployment, a steady stream of bankruptcies and a severe shortage of foreign exchange with which to buy much needed raw material and industrial machinery. In the first few years of the occupation American officials gave the economy relatively little consideration. Their efforts were focused on dismantling the military and industrial machinery that had been the foundation of the Japanese war effort and turning Japan into a parliamentary democracy. By the end of 1947, however, this policy began to be re-evaluated in the light of the growing confrontation with the Soviet Union and the success of the communists in the Chinese Civil War. An economically strong Japan was increasingly seen as a necessary bulwark against the expansion of communism in Asia. The work of the American Occupation Forces turned from reform to recovery. Basic industries such as coal and steel were given priority; the delivery of reparations was stopped; and American aid, mostly in the form of food aid to prevent starvation in the cities, was begun.

But the problems of a weak economy plagued by inflation and trade deficits that had to be underwritten by the American treasury persisted. In order to combat these problems, the American government announced a nine-point stabilization plan. A banker, Joseph Dodge, was sent out to implement it. The 'Dodge Line', as this programme of action became known, set out to introduce fiscal austerity by, among other policies, reducing domestic consumption and cutting government spending while at the same time promoting exports. The budgets for public works, welfare and education were cut. Subsidies and loans to priority industries were eliminated. In order to allow workers to be more easily laid off, labour laws were revised; the activities of labour unions, which had initially been encouraged, were severely curtailed; and communist leaders were driven out in the 'red purges' of 1950. The exchange rate was fixed at 360 yen to the dollar so as to stimulate exports and rules governing intercorporate stockholdings, mergers and multiple directorships were relaxed to allow the corporate sector to get back on its feet. But with a worldwide recession limiting any attempts at developing export markets and the Japanese domestic market contracting, Dodge's 'deflationary' policy produced such harsh economic conditions that there was a general sense of frustration and disaffection throughout the country. (Bowen 1984: 7; Dower 1999: 541; Johnson 1982: 200). Indeed, in the first half of 1950 every prediction about the fate of the Japanese economy was pessimistic in the extreme.

The Korean War had an immediate and dramatic impact on the severely depressed Japanese economy. In order to intervene in the Korean peninsula General MacArthur needed to put in place a secure supply line. Moving supplies from the United States across the Pacific by sea would take weeks and months while supplies could reach Korea from Japan in only hours and days. MacArthur and Washington wanted to move quickly. The obvious strategy was to use Japan's excess industrial capacity, close proximity to the battle lines and low-cost labour to support America's military campaign in Korea. Indeed, Japan was quickly turned into America's frontline base for its operation in Korea. Orders, or 'special procurements' were quickly placed with Japanese companies for everything from munitions to trucks, from cement to boots and mittens (Bowen 1984: 13–14).

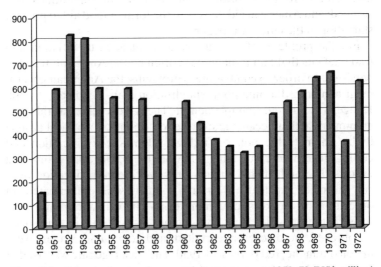

Figure 3.1   Japanese income from special procurement, 1950–72 (US$ million)
Sources: Data from Allen 1965: 278; and Schaller 1997.

This special procurement by the American military instantly injected much-needed dollars into the Japanese economy and acted as a catalyst for rapid economic growth. Estimates of the amount of money that the US military spent on the special procurements vary, but generally they suggest that dollar payments for special procurements totalled around US$2.5 billion over the course of the Korean War with overall spending on war-related supplies reaching US$3 billion. (Bowen 1984: 8–9; Dower 1999: 542; Johnson 1982: 23, 220; Nakamura 1981: 41). This boon to the Japanese economy was in addition to the US aid that had already been channelled into Japan and which, by the end of the Occupation in April 1952, added up to approximately US$1.7 billion dollars' worth of goods, mostly food and fuel (Adams and Hoshi 1972: 67).

The sum of dollars pumped into the Japanese economy through special procurements was enormous for the time and produced a veritable explosion in production. By the end of the war Japan was able to import nearly US$2 billion worth of goods annually while exports grew dramatically (Borthwick 1992: 244; Bowen 1984: 8). There is a wide consensus among those who have examined this period in Japan's history that the timely flood of capital, the introduction of new technology and the advent of a ready and voracious market were critical foundations for Japan's later rapid economic growth (e.g. Borden 1984; Hein 1990; 1993). For example, G.C. Allen (1965: 19) states that, 'It is scarcely possible to exaggerate the importance of these payments [special procurements] to Japan's economic recovery during the critical years after 1951', while John P. Bowen (1984: 53) asserts that, 'What Japan is today can, in large measure, be traced to the Korean War.'

The fruits of this economic upswing were distributed across a number of industries and had a dramatic and long-lasting impact on the Japanese economy. For example, during 1952, Nissan manufactured over 600 jeeps and nearly half the trucks it produced went to the US military. Toyota boosted its production by 40 per cent and the president noted that, 'These orders were Toyota's salvation' (quoted in Dower 1999: 542–3; see also Samuels 1994: 137; Tsuru 1993: 58). Shipbuilding, which had been a major industry in the 1930s, had been sidelined after the Second World War. But with a worldwide demand for new ships rapidly increasing and with the growing need for ships to carry supplies to the front lines in Korea, Japan's shipbuilding and repair capacity was quickly expanded and the industry was able to develop a solid foundation from which it went from strength to strength. Japan also supplied Korea with miles of steel rails, new and used locomotives, and rail cars giving a boost to the iron and steel industry and the machine tool industry. The demand generated by the war was especially important in helping to implement a planned rationalization of the iron and steel industry aimed at increasing capacity and efficiency. Overall, 'nearly 3000 companies had war-related contracts and many others arranged with US companies and the Defense Department to acquire new technology' (Schaller 1997: 48).

The impact of the Korean War boom and US special procurements also went well beyond the injection of dollars into key industries It stimulated an influx of new technology on which Japan's industrial development was later developed. For example, it was during the Korean War years that Japanese companies 'learned the fundamentals of standardized parts manufacturing, testing standards, and quality control' (Samuels 1994: 141). Major exporting companies of the future, such as Nissan, Toyota, Bridgestone and Kawasaki, were able to use the experience of filling special procurement contracts to incorporate new technologies into the production processes. Workers were trained to use the advanced technological skills that US procurement requests demanded.

Equally critical to the country's later rapid economic development were the formal political institutions that were created immediately prior to and during the Korean War years. The political battle that had emerged in the post-Second World War years between the socialists and communists on the one hand and the conservatives on the other was essentially resolved in favour of the conservatives. The Korean War confirmed the shift in the centre of gravity in Japanese politics to a new set of conservative politicians and bureaucrats. The Liberal Party, which, in 1955, joined forces with the Democrats to form the Liberal-Democratic Party (LDP), held power during the period of the war and was, therefore, associated with the initiation of the economic recovery and the regaining of independence. Indeed, setting a pattern for years to come, a sizeable portion of the Japanese population identified with the pro-growth, anti-communist, pro-American stance of the centre-right parties. At the same time the labour unions, an important vehicle for socialist activities, were put under considerable pressure by the unfolding of events. Along with the new constitution of 1947, General Douglas MacArthur, the Supreme Commander of the Allied Powers (SCAP), had been interested in bringing into Japanese political life some of the features of a free and democratic society, including free speech and rights for labour. However, the polarization of politics in Japan and the emergence of a relatively strong Communist Party increasingly backed by unions worried American occupation administrators. Their concerns increased as the Cold War gathered momentum with the Berlin Blockade and the communist takeover of China. As a result the decision was made to curtail the rights of labour and to rein in the unions. This approach was extended with the onset of the Korean War. Company unions with their emphasis on lifetime employment and seniority wage systems began to gain ground.

The Korean War and America's need for munitions, weapons and other war-related supplies boosted another key political player, the bureaucracy. The bureaucracy had emerged as the one political institution to survive the Second World War and the American occupation relatively unscathed. Moreover, because it was moulded to serve the imperial war machine, the bureaucracy had little difficulty adapting to America's special procurements demands. Interestingly, one of the most significant developments in the evolution of the bureaucracy occurred just prior to the Korean War. The Ministry of Commerce and Industry (MCI) was merged with the Board of Trade (BOT) to form the Ministry of International Trade and Industry (MITI). The combined responsibilities of the old MCI, which had been in charge of the planned industrial expansion of the 1930s and 1940s, and for munitions during the bulk of the Second World War, and the recently created BOT, which managed the import and export of goods under SCAP, then, gave the new MITI considerable powers (Johnson 1982).

The advent of the Korean War, the American military's special procurement policy and the return to Japan of its independence in April 1952 led to the crystallizing of MITI's authority. Along with the Ministry of Finance and the Bank of Japan, it occupied a central position in the powerful Japanese bureaucracy. MITI's responsibility for supervising the special procurements programme, begun at the outbreak of the Korean War, ensured that it was able to direct the foreign exchange that was earned into what were considered to be the most important industries. These industries included coal, iron and steel, mining, metalwork, chemicals, electric power generation, oil supply, transportation and shipbuilding. In addition, in August 1952, as the Japanese government reorganized the bureaucracy in the wake of SCAP's departure, MITI gained supervisory authority over all foreign exchange that was earned through trade; all imports of technology, including the all-important American technology that had begun to be employed as orders were placed under the special procurement plan; and all joint ventures. With the acquisition of these powers 'MITI came to possess weapons of industrial management and control that rivalled anything its predecessors had ever known during the prewar and wartime years' (Johnson 1982: 194).

The Korean War also led to the development of some key economic institutions. For example, the American military's special procurements had a major and long-lasting effect on the structure of Japan's banking system. Orders were being placed so quickly that Japanese firms found that they did not have access to enough capital to expand and fill the blizzard of contracts on offer. This need for capital led to what eventually became known as central bank 'over-loaning'. Individual firms would borrow capital well in excess of their immediate capacity to repay from the city banks who in turn would 'overborrow' from the Bank of Japan. This system, of course, gave the Bank of Japan considerable power over intermediate banks and afforded them a good deal of control over which sectors of the economy and which firms received loans and foreign exchange to buy raw materials, capital equipment and technology (Johnson 1982: 202–3; Packer 1994: 146; Wolferen 1989: 391). In 1951 the Japan Development Bank and the Japan Export Bank (later named the Japan Export-Import Bank) were set up to help with the financing done by ordinary financial institutions. Nakamura, for example, argues that 'Development Bank financing was highly significant in the long-term capitalization of key industries' (1981: 44). These, and other innovations of this period such as the Long-term Credit Bank Law, laid the foundation for the successful financing of Japan's phenomenal economic growth.

Parallel with the development of the new banking system was the reformation of the *zaibatsu*. After they were dissolved by SCAP immediately after the Second World War and forced to change their names, the Korean War boom and the advent of independence in April 1952 prompted the constituent members of the main *zaibatsu* to begin to reform with their old banks at the centre of the new conglomerate. Commonly referred to as *keiretsu*, three of the 'Big Six' conglomerates emerged out of old *zaibatsu*, while three others were new groupings of companies. Just as importantly, the Korean War boom accelerated the process by which the old set of generally conservative-minded managers were replaced in many companies by more aggressive high-growth-oriented, technocratic managers (Nakamura 1981: 65; see also Aoki 1987: 268–82).

It should not be assumed that the Korean War answered all of Japan's prayers. The economy lurched along as senior politicians and bureaucrats hotly debated how to manage the rapid rate of economic growth. Continued concerns were expressed about the possible resurgence of inflation and the need to deal with recurring balance of payments problems. However, the Korean War and the general Cold War environment were instrumental in the establishment of a number of what proved to be highly significant political and economic institutions. Certainly, the economic dynamism of the Korean War years laid both the economic and political foundations for the meteoric rise of the Japanese economy.

Significantly, the Korean War also set the course for Japan's regional and international relations. The war hastened the signing of the peace treaty with the US and more than forty other nations in September 1951. But Japan was also forced to sign a security treaty with the US that provided for the continued use by the US of bases on Japanese territory. In many ways the Korean War period tied Japan to the US both in economic and security terms for decades into the future. In addition, the entry of communist China into the Korean War in late 1950 and the subsequent Western embargo on commercial relations with the new regime meant that Japan had to give up any thoughts of trade with mainland China and North Korea, both of which had been major pre-Second World War trading partners. The result was Japan's promotion of economic linkages with non-communist East and Southeast Asia. Hence, the consequences of the Korean War, not only for Japan's domestic institutions but also for its foreign relations, were far-reaching and momentous.

The Korean War also 'saved' Taiwan. Certainly it saved Chiang Kai-shek and the Kuomintang (KMT) government of Taiwan, but in an important sense it also saved Taiwan, the future NIE. The economy was in a perilous state. It had been ransacked by the KMT as it fought to keep hold of mainland China. One estimate indicates that production levels had not only dropped 'far below pre-War Japanese production levels' but in the case of some sectors of the economy had 'sunk to the production levels of 1895' (Kerr 1965: 417). The population had swollen from 6 million to over 8 million in just a few years and was deeply divided. The increased demand for goods that this massive influx of people created, and the importation of large amounts of gold by Chiang Kai-shek and his associates, produced disruptively high levels of inflation. Moreover, the government was running substantial budget deficits as a result of reductions in revenue combined with massive military expenditures. In 1950 bank credit was rapidly expanded and the money supply doubled. Prices soared (Ho 1978).

The United States government, which had provided large amounts of aid to the KMT in its fight with the Chinese Communist

Party, became disillusioned with the corruption and incompetence of the Chiang Kai-shek regime and cut off funds. On 5 January 1950 President Truman issued a statement in which he indicated that the US would not give military aid or advice to Chiang Kai-shek nor would the US government get involved in the the civil conflict in China. In May 1950 the communists took over Hainan Island and the Chusan Archipelago between the mouth of the Yangtze River and Taiwan. Despite considerable support for Taiwan among Republicans and America's military community, it was clear that Taiwan was seen by many in the Truman Administration as just another of China's islands that would not be defended if attacked by the new government in Beijing (Fleming 1961: 593: Kerr 1965: 386–7).

The outbreak of the Korean War changed everything. On 27 June 1950, just two days after North Korean troops swept southwards down the peninsula, President Truman reversed US policy and announced that he had ordered the Seventh Fleet to prevent any attack on Taiwan. He also called on Chiang Kai-shek to cease all attacks against the mainland. Towards the end of 1950, aid money started to flow again as the US saw the need to bring some stability and order to Taiwan. Both decisions were vitally important to the future development of Taiwan. The military support gave the population a psychological boost while the massive injections of US aid helped to stabilize the economy, and lay some of the foundations for Taiwan's later rapid economic growth.

The initial period of foreign aid, from 1951 to 1955, was designed to meet the basic needs of the people, particularly in terms of food, and to curb inflation. Many of the capital goods brought in under the aid programme were farm implements and tools. The obvious aim was to feed the population while quickly developing the agricultural sector. The amounts of money funnelled into Taiwan grew rapidly so that in 1952 alone US$300 million was made available for economic aid (Kerr 1965: 417). The amounts of money were enormous and added up to around US$60 per person for the 1949–52 period at a time when the per capita income was just over US$100 per year (Ho 1978: 110; Taiwan Government 1955). The US also provided military aid which allowed more of the scarce domestic revenues and the limited foreign exchange that Taiwan earned from the export of sugar and other agricultural products to be ploughed back into reviving the economy. Overall, however, despite strict government controls, imports were about twice the value of exports with the average import surplus running at around US$107 million a year in the early years of the 1950s. Roughly 90 per cent of this import surplus was financed by US aid (Jacoby 1966: 97).

American aid and influence were crucial factors in the introduction of land reform in Taiwan. American advisors, through the Sino-American Joint Commission on Rural Reconstruction (JCRR), had failed to persuade the KMT to undertake a land-reform programme on the mainland after the surrender of the Japanese. Landed interests within the KMT had essentially vetoed the plan. Once the Chiang Kai-shek government retreated to Taiwan, land reform was given priority for a number of reasons. First, the Americans pushed hard, through the JCRR, for a land-reform programme. Their successful implementation of land reform in Japan and their assessment that land issues had helped the communists gain support in mainland China spurred them on. Second, the KMT government recognized that it needed to implement real land reform. It appreciated that its failure on the mainland had been in good part due to the mobilization of down-trodden peasants by the communists. It also acknowledged that if it was to have any chance of keeping social order in Taiwan, not to mention maintaining some level of US aid, effective land reform was necessary. Third, the KMT was able to redistribute land formerly held by the Japanese and land held by Taiwanese landlords with whom it had no links or to whom it had no obligations. Indeed, undermining the position of the local landlords served to reduce the chances that the indigenous Taiwanese elite could mount any meaningful opposition to KMT rule.

Three types of land reform took place in Taiwan. In 1949 farm rents were restricted to 37.5 per cent of the total annual main crop yield. Then, public land, mostly land formerly owned by the Japanese, was sold to tenants. Finally, the land-to-the tiller programme, begun in 1953, set an upper limit on the amount of land that could be held by any one household. Those who were forced to give up their land were compensated in the form of land bonds and stocks in government companies. The land acquired by the government was then sold to the tenants. While this process penalized those who had formerly been smaller landlords, it created a new pool of owner-cultivators. The real income of these small-scale farmers rose sharply as US aid money was channelled into the repair and upgrading of the rural infrastructure built during the Japanese colonial period, the introduction of improved farming techniques, and the development of new cash crops. As a result of the US aid, combined with the land reforms, agricultural production, which at the end of the Second World War 'had been reduced to the level of 1920', had, by 1952, 'regained its pre-War peak' (Ho 1978: 147).

The Chiang Kai-shek government was consumed by the problems of protecting its new base from the communists on the mainland and local opponents on Taiwan. Indeed, 'throughout the 1950s the economy operated on a war footing' (Haggard 1990: 262). Hence, while dealing with the land issue was crucial for the KMT, equally critical was coming to grips with the socially divisive and potentially debilitating economic chaos that had engulfed the island. Inflation was rampant. The New Taiwan Dollar, introduced in July 1949, quickly became overvalued, encouraging imports and discouraging exports. And production levels in all sectors of the economy, not just agriculture, were low. The new government tackled these problems directly. Rationing was introduced. Credit was closely managed and interest rates raised so as to entice more people to put their money into savings and thus lower the pressure on prices. Quotas were put on imports and rigorously enforced regulations governed all other exchange transactions. Finally, all industrial activity was brought under the direct control of the government (Ho 1987: 237).

Maintaining this pervasive control of the general economy and implementing land reform required an extensive and relatively skilled administrative structure. The key here was that the KMT government was able to take advantage of an existing, almost 'instant', well-developed administrative structure. On the mainland the KMT government had tried to maintain a strong centralized government administering a population of well over 500 million people. Of the 2 million KMT supporters and their families who fled to Taiwan in the late 1940s, many were government officials. They were re-employed to govern a population of a little over 8 million people. Just as importantly, the Taiwanese administrative structure the KMT government commandeered was a relatively efficient, highly centralized bureaucratic apparatus developed by the Japanese. In addition, through the vehicle of US aid, a relatively large contingent of highly trained Americans had a hand in developing many of Taiwan's key economic agencies and their policies.

Hence, both central economic planning institutions and implementing agencies at all levels owed their existence to both the KMT's and the American government's need to put Taiwan's economy on a firm footing in the face of the communist threat. For example, the JCRR, which was headed by a council of three Chinese and two Americans and had a well-trained staff of around 200, was instrumental in providing funds and technical assistance for land reform and other agricultural development programmes. It was later turned into the Council for Agricultural Planning and Development. Another example is the Council on US Aid (CUSA), which had the primary responsibility for the distribution of the American economic aid that 'constituted a large part of the economy's investment' and which 'was in effect a central planning agency' (Wade 1990: 199). CUSA later evolved into the Council for International Economic Cooperation and Development, then the Economic Planning Council and then the Council for Economic Planning and Development, each of which played a pivotal role in the development of Taiwan's later phenomenal economic growth. At the local level the implementation of the land-reform programme allowed the KMT government to reach down into every rural village and household on the island, through the Land Bank and the Provincial Food Bureau as well as the county- and village-level governing structures. In this way the KMT was able to ensure that its authority was accepted in every corner of Taiwan.

Throughout the first few years of the 1950s the KMT clearly established its political supremacy. President Chiang Kai-shek, under 'Temporary Provisions during the Period of National Crisis', employed a vast number of emergency powers. His party, the KMT, had a Leninist structure whereby members were assigned to cells that existed to control every facet of Taiwanese life. Their main function was to ensure that the KMT continued to control Taiwan and that party policies were properly executed. Supporting the KMT was also a network of party agents throughout the bureaucracy, as well as a large number of government security agencies including: the National Security Bureau; the Investigation Bureau; the Intelligence Bureau; the General Political Warfare Department; and the Taiwan Garrison Command (Gold 1986: 62–3). Essentially, 'party and state became inextricably intertwined' (Haggard 1990: 81). Moreover, Taiwan became a military society with the 600,000 military personnel making up 7.6 per cent of Taiwan's civilian population in 1951 (Jacoby 1966: 118). With the outbreak of the Korean War and the imminent threat of a communist invasion across the Taiwan Strait, there was no pressure from the Americans for the introduction of democratic reforms such as freedom of speech and assembly, fair elections, labour rights, or a free press.

For Taiwan, then, the Korean War heralded the sudden influx of massive amounts of American aid and an agreement between the US and KMT governments that priority was to be placed on security and internal stability. As a result the KMT, with the full support of Washington, put in place a strongly interventionist economic policy and a rigidly authoritarian political system. Economic stability and political order were sought at all costs. The institutions that were established as a result of these policies, then, were shaped in part by the legacy of Japanese colonialism but also, and even more importantly, by the imperatives of the Cold War and the threat posed by the new communist government on the Chinese mainland. The emergence of a powerful authoritarian regime in Taipei and the pervasive control exercised by the government over the economy during the Korean War years set the tone for later political and economic developments.

Malaya, Singapore and Thailand

The Korean War also 'saved' Malaya, Singapore and Thailand, although it did so in slightly different ways in each case. The most obvious impact of the Korean War was the sudden and dramatic rise in the prices of natural rubber and tin, two commodities which were widely viewed as essential to the war effort and which were crucial to all three economies. Increased international trade, that went along with the rise in defence spending in North America and Europe, also gave a boost to the economy of Singapore as an entrepôt and to the demand for Thailand's rice exports. The Korean War also brought Thailand, which had been on the side of Japan in the Second World War, firmly into the American Cold War camp with all the benefits that such a move conferred.

On the eve of the Korean War the British colonial government in Malaya was in serious trouble. The Malayan economy had slowly recovered in the post-Second World War years, but in June 1948 the government was forced to declare a state of emergency marking the beginning of a bitter guerrilla war with the Malayan Communist Party (MCP). As the British High Commissioner Sir Henry Gurney noted, 'Terrorism is the most expensive form of illness from which any community can suffer and becomes more so the longer it is permitted to drag on' (Stubbs 1974: 7). In May 1950 the high commissioner predicted that the Malayan reserves would be exhausted by the end of the year (Stubbs 1989a: 108). Moreover, the prospects for the two main export commodities, rubber and tin, were not good. Exploring for new tin deposits was curtailed by the guerrilla fighting and rubber production was down because of ageing trees and the reluctance of tappers to venture into areas frequented by the MCP guerrillas. In addition, the poor state of the economy, especially the high price of rice, the lack of employment and the government's strategy of using the army to search out guerrillas and punish those suspected of being their supporters, alienated many within the Malayan-Chinese community. It was this section of the Malayan society that the MCP depended on for support. In early 1950 government reports indicated that the situation was deteriorating steadily and that communism was getting a more and more serious hold (Stubbs 1989b: 93, 98).

The events in Malaya also affected Singapore. In many respects Malaya was Singapore's economic hinterland. For example, Singapore agency houses marketed Malaya's rubber production and Singapore was the main port for the export of both rubber and tin (Barlow 1978). Hence, the economic problems faced by Malaya reverberated in Singapore. Just as importantly, the guerrilla war on the peninsula created security problems for the Singapore government. The MCP had originally had its headquarters in Singapore and a significant portion of the MCP guerrillas had originally been Singapore residents. And because of the turn of events in mainland China there was much sympathy for the communist cause among portions of the predominantly ethnic-Chinese population. If the fighting intensified and expanded in scope or if it looked as if the MCP might win, tensions in the city-port would undoubtedly rise and the Singapore government would be placed in an extremely difficult position.

The Korean War, then, could not have come at a more opportune time for both Malaya and Singapore. Fear that the fighting might extend into Southeast Asia as well as the need to build up stockpiles of strategic raw materials led to a dramatic rise in the price of many commodities including the two pillars of the Malayan economy, rubber and tin. The price of rubber rose four-fold and the price of tin more than doubled (Stubbs 1974: 10). The resulting economic boom brought prosperity for all. With more than one third of Malaya's working population associated in one way or another with the rubber industry the incomes of estate workers and smallholders rose markedly. Profits in the estate sector of the rubber industry also increased significantly. As a result of this general rise in the level of prosperity, the government's finances improved dramatically. Expanded revenues from income tax, increased export duties on rubber and tin, and increased corporate taxes meant that the government's income more than doubled. The Korean War boom, then, gave the Malayan government the breathing space to rethink its counter-insurgency strategy and the funds to carry out the new plan (Stubbs 1974).

A key aspect of the new strategy was the resettlement of the rural Malayan-Chinese population that inhabited the jungle fringes and on whom the MCP guerrillas relied for much of their support. The idea was to bring the scattered rural population under the government's administrative control by grouping them in fortified centres. Fortuitously, the inception of the programme coincided with the outbreak of the Korean War and the government was able to fund this massive rehousing of a substantial portion of the Malayan population. Originally, it had been estimated that less than 300,000 people would have to be relocated; however, by the end of 1954 570,000 rural 'squatters' and landowners were living in resettlement areas at a total cost of over M$100 million or approximately 30 per cent of the government's total revenue for 1949 (Stubbs 1974). Without the revenues from the Korean War boom such an undertaking would have been impossible.

Resettlement proved to be vital to the government's ultimate success in defeating the communist guerrillas. Up to the beginning of 1952 the programme had not proved to be the success its advocates had hoped for. Moving created considerable hardships that tended to turn people against the government. The one mitigating factor from the point of view of those involved was the insatiable demand for labour and the high wages that could be obtained from working on rubber estates and smallholdings and in the tin mines. In February 1952 General Sir Gerald Templer took over as high commissioner in Malaya and instituted a new 'hearts and minds' approach to the prosecution of the guerrilla war in order to try to turn the momentum of events in the government's favour. A crucial aspect of the new strategy was to convert the resettlement centres into 'New Villages' with essential services such as schools, health facilities, community centres, places of worship, access roads, reasonable conditions of sanitation, and clean water as well as title to village land. Templer used the revenue surplus from the boom years of 1951 and 1952 to extend the programme into 1953 and 1954. The eventual success of the New Villages can be judged by the fact that at the end of the emergency few New Villages were abandoned, with most residents who left leaving only if forced to do so to find work. Most importantly, the more than 500 New Villages that were built changed the social and economic landscape of the country (Humphrey 1971).

Spurred on by the need to defeat the communist guerrillas and armed with a revenue surplus generated by the Korean War boom, the Malayan government began to implement a number of policies that had a long-term impact on the peninsula. First, in order to develop the services in the New Villages and successfully prosecute the 'hearts and minds' strategy the government had to expand the police force and the intelligence services. The civil service also grew rapidly. The staff of the District Offices were increased and key departments, such as Public Works, Education and Health, were quickly expanded. An enlarged bureaucracy was needed so that services could be provided to the New Villages and the government could exert administrative control over the population in order to separate the MCP guerrillas from their supporters. Second, railways were improved and roads built in order to be able to construct the New Villages along the jungle fringes and to give the police and the army access to strategic areas. This opened up new rubber-growing areas and made it much easier to move rubber and other crops to ports for export. Third, the government acknowledged that education was crucial in the battle against communism. Schools and especially teachers and the curriculum were more closely regulated and more government schools opened up for all sections of Malayan society. The Korean War boom, then, did not just save the Malayan economy and help reverse the fortunes of the Malayan government. It also contributed to the success of the Malayan government's 'hearts and minds' strategy in the guerrilla war and helped to lay the foundations for subsequent Malayan economic and political development (Stubbs 1989b).

For Singapore the Korean War proved to be a most welcome tonic. As in Malaya, during the post-Second World War years, Singapore was plagued by widespread unemployment, shortages of housing, low wages and poor working conditions. However, with

82   *Rethinking Asia's Economic Miracle*

42 per cent and 50 per cent of the total value of exports in 1950 and 1951 respectively coming from the export of rubber the four-fold rise in rubber prices had an enormous effect on the island's economy. As a consequence Singapore's total trade rose significantly and individuals who were in the rubber industry and their companies prospered. Increased economic activity, allied to the introduction of income tax in December 1947, also caused the Singapore government's revenues to sky-rocket to more than three times the pre-war levels. In both Singapore and Malaysia revenues from income and corporate taxes amounted to 30 per cent of total revenues in 1952 and 1953, and government revenues were a higher percentage of gross domestic product than in any other country in Southeast Asia (Stubbs 1989a: 523). The Korean War boom, then, allowed both British colonies to develop an efficient tax-collecting system that funded the expansion of their administrative and economic infrastructures.

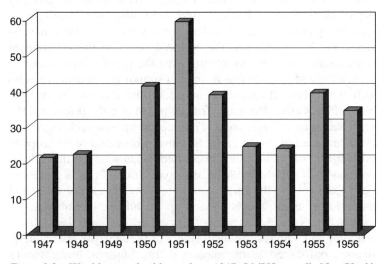

Figure 3.2   World natural rubber prices, 1947–56 (US¢ per lb, New York)
Source: Data from Federation of Malaya 1956.

For Thailand the outbreak of the Korean War both provided an immediate boost to a flagging economy and, critically, enabled the Thai government to move solidly into America's orbit. In the years immediately after the Second World War the Thai economy, like that of other countries in the region, faced inflationary pressures and low levels of production. The rise in rubber and tin prices, and the general regional economic prosperity induced by the Korean War spending, created considerable prosperity and stimulated industrial development, especially around Bangkok. Moreover, with a struggling economy and low revenues, the government had instituted, in 1946, an exchange control regime. Rice, rubber and tin exporters were forced to surrender export earnings to the Bank of Thailand at a fixed and highly disadvantageous rate. The rapid rise in both the prices for rubber and tin and the quantities of rice exported produced a balance of payments surplus and, by 1952, had increased the foreign exchange reserves to the equivalent of fourteen months of imports (Chomchai 1975: 137–8; Muscat 1994: 78). The Korean War boom had helped to turn the economy around and put the government on a firm economic footing.

In the post-Second World War years, the Thai government overcame its wartime alliance with Japan by engaging in intense diplomatic manoeuvring. In particular, the military-supported Phibun Songkhram, who had signed the December 1941 military alliance with Japan and was turfed out of office at the end of the Second World War, had to reinvent himself when he was returned to power not long after a November 1947 coup (Kingsbury 2001: 155). The Thai military attempted to obtain US military aid in 1947 but the Truman Administration, still wary of a country and army that had been so closely allied to the Japanese, turned the request down. To bolster his case to the US, Phibun pointed to communist-instigated guerrilla warfare in Malaya and Vietnam and the victory of the Chinese Communist Party, and emphasized that Thailand should be considered a frontline state in the battle against expansionist Asian communism. While talks did take place between the US and the Thai military in early 1950, it was the outbreak of the Korean War that was the deciding factor in propelling Thai–US relations forward. In the first months of the war, the Thai government authorized the sending of 4,000 troops and 40,000 tons of rice to help in the US fight against the invading North Koreans. By the end of the year, agreements had been signed for US military and economic aid. At the same time the World Bank had made its first loan to Thailand for rail and port upgrading and the building of a dam, while various UN agencies, such as the Food and Agriculture Organization, had initiated technical assistance programmes. By 1953 these programmes had started to make an impact. For example, US military aid provided equipment and training worth more than twice the country's military budget. The Korean War, then, gave the Thai government the chance to prove that it was firmly in the US camp and its reward was growing amounts of US aid (Muscat 1990; Muscat 1994: 50 Pusak and Baker 1995: 275).

South Korea

It may appear somewhat perverse to argue that the Korean War 'saved' South Korea. However, very much like Chiang Kai-shek in Taiwan, it certainly saved President Syngman Rhee's political fortunes. More importantly, by having the US make a clear long-term military and economic commitment to the country, the Korean War set the stage for the later emergence of South Korea as an NIE. There can be no doubt that Syngman Rhee was in political trouble. His government was widely seen as corrupt and incompetent. In addition, land reform, which had been instituted by the US Military government in March 1948 based on the sale of formerly Japanese-owned land to tenants, proved immensely popular. But Rhee and his landlord associates delayed further land-reform laws and then refused to implement any distribution of privately owned land. Not surprisingly his supporters in the Assembly were resoundingly beaten in elections held on 30 May 1950. Rhee's position as president was severely undermined and his political future bleak. At the same time the US was backing away from any commitment to South Korea as part of a defensive perimeter around East Asia. During late 1949 and early 1950 both Secretary of State Dean Acheson and a number of senior generals in the Pentagon publicly stated that the US could not guarantee support to South Korea in the face of a military attack. Indeed, there was, as D.F. Fleming has noted, 'a strong tendency in the United States to write off Korea as an indefensible liability' (1961: 592).

The Korean War 'came to Rhee's rescue ' (Haggard 1990: 56). Rhee presented himself as an anti-communist leader who needed to be wholeheartedly supported in the fight against the expansion of Asian communism. And given the context of the increasing Cold War tensions, the US government could not let the North Korean army sweep down through the peninsula unopposed. The decision to come to the aid of South Korea inevitably led to a decision to support the incumbent South Korean government. In the eyes of US officials it was not a good time to change leaders. Moreover, deploying such a large number of troops and resources essentially meant a long-term commitment to South Korea. This commitment was not only to ensure that, after the armistice of 1953, North Korea and China would not invade the South, but also to guarantee that Syngman Rhee would not act on his repeated claims to unite Korea by invading the North (Kotch 1983).

During and immediately after the Korean War a number of developments occurred which had a major impact on the role of the South Korean state and on the country's later economic growth. First, the South Korean army was greatly strengthened by the US and went on to play a crucial role in building the Korean state. US funds allowed the army to rapidly increase in size from 75,000 in 1950 to over 600,000 by the end of the War (Amsden 1989: 39; Cumings 1984a: 23). There was also a massive transfer of weapons so as to make the South Korean army as well equipped as possible.

Second, the US took advantage of the stalemate period of the war during 1952 and 1953 to pressure the South Korean government to push through land reform. With the North forcing many landlords off their land and a number of landlords killed in the fighting during the drive southwards in the early months of the war, resistance to land reform diminished substantially. The example of the popular land reforms put in place by the North Korean government also proved compelling. US administrators were able to use their influence to ensure that Korean-held land was fairly distributed in a programme very much like that introduced in Taiwan. The result was that the 'large landholders who once owned 90 per cent of the land were all but eliminated' (Jacobs 1985: 84). The land-reform programme, therefore, paved the way for a more equitable income distribution; increased the food supply, which in turn eased inflationary pressures; redirected idle capital away from land speculation towards investment in manufacturing; and totally undermined one of the most conservative elements in Korean society.

Finally, the war forced the US to put in place a long-term aid package for South Korea. From the end of the Second World War to the end of the Korean War, the US had spent US$1.17 billion in economic and military aid to Korea. David C. Cole points out that the average per capita economic aid 'for the eight years from 1946 through 1953 was about US$5 per annum, which was roughly equal to 10 per cent of per capita income in the prices of the time' (1980: 8). And calculations of these amounts of aid did not take into account the US$18 billion spent on the Korean War itself (Levin and Sneider 1983: 38). Having already sunk so many resources into the country, the US was not going to abandon South Korea. Immediately after the armistice was signed the US pledged a further US$200 million in economic aid as the first instalment of a US$1 billion aid package (Lyons 1961: 189). Indeed, the United States was to spend many billions of dollars more on South Korea in support of the economy and the military in the years to come.

Transforming Hong Kong

Hong Kong was not so much saved by the Korean War as it was transformed. The Chinese Civil War and the communist victory and then the entry of People's Republic of China into the Korean War in November 1950 changed Hong Kong from a war-ravaged entrepôt in the months directly after the Second World War into an increasingly successful exporter of manufactured goods by the middle of the 1950s. This transformation was not a planned economic strategy but one determined almost solely by the turn of geopolitical events.

In the months directly after the surrender of the Japanese, the British Military Administration (BMA) faced the daunting task of bringing the colony back into working order. There were numerous problems. For example, food, especially rice, was initially in short supply. As a result of the defeat of the Japanese, Chinese nationalism was on the rise. Unemployment was widespread and, for those who had jobs, pre-war wage rates did not take into account post-war inflation. The BMA, then, had to get the bureaucracy up and running; deal with the Triad gangs and more generally restore law and order; ensure that, as far as possible, the general population was properly fed and housed; reinvigorate the economy; and fend off the KMT government, which was expressing an interest in taking Hong Kong back. In short, the British administration found itself in a precarious situation (Snow 2003: 263–78, 296–301).

However, from late 1946 onwards, the face of Hong Kong changed dramatically as the colony became awash with refugees fleeing the fighting, corruption and general chaos of the civil war on the mainland. There were three main reasons why Hong Kong became the refuge of choice for so many. First, it was nearby and there were no restrictions on entry, making it a convenient sanctuary from both the advancing communists and the corrupt and incompetent KMT government. Second, it was an island of stability in a region where political strife and economic chaos seemed endemic. Britain's willingness to guarantee political stability and law and order were underscored when the garrison was increased from 6,000 to 30,000 troops and naval and air force reinforcements were dispatched to the colony (Snow 2003: 318; *New Chronicle*, 6 May 1949). And, third, with inflation consuming the mainland, Hong Kong provided a haven where the currency was stable; controls over imports, exports, foreign exchange and prices ensured supplies of key commodities; and the economy was expanding. As a result of these factors, Hong Kong's population grew from 600,00 at the end of the Second World War to 2.5 million by 1950 (Snow 2003: 317). Given this phenomenal growth in the colony's population M.J. Miners's (1975: 43) verdict is not unreasonable: 'Viewed objectively, Hong Kong was then one of the most unlikely places to be the scene of an economic miracle. The colony might well have seemed likely to become a vast refugee camp, surviving on international charity.'

Yet Hong Kong prospered. The colony's entrepôt trade regained its central role in the economy as the effects of the Second World War receded and East and Southeast Asia's regional trade began to pick up. Despite the economic problems faced by China, trade with the mainland was still crucial to Hong Kong's economy. Indeed, in mid-1949 entrepôt transshipments made up 66 per cent of Hong Kong's exports (*Financial Times*, 14 November 1949). Trading that had formerly been done through Shanghai was increasingly routed through Hong Kong as Shanghai became embroiled in the civil war and was eventually taken over by the communists. At the same time the savings that many of the more than 1.5 million refugees from mainland China brought to Hong Kong gave a massive boost to the economy. Rebuilding in the colony gathered pace as the refugees flocked in and the demand for housing shot up. Factories were also quickly set up in Hong Kong. The 366 factories at the end of December 1946 became more than 1,700 factories by December 1950 (*North China Daily News*, 1 March 1949; *Financial Times*, 3 May 1951).

But the most important development was the arrival of a group of Shanghai entrepreneurs who laid the foundation for Hong Kong's development as a manufacturing centre. During the period 1945 to 1947 cotton spinning mills in China that had not been destroyed by the fighting made large profits. However, from 1947 onwards, with inflation spiralling out of control, mill owners began to transfer their foreign exchange out of the country or to deposit in an account outside China. With their profits, the Shanghai textile manufacturers sought to buy new machinery from Britain and the US as well as large amounts of cotton yarn. But finding that Shanghai was increasingly caught up in the violence of the civil war they began to locate their new machinery in factories in Hong Kong. The first mill was set up in August 1947 and just over two years later there were thirteen sizeable mills in operation (*South China Morning Post*, 6 September 1953; Wong 1988: 44–50).

The total transfer of resources out of China into Hong Kong was massive and had a long-lasting impact on Hong Kong. Liu (1997: 588–9) records that between '1946 and 1950 no less than US$500 million poured from the Shanghai area into Hong Kong in the form of merchandise, securities, gold, and foreign exchange' (see also Snow 2003: 329). This amounted to an influx of funds equivalent to a phenomenal US$200 per person. As Stephan Haggard points out (1990: 118), 'approximately two-thirds of investment from 1947 through 1955, the period of Hong Kong's industrial take-off, was financed from abroad'. Moreover, many of those who found refuge in Hong Kong brought with them knowledge and skills that could be put to good use in the rapidly expanding economy. And, of course, the expansion of the manufacturing sector provided employment for Hong Kong's growing population.

While Hong Kong's manufacturing base was expanding rapidly, its entrepôt role was being just as drastically curtailed. Intriguingly, Britain's *Financial Times* (19 May 1949) noted in May 1949 that 'The Colony of Hong Kong is an entrepôt centre of immense importance and it can only survive as such.' However, in December 1950, just a few weeks after China entered the Korean War, the United States government placed an embargo on strategic goods that might find their way into the hands of the communists. Other Western governments followed suit and in May 1951 the United Nations banned the export of strategic goods to China. For the purposes of the embargo, Hong Kong, as a major transshipment point, was considered part of

China. The effect on Hong Kong's economy was immediate and devastating. Hong Kong's trade with China, which represented well over 33 per cent of its overall trade, slumped precipitously during 1951 as the embargo took hold (*New York Times*, 9 March 1953; *Christian Science Monitor*, 3 May 1952). By 1955 only 7.2 per cent of Hong Kong's exports went to China (Haggard 1990: 120).

In just a few short years, wars and geopolitics combined to turn Hong Kong from being primarily an entrepôt with a modest manufacturing capacity into an increasingly strong manufacturing centre with a diminished and uncertain entrepôt role. As the colony's entrepôt trade decreased, its exports of manufactured products, most importantly textiles, grew steadily and fairly rapidly. This transformation set Hong Kong firmly on the road to becoming a newly industrializing economy.

Conclusion

The Korean War had a major impact on each of the seven societies that eventually produced 'miracle' economies. Its influence was felt in two main ways. First, it created the conditions in which key resources were channelled into each of the seven societies. Critically, of course, large amounts of capital, mostly in the form of scarce American dollars, were made available to economies starved of funds and on the brink of collapse. Alleviating the severe capital shortages allowed these seven economies to develop a solid economic base. Japan profited from massive amounts of US government 'special procurements' and military and economic aid. Taiwan and South Korea also benefited from high levels of US military and economic assistance. In Malaya, Singapore and to a lesser extent Thailand, large amounts of capital suddenly flowed into their economies as a result of the rise in the prices for rubber and tin that was precipitated by the outbreak of the Korean War. Hong Kong was the beneficiary of the capital flight caused by the civil war in China. In addition, prompted by the need to mobilize resources and stop the spread of communism, US personnel based in East Asia imparted vital technical, administrative and organizational knowledge and skills to both the public and private sectors in Japan, Taiwan and South Korea. Overall, then, the injection of resources as a result of the outbreak of the Korean War and the civil war in China gave the seven future 'miracle' economies an advantage accorded no other developing economy at the time either in the region or in the rest of the world.

Second, by highlighting the threat from Asian communism and by freeing up resources the Korean War helped to centralize political power in each of the seven future 'miracle' economies. The devastation caused by the Second World War left the political institutions in East and Southeast Asia very weak. However, the destructive effects of war were followed by the formative effects of war. The enhanced risk of a communist-inspired invasion or internal subversion, underscored by the outbreak of the Korean War, created an environment in which there were calls for strong central political institutions to ward off the threat. During the Korean War period strong central political institutions began to appear in each of the seven societies. And crucially the growth of these institutions was possible because of the funds that the Korean War made available. In the case of Japan, the central political institutions developed around the bureaucracy which was the one institution that survived the Second World War relatively intact. The bureaucracy also expanded in Malaya and Singapore as the British colonial government moved to a strategy of attempting to win over the population by addressing some of their main grievances. In Taiwan, South Korea and Thailand, the central political institutions also included the emergence of a strong military as well as a revitalized bureaucracy. In Hong Kong, while the garrison was expanded, it was the bureaucracy that remained at the centre of the government. In other words, in each of the seven cases the Korean War promoted the initial expansion of the strong central governments that were to be a major feature of the years of rapid economic growth.

As Tilly points out (1992), it is important to appreciate the relationship between the supply of capital on the one hand and the state on the other and the implications of this relationship for the development of both the state and the economy. For Taiwan and South Korea, it is significant that the US supplied the capital which was largely fed into the economy by way of the state. In Japan, although capital ostensibly went to companies through special procurement contracts, state agencies used their tight control over foreign exchange reserves to exert considerable leverage in dealing with the business community and in developing the economy more generally. In Hong Kong, Singapore, Malaya and Thailand, the capital entered the economy through the private sector. In Hong Kong it was controlled by manufacturers, whereas in Singapore, Malaya and Thailand it was controlled by major rubber and tin companies and by trading houses. In these societies the state then used its taxing powers to mobilize the capital it needed to develop its security and economic policies.

The Korean War, then, had a timely and decisive influence on the initial economic and political development of what were to become the seven 'miracle' economies. However, while generally each of the seven societies benefited from the influx of large amounts of capital and the initial foundations of a strong state, in more specific terms each was also affected in a slightly different way. Each society differed in terms of the starting points of its economic and political institutions, the form of the capital influx, the culture context and the relationship between the capital and the state. Nonetheless, the general pattern was similar. The effects of the Korean War gave each of them a solid base on which to build over the next decade or so. This building process is the focus of the next chapter.

4

The Cold War Years

From the end of the Korean War to the middle of the 1960s, the Cold War dominated life in East and Southeast Asia. The United States and the seven societies that eventually produced the 'miracle' economies – Japan, South Korea, Taiwan, Hong Kong, Singapore, Malaysia and Thailand – feared that communism would take over the region. The immediate threat in most cases was thought to be an invasion by one of the communist countries. It was widely perceived that China, North Korea and – after the 1954 Geneva Agreement – North Vietnam, possibly in conjunction with the Soviet Union, were all capable of mounting an attack. Japan's sweep down through Southeast Asia in December 1941 and the North Korea's invasion of South Korea in June 1950 were invoked as examples of previous attacks that the unpredictable communists might emulate. The success of the People's Liberation Army in taking over China and fighting the Americans to a standstill in Korea was portrayed as clear evidence of how powerful the communists had become. There was also the pervasive fear of communist subversion destroying a society from within. The communist-inspired guerrilla wars in Malaya, the Philippines and Vietnam were widely seen as evidence that communism was trying to infiltrate the region by whatever means it could. Moreover, hand-in-hand with this ubiquitous sense of threat came a sense of vulnerability and insecurity. Few wanted a return to the chaos and destruction of the fighting during the war-years of the 1940s and early 1950s.

The significance of the Cold War and the influential presence of the US has, of course, been emphasized by those who advance an

American-hegemony explanation for the rise of the 'miracle' economies. They quite rightly point to the impact of US economic aid
on the 'miracle' economies and the way in which US advisors
tutored governments, such as those in Taiwan and South Korea, on
strategies for developing their economies. Others who employ a
version of the American-hegemony explanation also emphasize the
extent to which the US backed those authoritarian governments of
the region that remained steadfast in their opposition to the spread
of Asian communism. US military aid was clearly crucial in the
massive military buildup in East Asia and the general militarization of
a number of the 'miracle' economies. Yet the American-hegemony
approach does not provide a full explanation for the success of the
Asian economies. Most who use this explanation concentrate on
the economic rise of South Korea and Taiwan and ignore the
success of Hong Kong, Singapore and Malaysia. Moreover, many
of the analysts in this tradition are experts on international relations and few explore in any detail the way in which American
hegemony shaped the key domestic economic and political institutions and policies that drove the economic success of the seven
'miracle' economies.

Each of the other explanations of East and Southeast Asia's
economic success also helps to shed light on how the Cold War
influenced the development of the various economies, although few
allude to it directly. Like the proponents of the American-hegemony
approach the statists tend to concentrate on the way in which the
militarization of the region contributed to the emergence of the
strong interventionist state in Japan, South Korea and Taiwan.
However, they ignore the Cold War's influence over similar developments in the other successful economies. Advocates of the
Japan-centred approach note the re-emergence of the institutions
and policies that originated in the Japanese colonial period, but
tend to minimize the importance of the Cold War's role in providing the critical context for their revival. Some proponents of the
neoclassical economic approach acknowledge the contribution of
aid but, as was the case in the Korean War, most underestimate its
significance. The vast majority of analysts who adopt this line of
argument emphasize the switch to an export-oriented strategy in
places like Taiwan, South Korea and Singapore that came in the
mid-1960s. They appear unwilling, however, to recognize that the
import-substitution strategy of the 1950s and early 1960s, discussed

in this chapter, provided a valuable launching pad for the development of export-oriented industries. Finally, commentators who rely on cultural explanations are inclined to ignore the Cold War altogether, feeling that it had little impact on culture-based economic practices. Yet the cultural explanations provide an excellent reminder that no political or economic institution or set of policies would have lasted very long, or been very effective, had it run counter to prevailing cultural norms.

The key, then, is that the formative and reformative aspects of the Cold War be analysed in terms of each of the seven successful economies. Most significantly, there is a clear need to bring out the widespread sense of fear and trepidation that accompanied the Cold War and to explore the effects that this anxiety produced. Half a century later, it is perhaps difficult to understand fully the fear of communism and the omnipresent threat of war that gripped the region. Meredith Jung-En Woo-Cumings (1998: 335–6) in writing of this period describes, 'the intense, emotional loathing of communism that was so successfully drilled into every child, the constant drumbeat of admonition that national survival was contingent on economic development and military preparedness that demanded personal sacrifice'. She says that this view of the world was 'bred in the bones of anyone growing up in post-1949 Taiwan or postwar South Korea'.

Other parts of East and Southeast Asia experienced similar fears. In the preface to his book on national security and the technological transformation of Japan, Richard J. Samuels (1994: ix–x; see also Donnelly 2004) writes that after speaking to a group of Americans he was asked to 'sum up in one word what makes Japan tick'. His answer was 'insecurity'; He pointed out that among Japanese there is 'a pervasive anxiety that Japan must compensate for its special vulnerabilities in a Hobbesian world. This feeling of insecurity and vulnerability has been articulated repeatedly throughout Japanese history.' Certainly, Japan's sense of insecurity was exacerbated by the hostile environment in which it found itself in the post-Second World War period when it was equipped with neither a strong army nor a strong economy. In the same vein, Michael Leifer (2000: 4), in a book on Singapore's foreign policy which is subtitled *Coping with Vulnerability*, comments that the island nation's policies are 'rooted in a culture of siege and insecurity'. For Singaporeans the concern was not only the external and internal threat of communism but also the fact that their country is a small, mostly Chinese, society surrounded by the relatively large, predominantly Malay, populations of Indonesia and Malaysia (H.C. Chan 1971). Moreover, Alex H. Choi (1999: 144) argues that 'Political insecurity was the hallmark of colonialism in post-war Hong Kong.' He makes the point that, 'Hong Kong's political status did not depend solely on the expiration of the New Territories Lease but also on the rise and fall of the great powers and Cold War politics.'

These observations indicate the profound sense of apprehension and, in many cases, fear felt across East and Southeast Asia. The Cold War and the possibility of the spread of communism posed such a threat to the various communities of East and Southeast Asia that it became the defining issue through which all policies were filtered. Collectively preparing to face the external threat was a key motivating force in the drive for economic development. It was also the justification for the rapid rise in nationalism and the attendant expansion of the coercive aspects of the state – the military, police and intelligence agencies – as well as the increasingly interventionist role that the state played in the economy. This 'securitization' of state policies became institutionalized and, because the threat lasted for so long, deeply embedded in the life of the societies which are the focus of this study (Buzan, Waever and Wilde 1998: 23–9). As Meredith Woo-Cumings (1999: 23) has pointed out, the 'genius' of the 'security states' was 'in harnessing very real fears of war and instability toward a remarkable developmental energy, which in turn could become a binding agent for growth'.

This chapter will explore the effect of the Cold War years on the development of the political and economic institutions that supported the 'miracle' economic growth of Japan, Hong Kong, Taiwan, South Korea, Singapore, Malaysia and Thailand. In each case the progress of the political and economic institutions in each society, from the end of the Korean War to the middle of the 1960s, clearly builds on the initial developments made during the Korean War. The Cold War years, therefore, saw the consolidation of the initiatives undertaken during Korean War's critical-juncture period. The one major departure from the trajectory for economic development set out during the early 1950s was induced when the import-substitution policies in Taiwan, South Korea and Singapore became untenable and required a reorientation around an export-oriented strategy.

Japan

The end of the Korean War to the mid-1960s was a period of rapid economic growth for Japan. With no domestic appetite to re-militarize and build a 'strong army', the country's leaders vowed to construct a 'rich nation' that would be as resilient as possible in a menacing world. 'Catch-up' with the West, especially the United States, was the rallying call and the means to achieve this goal were, to import technology, expand the domestic economy and export manufactured goods. During the dozen years after the Korean War, a series of booms and periods of restraint produced growth rates that averaged just under 10 per cent per year. This rapid rate of growth was a remarkable achievement given the ruins in which Japan lay at the end of the Second World War.

In the post-Korean War, Cold War years, the United States continued to furnish Japan with a number of benefits. The US–Japan security treaty, signed in 1952, provided for the stationing of American troops on bases around Japan and essentially guaranteed that the US would come to Japan's defence in case of an attack. America's commitment of troops to Japan also meant that in 1954 Japan's military, which had emerged out of the National Police Reserve Force, numbered around only 200,000. The limited size and slow growth of the military saved the government from a barrage of attacks from widely supported pacifist groups and from the need to spend large amounts of money on a greatly expanded National Defence Force. In addition, the Americans signed a Mutual Security Assistance agreement in May 1953 that saw the transfer of US military technology and financial assistance to Japan. Just as importantly, the Japanese government won a concession that these funds could be used for civilian purposes when appropriate (Samuels 1994: 150).

The US government continued to pump massive amounts of money into the Japanese economy. It persisted with its 'special procurement' programme even after the end of the Korean War so that even as late as 1960 special procurements amounted to US$549 million or over 12 per cent of imports (Allen 1962: 214). John Dower (1999: 542) notes that 'this prolonged windfall enabled Japan to increase imports greatly and virtually double its scale of production in key industries'. These key industries included machine manufacturing and the auto sector which were later to become so crucial to Japan's success as an exporter.

The Cold War also provided the backdrop to the development of Japan's political institutions. The period from 1953 to 1960 was politically turbulent as the country debated the best path to follow. Those who wanted a rearmed Japan to guard against the threat from communism were pitted against those who wanted to put all the emphasis on economic development. Prime Minister Yoshida Shigeru, the most influential figure of the early 1950s, pushed for the country to concentrate on economic growth. He was challenged from various quarters. When the Liberals and the Democrats, the two parties that had led most post-Second World War governments, merged in November 1955 to form the right-of-centre Liberal Democratic Party (LDP) the tussle continued within the new party. The tensions came to a head during the 1960 renegotiation of the 1952 Security Treaty. Old pre-Second World War and wartime antagonisms were part of the problem but so were concerns about the US and their bases in Japan. In the end, despite large-scale demonstrations on the streets of Tokyo, the new treaty was ratified by the Diet. A compromise granted Japan greater powers in determining the use of American bases in the case of war. However, Prime Minister Kishi Nobusuke, whose reputation was damaged by the battle over ratification, resigned and was replaced by Ikeda Hayato. Ikeda pursued a much less confrontational course than his predecessor.

Yoshida's view that the external and internal threats to Japanese security were best countered by an economically strong society became the consensus view among the country's conservative powerbrokers by the early 1960s. Acting on this approach, Ikeda had begun to work in 1959 on an Income Doubling Plan. The idea was to double both the national income, measured in terms of GNP growth, and individual incomes measured in terms of increased consumption (Allinson 1993: 123). Once he became prime minister, Ikeda unfurled the Income Doubling Plan and made it the centrepiece of his government. While there are mixed views about the Plan's concrete economic impact, it gave all sectors of society a project around which to rally. In the end, the aim of having an average growth in GNP of 7.2 per cent was greatly exceeded (Tsuru 1993: 96).

A former bureaucrat, Ikeda used his personal links to top administrators in key ministries and agencies and his connections to the many other former bureaucrats who had moved into leadership positions in the major corporations. The resulting emphasis on 'administrative guidance' to steer the economy underscored Chalmers Johnson's (1982: 154) point that 'The politicians reign and the bureaucrats rule.' The politicians set out the goals, created the national consensus and gave the bureaucrats the political space to write the rules and implement the policies needed to reach the goals. Increasingly, through the 1960s, as liberalization took hold and ministries lost the power to force edicts on enterprises, bureaucratic rule was exercised by means of request, warnings, suggestions and encouragement rather than enforceable directives. In many ways the 'embedded' bureaucracy continued practices that went back to the 1930s, and had re-emerged during the Korean War years, but employed a lighter touch. Leading the way was the Ministry of International Trade and Industry (MITI) as the 'pilot' agency. Using its knowledge of various industries, domestic and international markets and the overall strategy of the government, MITI, in conjunction with other key ministries and the business sector, decided which sectors would be developed in which direction, brought businesses representatives together and successfully managed the push to rapid economic growth.

The Japanese approach to the role of the state in developing the economy was one of 'developmental interventionism'. Some industries and sectors remained protected but those which were opened up to domestic and international competition were supported as they came to grips with market forces. The full array of institutions that emerged during the Korean War years was used in this developmental interventionist approach. For example, the banking and credit distribution systems which brought the state, the banking system and industry together to mobilize and 'allocate investment capital to export winners and away from domestic consumption' was a key component in the high-growth strategy (Cerny 2004: 105). Moreover, the *keiretsu*, the trade promotion agencies and the means of screening of foreign capital all played a part in the rapid growth of the late 1950s and early 1960s. Similarly, socioeconomic institutions such as the enterprise unions, the subcontracting systems, lifetime employment and forced savings to compensate for the lack of a welfare system contributed to the development of Japan's rapid economic growth. And just as importantly, the changes made in various sectors of the economy produced a synergy that helped to propel the economy forward. For instance, land reform and high prices for rice gave a large number of owner-farmers the funds to introduce technology and raise levels of production. The increased efficiencies in farming freed labour to move from the countryside into the towns and cities where manufacturing jobs were being created at a rapidly expanding rate. At the same time significant 'administrative' investments were made in urban housing, railways, roads and the electricity supply to support the increase in industrial activity (Allen 1965: 36).

Overall, then, galvanized by the insecurity and sense of vulnerability created by the Cold War, Japan moved from success to success. Certainly, the Cold War environment aided the conservative block in taking over full control of Japanese politics. Under the conservatives' guidance the political institutions recovered from the US Occupation and solidified their position at the centre of Japan's economic prosperity. The economy, which had been set on its course by Dodge's export-oriented philosophy as well as the boost from the Korean War boom and the subsequent opening up of the American market, grew at an accelerated rate. Hence, although there were some problems along the way, the political and economic institutions that underwrote the country's economic development produced results. As a consequence, they were fused in place. The positive feedback reinforced the commanding role played by the institutions that were driving the economy forward.

Taiwan

Thomas B. Gold (1986: 72) observes that 'In the critical 1950s, the KMT (Kuomintang) regime, guided and supported by the United States, institutionalized the structure within which Taiwan's economy, society and politics would evolve.' During the 1950s and well into the 1960s, the Cold War played a central role in the development of the institutions and structure to which Gold refers. The KMT dominated the various agencies of the state and used them to impose its political will on all parts of the society. State agencies also dominated the economy. The state allocated capital, regulated trade and picked the industries and companies that would be supported. After the 'loss' of China, the US decided that Taiwan had a key role to play as a vital ally in the fight against the spread of Asian communism and so gave the KMT its full support. The US government's commitment to Taiwan was demonstrated in a number of ways. It showed it was willing to deploy the US Seventh Fleet in the waters between Taiwan and mainland China, and to threaten the use of a nuclear strike against China whenever tensions increased over the Taiwanese outposts of Quemoy and Matsu. It also signed the December 1954 'Mutual Defense Treaty' which came into force in March 1955. As a result, the American government essentially underwrote the KMT's command of Taiwan's society. It was made clear that the US would not interfere with the KMT's often brutal suppression of the local Taiwanese or any other dissenters and only slowly did it press for a more open economy.

Building on the coercive institutions developed during the Korean War years, the KMT reinforced its total control over the state apparatus and Taiwanese society. Concerned about both the external threat from Communist China and the internal threat from 'subversion', the KMT government built up a massive military force that became the seventh largest land army in the world and the fifth largest among non-communist countries by the late 1950s (Woo-Cumings 1998: 331). Taiwan was, in Robert Wade's (1990: 253) terms, 'a militarized society' with the armed forces inculcating 'military notions of discipline, authority, and vigilance'. The reason that the Taiwanese government was able to build such a large military was because of the high levels of military aid from the Americans. It amounted to more than US$2.5 billion between 1950 and the mid-1960s, with most disbursed in the form of grants rather than loans (Ho 1978: 110; Jacoby 1966: 118).

But the impact of US military aid went beyond simply expanding the Taiwanese military and equipping it with modern weapons systems. Two examples illustrate this point. First, it was an important channel for the transfer of key technologies. For instance, the textile industry benefited from the transfer of technology to make better military uniforms and the electronic industry was helped by the transfer of technology in the radar and avionics sectors (Wade 1990: 83). Second, a portion of military aid was used to build airfields, roads and telecommunications facilities and to develop training programmes in language and mechanical skills. The expansion of the infrastructure and the pool of human capital had long-term developmental benefits. In addition, given that the KMT government was so intent on building up its military for an eventual return to the mainland and spent such a high proportion of its budget on

Taiwan's armed forces, without US military aid, little would have been spent on developing the economy (Jacoby 1966: 120).

Apart from the KMT and the military, the other major political institution of consequence was the bureaucracy. At the top were a small number of highly able technocrats such as K.Y. Yin (Yin Chung-yung) and K.T. Li (Li Kwoh-ting), who were fully supported by Chiang Kai-shek, Chen Cheng and other senior members of the KMT, and who pushed through a series of economic reforms. Just as importantly, Taiwan had an unusually strong mid-level cohort of refugee mainland Chinese bureaucrats and Japanese-trained Taiwanese bureaucrats who were fully capable of working out the details of policies and putting them into effect. They proved to be especially useful in moving from an import-substitution strategy in the years up to 1958 to a greater emphasis on exports in the period from 1958 to the mid-1960s. The three main political institutions of the KMT, the military and the bureaucracy together maintained domestic political stability while simultaneously planning and implementing economic development.

During the Cold War years, from 1953 to the mid-1960s, Taiwan built on the revival of the economy it had achieved during the Korean War years and set in place the foundations for its later, remarkable economic success. A fundamental feature of the island's economic development during this period was US economic aid and advice. US aid officially ended on 30 June 1965, but supplies previously approved by the US government and agricultural surpluses sent under PL480 continued until 1967. From 1953 to 1967 Taiwan received US$1.3 billion in US economic assistance mainly in the form of grants. If economic and military assistance are combined during the same period then total US assistance came to US$3.64 billion. Between 1953 and 1967 US aid, therefore, amounted to roughly US$365 per capita, an extraordinary sum given that the annual per capita income in 1960 in Taiwan was only US$110 (Ho 1978: 110–11).

US advice and the Cold War context also had a significant role in the evolution of Taiwan's overall economic strategy. Having been forced to adopt an import-substitution strategy during the late 1940s and early 1950s in response to the problems created by high inflation and shortages of foreign exchange, the KMT government, building on its policies during the Korean War years, set out to get the most out of the economy. The government's import-substitution policies included tariffs, import controls and multiple exchange rates. In addition, the agricultural sector was expanded based on US-supported land reform and US economic aid – 21.5 per cent of which went to agriculture – and the surplus used to subsidize import-substitution industries (Cheng 1990: 142; Ho 1978: 118; Yager 1988). Import-substitution industries such as textiles, synthetic materials, rubber goods, wood products and plastics were given priority by the government (Gold 1986: 72; Wade 1990: 79–81).

As the 1950s wore on the import-substitution strategy started to run aground. The domestic market in key sectors was becoming saturated and the economy showed signs of slowing down. Corruption became a problem as battles took place over the allocation of foreign currency and quotas. Businessmen called for the government to provide more assistance to import-substitution industries and to impose cartels to limit production. Others argued for the development of secondary import-substitution industries such as chemicals and autos (Haggard 1990: 90–1). A number of technocrats, however, spurred on by advice given to the government by an IMF mission in 1954, advocated turning to an export-oriented strategy. The large US aid contingent in Taiwan also pushed for a reform package that relied more on exports. Among other benefits, it was argued, an export-oriented approach would help with the increasing problems associated with a chronic shortage of foreign exchange.

A crucial catalyst for the shift from import-substitution to an emphasis on exports was a key flash-point in the Cold War. During August, September and October of 1958 the People's Republic of China (PRC) maintained an incessant artillery bombardment of two islands, Quemoy and Matsu, which were occupied by Taiwan and were only a few miles from the coast of the mainland. The US sent in the Seventh Fleet and announced that it would support Taiwan in defending the islands. America's emphatic intervention surprised China and effectively ended the confrontation. But the crisis brought to a head questions about Taiwan's future. In supporting Taiwan in the crisis the US made it clear that the KMT's dreams of unification through military action were untenable. The US also emphasized that it strongly favoured a development-oriented economy in which private investment would play a greater role. For its part the KMT government recognized that it needed to be more self-reliant and to become economically stronger in order to fend off the threat from the PRC. In the political fallout from the crisis, those who endorsed shifting from a total emphasis on import-substitution to an emphasis on both import-substitution and export-led development won out. In 1959 the US Agency for International Development (AID) proposed relaxing government controls and encouraging private investment. These proposals were picked up by the economic reformers within the Taiwanese government and developed into a Nineteen-Point Program for Economic and Financial Reform. They were also incorporated into the Third Four-Year Plan for 'accelerated economic development'(Jacoby 1966: 135). The US offered a US$20–30 million incentive package to encourage the implementation of the reforms.

Over the next half-dozen years the reform package was implemented and US aid phased out. Regulation of foreign investment was eased and the multiple exchange rate was slowly simplified until there was one, devalued single rate. In addition, trade and exchange controls were relaxed. At the same time regulations were introduced aimed at encouraging domestic savings and private investment, subsidies in import-substitution sectors were reduced, and export promotion schemes and concessional export credits were implemented. As a result, exports gradually increased, rising from US$120 million in 1958 to US$496 million in 1965 (Ho 1978: 134).

Overall, then, by the mid-1960s the KMT had embraced economic development as a hegemonic project which could create a base for a strong military to defend the island from any attack from the mainland. Administratively, the government had prepared for the end of US economic assistance by merging the Council on US Aid (CUSA) into a new Council for International Economic Cooperation and Development (CIECD). The CIECD continued to provide the central planning and coordination necessary to develop the domestic economy and link it in to the world economy (Gold 1986: 78). With policies encouraging both more private investment and export-led growth, the economy continued to flourish. The share of public ownership in total industrial production and the share of public enterprise in manufacturing were both slowly being reduced (Li 2002: 85). And agriculture was playing a more limited role in the overall economy. But the extent to which the new approach to development, and especially the export-oriented strategy, would be a success was still in doubt. Taiwan had reached a critical point in its economic development.

South Korea

Although the Korean War came to an end with the signing of the Korean Armistice Agreement in 1953, formally the two Koreas remained at war with each other. The threat of a return to open conflict hung over the peninsula. For the Americans, having spent both blood and treasure in fighting the Korean War, there was every reason to maintain their full commitment to the stability and security of one of their major allies in the battle against Asian communism. Indeed, the US needed South Korea as much as South Korea needed the support of the American government. It was in the Cold War context, then, that the political and economic institutions in South Korea emerged during the 1950s. President Syngman Rhee, who headed a corrupt and increasingly discredited political system that slowly unravelled as the years unfolded, proved a master at maintaining the support of the Americans even though they distrusted him intensely. The economy, essentially based on an import-substitution approach, drifted along, propped up by massive amounts of US military and economic aid. However, underlying this seeming political and economic stagnation, changes were taking place in South Korea's social, political and economic life that eventually led, in the early 1960s, to a crisis. The outcome of the crisis reoriented the political and economic direction of the country.

During the years between the end of the Korean War and the 1961 coup, South Korea's political institutions remained weak and ineffective. An autocratic but ageing President Rhee operated within an ostensibly democratic framework. Political parties remained legal and functioned in a competitive political system, but were often suppressed by a regime that used anti-communism and national unfication as an excuse for organized violence (Cheng 1990: 148). The constitution was repeatedly revised to keep Rhee in office and a small coterie of trusted advisors around the President used corruption, mainly tied to the distribution of US aid, the threat of force through the brutal actions of the police, and intrigue to maintain their increasingly unpopular hold on power. The bureaucracy, which had a strong centralizing role during the Japanese colonial period and remained relatively large, suffered from the political infighting and high levels of corruption that characterized the Rhee regime and was not as dominant a player as its history might have suggested.

The one political institution that gained in strength and stature during the 1950s was the military. By 1956 the military numbered around 700,000 and was one of the largest armies in the world (Cole and Lyman 1971: 35). Maintaining a strong military was vital for the US government which wanted a stable, impregnable fortress to keep Asian communism at bay. In order to accomplish this task the US pumped massive sums of military aid into South Korea. US$4.1 billion in military aid was supplied to South Korea by the US government between 1953 and 1969 (Cole 1980: 12). As a result, the South Korean armed forces had some of the most up-to-date military equipment and weapons systems in the world at that time. In addition, military assistance provided training for military personnel and encouraged professionalization among the upper ranks. The US command structure tied the Korean forces to the Commander in Chief UN Command (CINCUNC), an American, and ensured that the military was in many respects beyond the influence of the machinations of the Rhee regime. As a result 'the autonomous military became an alternative source of authoritarianism' to that practised by Rhee (Cheng 1990: 149).

As in Taiwan, the US military assistance programme also had wider consequences for the general economy. Many enlisted men, who received training in organizational, management and technical skills, took their newly acquired knowledge and skills into private-sector and government-owned enterprises when they left the military. Moreover, military assistance went into the construction of roads, bridges and other forms of needed infrastructure in order to allow units access to key military positions (Cole 1980: 13). This was especially important around Seoul and the demilitarized zone. Indeed, the reconstruction of South Korea's infrastructure after the Korean War was an important ingredient in getting the country's construction industry off the ground.

When the economic aid provided by the US is added to the military aid, the resulting sum is truly phenomenal. There can be no doubt that US aid was vital to the survival of South Korea and to its later remarkable economic growth rates (cf. Cole 1980: 16; Haggard 1990: 55; Scalapino 1980: ii; Woo 1991: 212) Overall, between 1946 and 1976, the US supplied US$12.6 billion in economic and military assistance while Japan supplied US$1 billion and international financial institutions contributed US$2 billion. This amounted to roughly US$600 per capita for South Korea compared to about US$425 per capita for Taiwan. To put these figures into perspective, South Korea's haul of aid was much greater than given to any other country in the world except South Vietnam and Israel. The amount of aid for this one country was comparable to the amount of aid received by the whole of Africa and was only just under half the aid given to all of Latin America over the same period (Cole 1980: 1; Cumings 1984a: 24; Woo 1991: 45).

US aid underwrote the stabilization of the South Korean economy and its adoption of an import-substitution approach to economic management. During the main import-substitution years, from 1953 to 1962, 'aid financed nearly 70 per cent of total imports' and 'equalled 75 per cent of total fixed capital formation' (Haggard 1990: 55; Cole 1980: 28–9). The bulk of US aid projects were heavily concentrated in the areas of transportation and electric power – in other words in infrastructure projects – and in manufacturing. Hence, although the agricultural sector was slow to get back on its feet and the overall economy grew at only 4 per cent per year between 1954 and 1960 – below the world average and well below Taiwan's 7.2 per cent – the industrial manufacturing sector thrived, growing at over 11 per cent per year (Cheng 1990: 146: Woo 1991: 59). Many undervalued state-owned enterprises were sold off cheaply to politically well-connected entrepreneurs who used their political relationships to acquire valuable foreign exchange and expand their companies. Aided by high tariff barriers, firms in the textile, milling and light consumer goods sectors all developed rapidly. So did the construction firms that gained contracts for US aid infrastructure projects (Woo 1991: 59).

However, despite the successes in the manufacturing sector and the massive influx of aid, the country's economy drifted along. The import-substitution approach ran into increasing problems. Inflation proved corrosive, the currency was overvalued, bank interest rates were set unrealistically low and tax collection was ineffective (Kuznets 1980: 63). The need for large quantities of chemical ferti- lizers to keep the long-established intensive farming practices producing rice and other foodstuffs exacerbated the problem of the already significant shortages of foreign exchange. And the political turmoil created by Rhee's weakening authority served to only magnify the country's deepening economic problems. By 1960 the GNP growth rate had declined to 2.3 per cent, unemployment was estimated at one fifth the total labour force, and the per capita income was less than $100, or about the same as India, one quarter Japan's and two-thirds of Taiwan's (Amsden 1989: 48: Woo 1991: 59).

The stalling economy, the political corruption and the increased violence of the Rhee regime produced a crisis. Student-led riots forced Rhee's resignation and the installation of a new government under Chang Myon in April 1960. When the new government proved just as inept and corrupt as its predecessor, a coup in May 1961 placed General Park Chung Hee in power. After some initial hesitation, the US backed the coup but registered its intent to reduce both economic and military aid and expressed its wish that power be transferred back to a civilian authority at an appropriate time (Kim 1990: 68).

Park's new military government quickly centralized power. The National Assembly was dissolved as were all existing political organizations. Labour unions were reorganized and any group that might have espoused a 'left' or 'quasi-left' approach was brutally shut down (Cole and Lyman 1971: 38). The commercial banks were nationalized and all financial intermediaries were brought under the direction of the Ministry of Finance (J.-E. Woo 1991: 84). Business leaders were fined for their dubious activities under the previous regimes and brought firmly under the government's control. In addition, new business organizations were established with close ties into the new regime. Foreign-trained – mostly in the US – Korean technocrats and academics were drafted in to bolster the bureaucracy, especially in terms of planning and implementing economic policy. Central to economic planning was the Economic Planning Board, which also had responsibility for national budgeting, foreign capital management and statistics and was headed after 1963 by the deputy prime minister. In addition, there was an Office of Planning and Coordination under the prime minister and a Planning and Management Unit in each ministry (Song 1990: 141; Whang 1987: 3). President Park also established a presidential secretariat to oversee policy making. And the Korean Central Intelligence Agency (KCIA), which was created in 1961, proved to be 'perhaps the most powerful instrument of social and political control'. It was responsible to the executive and its 'significance in all matters – ranging from intelligence gathering and secret police functions to the implementation of economic policy and interbureaucratic coordination – cannot be overestimated' (Haggard and Moon 1983: 142).

After an initial, false start, during which the government went on a spending spree that rekindled inflation, accentuated the growing balance-of-payments difficulties, and aggravated the problems created by the poor harvests of 1962 and 1963, an export-oriented approach to economic development was given priority. The US was a major reason for this change in strategy. In order to ensure that the US covered the food shortage and did not turn off the aid tap immediately as it indicated it was intent on doing, the Park government responded to US pressure. It devalued the currency and established a unitary exchange rate, reduced restrictions on imports, severely constrained credit expansion and balanced the budget. It also raised bank interest rates and introduced measures to encourage export expansion. Although forced to make this abrupt change in economic policy by the emerging crisis in the economy and the heavy pressure from the US, Park's military junta recognized that an export-oriented strategy had the potential to move the country away from dependence on the US while at the same time developing a strong economic base for confronting the North.

By 1965 South Korea was very much in the same position as Taiwan. With a deepening crisis in the economy brought on by declining foreign currency reserves and facing pressure from American advisors who wielded the aid stick, the Park government switched from an import-substitution to an export-oriented economic strategy. Relatively insulated from societal pressures and facing a weak, fragmented and poorly organized opposition, the government had considerable leeway in implementing its new policy. Yet there was a good deal of trial and error in the implementation of the new approach. There was certainly no guarantee of success. Like Taiwan, South Korea had reached a pivotal point in its development.

Hong Kong

From the end of the Korean War to the middle of the 1960s, Hong Kong's export-oriented economy, whose basic trajectory had been determined by the Chinese Civil War and the Korean War, prospered. As a British colony it was essentially outside the US protective umbrella. Hong Kong, therefore, relied for its relative stability and security on a small British garrison paid for by the British government, the acquiescence of the Chinese population that had sought it out as a haven of tranquillity and economic opportunity, and the unwillingness of the People's Republic of China to push for the colony's premature return. Both Britain and China valued the colony for the same reason: foreign exchange. For Britain, which had depended on Malaya as the major dollar earner through to the end of the Korean War, Hong Kong exports were an invaluable source of US dollars, which were much needed as sterling went through crisis after crisis. For China it was a window on the outside world which also brought in increasing amounts of foreign currency that could be used to purchase imports from the non-communist world (Choi 1999: 146–50: Miners 1975: 18–19). As a result of this implicit agreement among the major powers to maintain the status quo, Hong Kong occupied a curious niche in the Cold War as long as its export economy thrived and it was not totally shut off from the mainland.

The one political institution of any consequence in Hong Kong was the administrative bureaucracy headed by a British-appointed governor. The governor and the bureaucracy answered to London, although they were given considerable autonomy. While there were, of course, links into the European business community and advisory roles for the Legislative Council and the Executive Council, the colonial administration was also relatively immune from local pressure. The financial secretary, backed by the governor, tended to steer a relatively conservative course that ensured that Hong Kong's foreign exchange reserves kept on increasing and could be sent to London for safe-keeping. Overall, during this period the bureaucracy was remarkable, when compared to most bureaucracies in developing countries, for its 'continuity, stability, efficiency in delivering services, respectable status in society, relative freedom from corruption and political legitimacy' (Lau 1983: 25).

What was the Hong Kong government's role in the economy? There has been considerable scholarly debate over the degree to which the Hong Kong colonial administration followed a *laissez-faire* economic policy. Advocates of a *laissez-faire* interpretation, encouraged by Sir John Cowperthwaite, who was financial secretary during the 1960s, point out that from the 1950s onwards there were no tariffs, no control over capital movement, no minimum wage legislation for workers, very limited government regulation, and low taxes (Friedman 1981; Chow and Papanek 1981). However, this view ignores the extent to which the government intervened to facilitate the development of the colony's export-oriented economy. Certainly, the administrative bureaucracy in Hong Kong engaged in 'developmental interventionism', although not to the same extent as in Japan and Taiwan.

The most obvious way in which the Hong Kong administration intervened to support the development of the export economy was in ensuring a good, stable supply of cheap labour. This was achieved through various means. Most importantly, it provided housing on a large scale. The Hong Kong Housing Association was set up to provide housing for squatters and the steady flow of refugees who entered the colony. Between 1954 and 1960 new housing, including nine multi-storey blocks of flats, was built to accommodate 310,000 people (Great Britain 1960: 15). The construction of housing for refugees and others continued on until 40 per cent to 45 per cent of the population lived in subsidized housing (Castells 1992: 48; Youngson 1982: 128). At times rent controls were also applied to non-government-owned flats in order to ensure that housing remained affordable (Miners 1975: 47–8).

Other forms of subsidies for labour were also developed over the 1950s and 1960s. The Hong Kong government provided a system of public education, including public universities; a public health care system geared mostly to the lower-income groups; social services; publicaly subsidized mass transportation; and subsidized foodstuffs, especially rice, some of which was even made available by China. One study indicates that by the early 1970s these government policies created a 50 per cent subsidy for each blue-collar household while another study indicates that the public housing subsidy provided 'a transfer-in-kind to the average public housing tenant equivalent to 70% of the household income' (Schiffer 1983 and Yu and Li 1985, both quoted in Castells 1992: 49). In addition, during the 1950s and 1960s a steady stream of refugees entered Hong Kong pushing the total population above 3 million. Although greater restrictions were imposed on refugees during the 1960s, there was no shortage of labour that might force up labour costs. Moreover, given the administration's concerns about political action linked to either mainland China or Taiwan, the activities of unions in the colony were severely proscribed. In general, then, during the 1950s and early 1960s government intervention served to support an expanding, relatively docile, low-cost pool of labour for which business had to provide very little except a basic wage.

But labour was not the only area in which the Hong Kong government intervened in the economy. The government owned all the land in the colony and as a result was the monopoly supplier of this valuable commodity. Hence, through its sale of specific pieces of land it had a significant influence over where and when industrial development took place as well as what kind of enterprises were developed. For example, the government pushed for industrial diversification towards the end of the 1950s as the textile and clothing industry ran into resistance from the colony's traditional markets. It also limited competition in some utilities and services to ensure that the initial investment required to develop the needed infrastructure was put in place. Moreover, from the 1950s onwards the colonial bureaucracy sought to promote Hong Kong's industrial products overseas. And in 1964 the banking sector was more tightly regulated under a revised Banking Ordinance, and an Interest Rate Agreement was instituted which sought to rein in excessive competition over interest rates and stabilize what had become a dangerously volatile market. Overall, although the administration in Hong Kong intervened in the colony's economy much less than did the governments of the other six 'miracle' societies, there were still areas where it employed a 'developmental interventionist' approach to facilitate the growth of the business community (Castells 1992: 46–8; McGurn 1996: 62).

During the 1950s and into the 1960s, Hong Kong's industrialization proceeded apace. As a result not only of the US embargo on trade to China but also China's increasing preference for trade with other communist countries and direct bulk agreements with foreign governments, Hong Kong's entrepôt facilities were ignored and Hong Kong's exports to China fell steadily to less than 5 per cent of total exports by 1958. Hence, the colony's business community had little option but to adapt its entrepôt facilities to serve trade between other parts of the world and more particularly to become one of the earliest export manufacturing enclaves. By 1959 domestic exports accounted for 70 per cent of total exports, with the US, the United Kingdom, Malaya and Japan the chief recipients (Great Britain 1960: 5–6). During the 1950s the textile and clothing sector were at the centre of Hong Kong's manufacturing industry. By the late 1950s plastic flowers and later plastic toys started to be produced and the industry grew quickly. Similarly, in 1959 Sony began to assemble transistor radios in Hong Kong, later expanding its operation to include FM radios and television sets. Other companies followed suit in order to cope with the competition. Overall, Hong Kong's adoption of an export-oriented development strategy, forced on it by the changing geopolitics of the region, served the colony well in the dozen years following the end of the Korean War.

Malaysia and Singapore

From the end of the Korean War to the mid-1960s the fortunes of Malaya/Malaysia and Singapore were very much intertwined. The political development of both countries was shaped in crucial ways by the overarching Cold War and the fight against communism. The foundations of the political institutions that have run both countries up to the present time were laid during this period.

In 1948 Malaya was reconstituted as a federal system with a relatively weak central government and relatively strong state governments that were given control over key policy areas such as land and agriculture. During the next fifteen years or so Malaya/Malaysia retained its federal system but the central government became strong and the state governments weak. The catalyst for this shift in power between the two levels of government was the counter-guerrilla campaign that the Malayan government waged against the Malayan Communist Party (MCP) guerrillas and the general Cold War insecurities that permeated the region. Three dimensions of this shift in power between the federal government and the state governments are key (Stubbs 1997).

First, the federal government in Kuala Lumpur had to generate the necessary funds to wage the increasingly costly guerrilla war against the MCP. Immediately following the Second World War the British insisted that Malaya be self-financing. Corporate taxes were revised and Inland Revenue personnel were sent out from Britain to train Malayan officials in tax collection. The onset of the boom generated by the Korean War permitted the federal authorities to raise taxes on the export of rubber and tin. These revenues, along with the corporate and income tax, allowed the government to triple its income from 1948 to 1951. The tax laws were once again revised in

1957 immediately after independence. As a result of these initiatives, by the early 1960s, the Malaysian government was able to mobilize a very creditable 18 per cent of GNP through taxation and a further 3 per cent through domestic borrowing (Esman 1972: 96). Armed with these funds, the central government was able to bring the chronically cash-strapped states to heel by offering them funds to implement Kuala Lumpur's policies.

Second, political developments, shaped by the communist guerrilla war and the general Cold War environment, gave the federal government the upper hand in dealing with the states. The British colonial administration opened up the political process from 1952 onwards with the first federal elections taking place in 1955. It refused, however, to grant independence until all races in the country were united. The Malay political elites at the state level backed the multiracial Independence of Malaya Party (IMP). But the group that swept the polls at state and federal elections was a coalition of individual parties, each of which represented a major racial group – the United Malays Nationalist Organization (UMNO), the Malayan Chinese Association (MCA) and the Malayan Indian Congress (MIC). As a result the state elites were left on the sidelines. The success of the essentially right-of-centre Alliance Party, as the coalition became known, necessitated negotiations among the leaders over policy and the assignment of constituencies in which each party would run. This process, which was dominated by the UMNO, tended to centralize power in the leadership in Kuala Lumpur. At the state level Alliance Party members were guided by those at the federal level, even to the extent that a chief minister in an Alliance Party-controlled state government had to have the approval of the Federation's prime minister – always the leader of UMNO – in his capacity as head of the Alliance Party. From 1955 to the present, the multiracial coalition lead by UMNO has won every election (Stubbs 1997: 63–4).

However, the political development that was most important in crystallizing the centralization of power was the new constitution that came with independence in 1957. With the guerrilla war, or emergency, still in effect, the federal government argued that it needed considerable centralized coordinating authority if it was to finally defeat the MCP guerrillas and to ensure that any resurgent communist threat could be contained in the future. As a consequence a number of powers were transferred from the states to the federal government when the constitution for the newly independent state was proclaimed (Means 1976: 182–6). The result was to give the federal government 'truly formidable' powers over the state governments (Milne and Mauzy 1978: 105).

Third, the central government in Kuala Lumpur benefited from the need to expand the police, the armed forces and the bureaucracy in order to implement the 'hearts and minds' strategy. Indeed, when the emergency was declared over in 1960 the government had built up a substantial and relatively efficient security apparatus. The police had become a sizeable and reasonably well-trained organization and the Special Branch had gained a deserved reputation as an intelligence-gathering agency (Zakaria 1977). Although British and Commonwealth troops provided the bulk of the military component of the counter-insurgency operations and the Malayan armed forces were, as a consequence, relatively small, they were also well-trained and effective. Backing up this impressive institutional power was the Internal Security Act which replaced the emergency regulations in 1960. It gave extensive powers to security forces, and the government more generally, on the presumption that they would be needed to combat any future communist threat.

The Malayan government's strategy of addressing the population's grievances in an effort to wean them away from supporting the MCP guerrillas required the expansion of the administration. Enlarging the bureaucracy occurred at both the local level and in departments dealing with the delivery of programmes like education, health services, public works, and drainage and irrigation. The emergency generated a spectacular three-fold increase in the size of the Malayan bureaucracy from 1948 to its close in 1960 (Stubbs 1989b: 263). By 1965 it had expanded to a workforce of 228,000, 'a high figure comparable to such countries as the United Kingdom and Denmark' (Esman 1972: 70–1). Significantly, the expansion of the administrative structure took place at the same time as the political parties were evolving. A substantial number of those who ran as candidates for the UMNO had been government employees of one sort or another. Overall, the fusion of the Alliance Party, especially the UMNO, and the bureaucracy underscored the transformation of the Malayan government into what was, by comparison with other developing countries, a relatively strong, centralized political institution. It led one commentator to label Malaysia – as Malaya became known after 1963 – an 'administrative state' (Esman 1972: 62–6).

Singapore's development during the period from 1953 to the mid-1960s was closely tied to events in Malaya. Until 1941 Singapore was the administrative centre of British Malaya. However, in the immediate post-Second World War period the British government became concerned both about the possible racial tensions between Singapore's Chinese majority and the Malay majority in peninsular Malaysia and about the rising tide of communism inside Singapore's unions and Chinese middle schools. So in April 1946, for essentially strategic reasons, Singapore was divided off from Malaya and administered separately. Despite this division, the futures of Singapore and Malaya remained locked together.

During the first few years of the emergency many of Singapore's communists went into the Malayan jungle to fight the guerrilla war against the British. The absence of communist activists combined with the Korean War boom to produce a period of relative calm in the colony. However, by 1953 it was becoming obvious that the MCP's guerrilla campaign was running into difficulty. A number of communists filtered back from the jungles of the Malayan peninsula and joined the growing band of communist sympathizers who were becoming more and more active in Singapore politics. Recognizing that eventually they would have to grant independence to Singapore and wanting to capitalize on the increasing success of the Malayan government against the MCP guerrillas, the British slowly opened up the political process. The communists sought to take advantage of the opportunities this development offered. Their plan was to expand their base of support especially among Chinese-educated Singaporeans to whom the franchise was gradually being extended and take over an independent Singapore through their manipulation of front organizations and political parties.

With the first major elections set for April 1955, a number of new political parties were launched. The two most important parties were the Labour Front (LF) and the People's Action Party (PAP). The LF was a moderate left-wing party which captured the most seats in the 1955 election and in a coalition with some smaller parties formed the first locally elected government. The PAP was established in November 1954 and was made up of a moderate, anti-colonial, English-educated faction led by Lee Kuan Yew and a radical pro-communist trade union and Chinese student faction. The PAP was clearly situated well to the left on the political spectrum and had as its main goals 'to oppose colonialism and to create a united, democratic, non-communist, socialist Malaya with Singapore as a component' (Chan 1987:149). In the period between the 1955 elections and the 1959 elections that came with the granting of limited independence, the factions battled for power while at the same time rapidly developing the PAP's base of political support throughout Singapore. The moderates retained power through some timely arrests by the government, backed by the British, of those in the opposing, communist-front faction. After a vigorous campaign the PAP won the 1959 elections, claiming 43 of the 51 seats with 53.4 per cent of the total vote (Chan 1987; Lee 1998; Milne and Mauzy 1990: 47–52; Rodan 1989: 58–63).

Yet the battle against the communists was far from over. The new prime minister, Lew Kuan Yew, and the moderate faction within the PAP had to confront both the opposing pro-communist faction within the Party and the emergence of a new left-wing party, the communist-infiltrated Barisan Sosialis. With some astute manoeuvring and a major roundup of 107 communist and other dissidents in February 1963, Lee was able to limit the powers of the communists, their front organizations and their sympathizers. An important ingredient in the ensuing battle was Singapore's merger with Malaya, Sabah and Sarawak in 1963 to form Malaysia. The PAP mobilized public opinion behind this move by emphasizing that it would allow for the development of an import-substitution strategy in a larger market. Moving into Malaysia, it was argued, would alleviate Singapore's economic woes and help to create a vibrant economy. For the moderate PAP faction, joining Singapore and Malaysia also meant that the communists had to deal with Kuala Lumpur's Internal Security Act wielded by a Malay-dominated government. Importantly, the government in Kuala Lumpur was indifferent to the nuances of Chinese politics in the new part of the federation and very concerned about the role of Singapore communists in Indonesia's aggressive policy of armed confrontation against Malaysia. Indeed, one of the reasons why the Malayan Prime Minister Tunku Abdul Rahman had wanted to form Malaysia was to ensure that Singapore did not become a communist enclave on its borders. In this he was strongly supported by the British.

But the merger did not work. Conflict quickly engulfed the new political arrangement. The Alliance Party was conservative and the main party in the coalition, the UMNO, was intent on maintaining the political dominance of the Malays. The PAP had an essentially socialist agenda and wanted a multiracial society in which Malaysia's large ethnic Chinese community was given a better political deal. On top of this, the respective leaders of the Alliance, Tunku Abdul Rahman, and the PAP, Lee Kuan Yew, could not get along. Extremist rhetoric on both sides managed only to increase the racial animosity and resulted in race riots, deaths and casualties. In August 1965 it was announced that Singapore would separate from Malaysia. Singapore, an island of only 1.5 million people, was on its own.

As the Lee Kuan Yew faction of the PAP took over the reins of government in the newly independent Singapore, it was heavily influenced by the war of attrition the PAP had waged against various opponents during the preceding decade. The PAP leadership were fiercely anti-communist. It headed an ostensibly mass party but one that was, in fact, run by a twelve-member Central Executive Committee, and one from which any real opposition had been largely vanquished. In the September 1963 election the PAP won 37 of 51 seats with 47 per cent of the vote. The PAP dominated the legislature. The Singapore City Council was abolished in 1959 and its powers moved to the central government. The civil service was largely localized and, after some initial conflict, came to value the approach of the moderate wing of the PAP. And the trade union movement was brought under control when the communist-dominated Singapore Association of Trade Unions (SATU) was closed down after its application for registration was rejected in 1963 and the PAP-sponsored National Trade Union Congress (NTUC), which became the national organization to which all trade unions belonged, was set up in 1964. At the end of 1965, then, the PAP government of the unexpectedly independent Singapore was relatively autonomous of societal influences and could face its new responsibilities unencumbered by obligations or unpaid political debts (Rodan 1989: 30). It had also inherited from the British a well-trained civil service which allowed for the buildup of a very effective and relatively autonomous 'administrative state' (Chan 1975: 223).

In both Malaya/Malaysia and Singapore economic development from the end of the Korean War to the mid-1960s was uneven. In Malaya/Malaysia economic policy revolved around a series of five-year economic plans which began in 1950. The government thus adopted 'a broadly interventionist role' (Drabble 2000: 162) which was reinforced by its willingness to become involved in the economic and social lives of Malayans/Malaysians in order to address the grievances of the rural population and, hence, ensure that they did not support the MCP guerrillas. During the 1950s this involvement included rubber-replanting schemes and rural development projects. The education system was expanded, and new roads, railways, port facilities and electrical power stations were constructed. Also, new dormitory towns, such as Petaling Jaya, were built around the major centres to accommodate the influx of people leaving the rural areas to escape the guerrilla war.

After independence in 1957, the conservative Alliance Party, led by Prime Minister Tunku Abdul Rahman and Deputy Prime Minister Tun Razak, intervened to fund and direct rural development policies designed to maintain the support of the politically crucial rural Malays. Land resettlement was made available for Malays under the Federal Land Development Authority, the rural infra-structure improved to facilitate agricultural output, and living conditions improved in villages and towns in Malay areas. There was also a concerted attempt to scientifically upgrade rubber production through the Rubber Research Institute. In addition, commodity production was diversified beyond rubber and tin to palm oil, tropical hardwoods and pepper. Indeed, Malaysia essentially remained a commodity producer and, while growth rates in the early 1960s averaged a respectable 4.7 per cent, in any one year its economy prospered or languished depending on the prices of its key raw materials (Drabble 2000: 187). In terms of industrialization, during the early and mid-1960s the government, led by the Economic Planning Unit in the prime minister's department which was given responsibility for national economic planning in 1959, gradually raised tariffs and provided incentives for the development of import-substitution industries. Increased private investment in import-substitution industrialization was also apparent after the domestic market was expanded with the formation of Malaysia in 1963. The new political arrangement certainly produced a noticeable increase in the manufacturing sector's share of GDP, which moved from 6.3 per cent in 1957 to 10.4 per cent in 1965 (Jomo 1997: 90).

In Singapore, the PAP's accession to power in 1959 saw a shift in emphasis in the government's economic policy. Between 1953 and 1959 Singapore's economy continued to be almost solely based on its entrepôt role. However, it became obvious that Singapore could not continue to rely on entrepôt trade, which only grew by 1 per cent per year between 1956 and 1960, to absorb the island's growing workforce. To do so was a recipe for continued high levels of unemployment and social and political discontent (Haggard 1990: 108). Guided by a report developed by a UN Industrial Survey Mission, the new PAP government began to prepare the ground for import-substitution industrialization. The UN report's recommendations, which heavily influenced Singapore's 1961–4 State Development Plan, urged the government to make Singapore an attractive site for foreign investment. As a result, among other initiatives, the PAP government improved and expanded the physical infrastructure; set up a system of industrial estates; and established an Economic Development Board, which was charged with coordinating industrial development. One of the key features of the UN report was its emphasis on the need to provide a more educated, less fractious, low-cost supply of labour. The government's successful abolition of the communist-infiltrated SATU and the setting up of the NTUC helped to bring about greater labour peace. At the same time government investment in low-cost housing and education increased massively. The resulting boom in construction and the boost to import-substitution industrialization brought about by Singapore's integration into the larger Malaysian market in 1963 more than made up for the drag on entrepôt trade created by 'Confrontation' with Indonesia. The economy was propelled forward at a creditable average annual 5.7 per cent growth rate from 1960 to 1966 (Huff 1994: 302).

Having started down the import-substitution road to industrialization, both Malaysia and Singapore were forced to rethink their strategies in light of the traumatic events of August 1965 when Prime Minister Tunku Abdul Rhaman decided that Singapore had to leave Malaysia. For Malaysia the consequences were not nearly so troubling as they were for Singapore. Malaysia had a growing commodity export sector and a larger population than Singapore, although it was still relatively small at just less than 10 million people. For Singapore, the separation was clearly a major crisis. Having embarked on an import-substitution strategy it was suddenly faced with a domestic market that could not support any sort of sustained economic growth. A reorientation in its economic policy was necessary, but where would it get the resources to undertake such a manoeuvre? And could a new strategy be developed in time to save the newly independent country and the PAP government from disaster?

Thailand

Although fighting stopped on the Korean peninsula in 1953, the US government continued to be concerned about the possibility of China extending its influence southwards into Southeast Asia. The Thai government was able to portray the country as a frontline bastion against any communist encroachment. The US agreed with this depiction of Thailand's strategic position and proceeded to make Bangkok the headquarters for the US-sponsored Southeast Asia Treaty Organization (SEATO) (Caldwell 1974: 42). Preoccupied with the region's security and determined to ensure that Thailand was capable of defending itself against an external communist attack and internal subversion, the US increased both its military and economic aid. It gave little thought to continued centralization of power this might entail. Indeed, when, in 1957, Field Marshal Sarit Thanarat staged a bloodless coup against Phibun's government – following a series of scandals and a patently fraudulent election – and then in 1958 annulled the constitution and imposed a harsh, personal dictatorial rule, the US quickly confirmed its support for his anti-communist regime. Most importantly from the Thai point of view, US aid continued to flow.

American aid during the period from the end of the Korean War to the mid-1960s prompted a marked increase in the size and effectiveness of Thailand's two main political institutions, the military and the bureaucracy. Between 1953 and 1965 the US provided US$540 million in military assistance, almost all in grants, to Thailand (United States Senate 1969: 633). As a result of this funding the Thai armed forces expanded from 45,200 in 1955 to 134,000 in 1961 and around 160,00 by the mid-1960s (Chai-Anan *et al.* 1990: 22–31; United States Senate 1969: 708). As well as increasing the size of the Thai armed forces, US military aid went to extensive training, upgrading the armed forces' professional standards – although it did not dent the military's insistence on playing a leading role in Thai politics – and supplying modern equipment. Beginning in 1957 the equipment and training of the police force were also improved courtesy of the US Central Intelligence Agency. During this period – from 1953 to 1965 – the US also supplied US$343 million in economic aid (Muscat 1990: 295). A substantial portion of this aid went towards upgrading Thailand's public administration. Between 1954 and 1965 the USAID sponsored over 3,200 students who undertook periods of study in America. A large number of these students returned to work in the Thai bureaucracy. In addition, budgeting, financial and accounting procedures were modernized and a school for upper-level bureaucrats established. Departments and agencies were set up which allowed the Thai government not only to play a relatively strong role in the aid process but also to manage the expanding economy better. Most notable among these new institutions were the Budget Bureau of the Prime Minister's Department, National Statistical Office, National Economic Development Board (later the National Economic and Social Development Board), the Board of Investment and the Office of Fiscal Policy in the Ministry of Finance (Muscat 1994: 92; Pasuk and Baker 1995: 128). Indeed, so much modernization of the bureaucracy took place during this period that one observer, with perhaps just a slight hint of hyperbole, argued that Thailand has a 'strong and effective government' and the 'most efficient civil service in Southeast Asia' (Nuechterlein 1967: 126).

Sarit's ascendency to power brought about major changes in Thai economic policy. Indeed, 'The Sarit coup brought into line the strategic interests of the US, the dictatorial aims of the Thai military, and the commercial ambitions of domestic capital' (Pasak and Baker (1995: 127). The Phibun government had followed a state-led, economic-nationalist strategy through to 1957. However, once Sarit took over he abandoned this approach in favour of economic growth based on private capital. He was urged to undertake this new strategy by an International Bank for Reconstruction and Development (IBRD) report published in 1959 which was strongly backed by the US government, USAID officials in Thailand and Thai technocrats who had recently returned from studying in the US. The new strategy centred on import-substitution. As a result state-enterprises were dismantled or sold to private investors, high rates of import tariffs were maintained on consumer goods and lower rates on capital goods and inputs, and private investors were encouraged, through incentives, to put their capital into a wide range of enterprises, from textiles and automobiles to refined sugar and cosmetics. Labour was plentiful, urban rice prices were subsidized and labour organizations prohibited. The major beneficiaries of this import-substitution strategy were the domestic 'developing industrial conglomerates and their financial partners, and most notably the fifteen to twenty families who dominated the highly protected domestic commercial banks' (Hewison 1997: 103; Hewison 1989; Suehiro 1985).

But the relatively high growth rates of about 7 per cent during the early 1960s could not have been achieved without the massive amounts of US military and economic aid and the IBRD loans that funded the country's expanding economic and social infrastructure. Between 1951 and 1965 about US$350 million was spent on highway construction (Surachat 1988: 125). As a consequence by the mid-1960s Thailand had developed a national road system where none had existed before; constructed a deep water port at Sattahip to alleviate congestion in the Port of Bangkok; and, as a side-effect, acquired a relatively capable civil engineering sector. In addition, substantial US aid was put into electrical generation so that by 1960 65 per cent of Thailand's total power supply was provided by US-financed generating capacity (Muscat 1990: 110). And as the country was opened up and rural and agricultural aid projects developed so marked increases in rice and corn production were realized. Overall, then, by the mid-1960s, Thailand's political and economic institutions were starting to modernize as US aid, security needs and development thinking, driven by the imperatives of the Cold War, began to have an impact.

Conclusion

From the end of the Korean War to the mid-1960s the Cold War, and its associated regional wars, had an enormous impact on the development of the institutional state in what were to become the 'miracle' economies. For the American government, fighting the Cold War meant setting up Japan, South Korea, Taiwan and Thailand as frontline fortresses in the battle to contain the spread of communism. The British also saw communism as an evil to be defeated by all means available and made every effort to eradicate communism from Hong Kong, Singapore and Malaya. For both the Americans and the British, strong centralized governments in these seven societies were viewed as a necessity. And for large portions of the populations of these Asian societies, the external and, in some cases the internal, communist threat warranted the concentration of power in the hands of the government. As psychologists consistently point out, in times of crisis people are all too willing to cede power to those able to demonstrate their capacity to successfully deal with the problems that threaten the group.

During this period, the massive influx of aid into Japan, South Korea, Taiwan and Thailand; immigrant skills and capital into Hong Kong; and the war-driven commodity booms in Malaya and Singapore fuelled the rapid growth of the coercive and the administrative institutions of the state. Armed forces, police and intelligence agencies were formed into reasonably effective instruments for bringing about and maintaining social order and, when necessary, for providing a show of strength to ward off external threats. Also helped by the flow of funds into the seven Asian societies, bureaucracies were expanded and upgraded to implement successfully the economic policies of the increasingly centralized governments. Moreover, key political parties which continue to dominate their societies to this day – the LDP in Japan, the PAP in Singapore, and the Alliance Party/Barisan Nasional in Malaysia – emerged as central players. Overall, then, this was a crucial formative period in the development of the key political institutions of the seven 'miracle' economies.

Just as importantly, the Cold War provided the political justification not only for the strong state but also for the mobilization of each country's population around a national hegemonic project (Jessup 1982: 243). This is not to suggest, as many analysts have, that the economic strategies of each of the seven 'miracle' economies were fully thought out from the start. As Tun-jen Cheng (1990: 141) notes, 'in reality, the course of development is shaped more by numerous improvised decisions or ad hoc policy changes than by some predetermined national grand design'. The Cold War context, including at times pressure from US advisors, hedged-in policy makers and steered policy in the direction of development through growth as leaders attempted to ensure their society's ability to withstand the internal and external communist threat. It was such pressure, for example, that provided the rationale for the depoliticization of labour and, in South Korea and Taiwan, the impetus to move from an import-substitution strategy to an export-oriented industrialization strategy. The communist threat also allowed for the opening of markets, especially those in the US. In other words, the economic policies of the seven 'miracle' governments during the dozen years from 1953 to the mid-1960s cannot be fully understood without reference to the pervasive influence of the Cold War.

In addition, the Cold War had a critical, direct impact on the economies of these Asian societies. It provided both the resources and the *raison d'être* for the emerging emphasis on rapid economic growth. Prompted by the requirements of the Cold War, the increased flow of funds, including military and economic aid, allowed for the foundations of industrialization to be laid. These foundations included the emergence of key manufacturing sectors. Considerable investments were made in infrastructure projects, often for military reasons, to allow the armed forces access to areas of the country considered strategically vital in a guerrilla war (as in the case of Malaya) or any possible future war (as was the case in South Korea and Thailand) against communism. However, the crucial point is, of course, that this infrastructural development – roads, railways, bridges, ports, electrical power capacity, and so forth – proved to have dramatic and long-term benefits for economic expansion. The same was true of investment in human capital. Education systems were expanded, skills-training given priority, rural development promoted and subsidized housing built.

In terms of their industrial strategies, each of the seven economies was at a different point in its decision to de-emphasize import-substitution and give a high priority to the export of manufacturing products. Hong Kong and Japan had adopted this approach in the late 1940s and early 1950s and by the mid-1960s had achieved some measure of success. Taiwan, South Korea and Singapore had made a commitment to an export-oriented strategy by the mid-1960s but were not guaranteed success. Malaysia was moving slowly towards a greater commitment to export industrialization while Thailand was still attempting to get industrialization of any sort off the ground. No one was yet describing any of these seven societies as having a 'miracle' economy. At this point their future prosperity was by no means preordained.

5

The Vietnam War as Economic Catalyst

In early August 1964 the US claimed that American naval ships operating in international waters in the Gulf of Tonkin were attacked in two separate incidents by North Vietnamese torpedo boats. President Johnson immediately ordered retaliatory air strikes against North Vietnam. He sought and received authorization from Congress to use military force to counter what was seen as an increasingly successful communist campaign to take over South Vietnam. In February 1965 the first regular US combat troops arrived at Da Nang air-base in South Vietnam. A few months later they were fully engaged in the fighting. From that point on, troops were quickly deployed to the region. By early 1969 there were over 540,000 US soldiers based in Vietnam. Towards the end of 1969, discouraged by the obvious lack of success in combating the communists, the US began a 'Vietnamization' of its war effort. By the end of 1971, it had reduced the number of US soldiers stationed in Vietnam to 139,000. On 27 January 1973 a peace agreement was signed with North Vietnam and by March, America's military participation in the war had essentially come to an end.

In strictly economic terms, the Vietnam War was the second most expensive war in US history after the Second World War (United States Senate 1971: 1). The full cost of the Vietnam War has officially been estimated to be in the region of US$140 billion with the incremental costs – costs attributed to the Vietnam War that would not otherwise have been incurred – estimated at approximately US$112 billion. Other estimates are higher (Littauer and Uphoff 1972: 100; Stevens 1976: 166). In contrast to what happened during the Korean War, a substantial portion of the procurement of goods and services took place in the US itself rather than in East and Southeast Asia. Nonetheless, the impact of US spending on the war was hugely significant for the economy of the region.

Yet, surprisingly, the Vietnam War and its economic consequences for the Asian 'miracle' economies have been largely ignored by those seeking to explain the region's success. With one or two notable exceptions (e.g. Woo 1991), analysts who adopt an American-hegemony explanation for the region's economic success, while generally stressing the determining role played by the US in shaping the region's security and political economy, fail to detail the way in which US spending on the Vietnam War boosted regional economies. Perhaps most intriguingly, they neglect to explore why the economies of some of Vietnam's Southeast Asian neighbours – such as Singapore, Malaysia and Thailand – benefited from the war and others – such as the Philippines and Indonesia did not. Nor do they specify the political effects of the war, which were often significant. For some leaders, at least by 'holding the communists at bay' the Americans were seen as providing a 'respite' that was crucial to the political and economic progress and prosperity of the region (Jayakumar 1966: 16; Stockwin 1975: 53). And the overall regional prosperity induced by spending on the war was important in ensuring the continued performance legitimacy of most regional governments.

The other explanations for the East and Southeast Asia's economic success similarly overlook the catalytic effects of the Vietnam War on Asia's 'miracle' economies. The vast majority of those advocating a neoclassical economic perspective focused almost exclusively on the virtues of the export-oriented approach adopted by Taiwan, South Korea and Singapore during the 1960s and the benefits of market-driven policies. The statists sought to counter the neoclassical economic perspective by detailing the positive interventionist role of the state in promoting economic development. Apart from some passing references (Wade 1990: 96), neither group has been especially interested in placing their analyses in the larger context of the economic and political impact of the Vietnam War. Likewise, the proponents of the cultural and the Japan-centred explanations of Asia's economic success see the war as irrelevant. Indeed, both groups have tended to concentrate on the rapid economic growth of the 'miracle' economies from the 1970s onwards – in other words, after the war was over. None of the five sets of explanations for

Asia's rapid economic growth, then, takes into account the full economic effects of the Vietnam War. There is clearly a need to rectify this oversight.

It needs to be emphasized that the purpose of this chapter is not to debate the merits of the American involvement in the Vietnam War. Rather it is to explore the economic consequences of the war. It is not the intention here to underestimate the devastation that the war brought to Vietnam. It was disastrous for both North and South Vietnam. Estimates suggest that nearly five million people were killed or wounded and close to a third of South Vietnam's population made homeless at one time or another (e.g. Kingsbury 2001: 2496). The war was also calamitous for the US. Over 58,000 Americans were killed and more than 153,000 severely injured. Yet, despite the loss of life and the widespread devastation, the Vietnam War had an enormous positive economic impact on the seven future 'miracle' economies of East and Southeast Asia – Japan, Taiwan, South Korea, Hong Kong, Singapore, Malaysia and Thailand.

Although Vietnam itself suffered from the destructive and disintegrative aspects of war, the 'miracle' economies benefited from the war's formative and developmental effects as well as its reformative and redistributive effects. The economic boom created by the Vietnam War solidified existing institutions and made possible the successful development of new economic and political institutions. Certainly, the massive economic boost from US spending on the war provided a positive feedback for the economic and political institutions in the Asian societies on which the war-induced prosperity was built. The war confirmed the industrializing, development trajectory that the 'miracle' economies had set for themselves and further entrenched within their societies the institutions and policies that made rapid economic development possible.

Japan

Although the Vietnam War did not have as great an impact on the Japanese economy as the Korean War, it was still significant. American military procurements increased markedly over the eight years of US involvement in the war. At the same time Japan benefited from being able to export materials, supplies and components to companies in other regional centres, such as South Korea, Taiwan and Thailand, which were filling their own procurement contracts. Of course, Japan's exports to South Vietnam also rose quickly. Indeed, Japan became the largest Asian supplier of goods for the Vietnam market (Naya 1971: 41). And all this was in addition to the many American troops who spent money in Tokyo during their rest and recreation (R&R) visits. (EUI 1968: 13; Havens 1987: 101). While Japan's economy was boosted by US spending in East and Southeast Asia it was also given a major lift by the increase in the value of Japanese exports to the US. With so much spending on the Vietnam War, the US economy quickly heated up and absorbed increasing amounts of imports. The general consensus is that from 1965 to 1972 Japan earned, on average, at least US$1 billion a year from the Vietnam War, with some estimates putting the figure as high as US$1.5 billion (Havens 1987: 96; Schaller 1997: 198).

But it is was not just the absolute amounts that were important. The wide variety of goods that were in demand because of the Vietnam War stimulated specific sectors and industries. The new procurement funds were a boon to the young industries which obtained US contracts (Havens 1987: 96). Initially, relatively small Japanese businesses that could gear up quickly for the new market prospered. Later, as camps were built, larger firms that had the capacity to fill a variety of orders for such items as cement, cranes and jeeps received an increasing number of contracts. There was also a growing demand for consumer goods. Japanese beer and gum as well as television sets were shipped to American camps in Vietnam to keep the troops happy. And as the money poured into Vietnam so there was an increasing demand among urban Vietnamese for radios, motorcycles, scooters and a wide range of other consumer items (Havens 1987). The variety of goods that were in demand, because of both regional prosperity and the insatiable US home market, proved to be a valuable incentive to the development of many parts of the Japanese economy but especially to the newly emerging consumer goods sector.

For the Japanese economy, then, the Vietnam War years proved to be a watershed period. It helped pull the economy out of the downturn of 1965 and reinforced Japan's strategy of export promotion. Indeed, overall, exports quickly grew from US$8.15 billion in 1966 to US$24 billion in 1971 with chemicals and heavy industrial products – a large portion of which went to the US – leading the way (Havens 1987: 95; IMF 1971; IMF 1978; Nakamura 1981: 212).

Particularly noteworthy was the increase in the number of vehicles exported by Japan. It was during this period that Japan's trade surplus with the United States began to mount to significant proportions. From a trade deficit with the US of just over US$240 million in 1964 Japan moved to a surplus of over US$4 billion by 1972 (IMF 1971; IMF 1978; Schaller 1997). And the Vietnam War paved the way for greater Japanese links to Southeast Asia. US procurements in places such as Singapore and Thailand, combined with the general regional prosperity generated by US spending on the war, increased markets for Japanese goods. Within Japan the economy had reached 'maturity' by the late 1960s and the general pattern of rapid economic growth had been firmly established. The boost from the Vietnam War underscored the validity of the government's general approach to economic development. In particular, it reinforced the political and economic institutional structures that underpinned the country's overall economic success.

Hong Kong

By 1965 and the beginning of the Vietnam War, Hong Kong, like Japan, had developed a strong export-oriented economy. With no US economic or military aid going to Hong Kong, the major impact of the war on the British colony came in the form of profits from the massive influx of US sailors and soldiers on R&R and the rapid rise in exports to the war-fuelled US economy. Hong Kong's population of only 3.6 million in 1965 welcomed the general regional prosperity that US spending on the Vietnam War generated, especially as a counter to the severe economic and social disruptions produced by the Cultural Revolution in mainland China during the second half of the 1960s. Certainly, in the first few years of the Vietnam War, the boost to the economy was the silver lining in the dark cloud of anxiety that hung over Hong Kong where the fear was that 'the war might escalate into a major conflict between the US and China, potentially affecting the status of the colony' (Choi 1999: 145).

Hong Kong was the preferred destination for US military personnel on their one-week regional leave. Hostess bars were packed with American sailors (*The Times*, 20 January 1966). One estimate indicates that in 1967 2 out of every 7 of the 500,000 or so tourists who arrived in Hong Kong were US personnel on leave. Overall,

Hong Kong appears to have earned well over US$80 million per year from R&R (EIU 1968: 13–15). An added consequence of the US 'invasion' was that Hong Kong became the leading souvenir producer in Asia and booming sales gave a major boost to the already thriving clothing, plastics and electronics sectors (Miller 1968). Hong Kong's exports to South Vietnam did increase, but the volume was so small as to make little difference to the colony's overall trade (Naya 1971).

The major rise in Hong Kong's trade was with the US. As an exporter of manufactured goods, Hong Kong, like Japan, benefited from the increased demand in the US as the economy was stoked by the American government's domestic war-related spending. In 1965, spurred on by 'the effects of the Vietnam War', Hong Kong's 'cotton textile exports to the US expanded phenomenally' (*The Times*, 14 April 1966). Moreover, as manufacturers made greater use of man-made fibres and up-graded the quality of their products, exports continued to expand into the early 1970s. The other major export from Hong Kong to the US was electrical goods. Foreign direct investment from both the US and Japan flooded into Hong Kong so that the number of factories manufacturing electronic goods leaped from 31 in 1965 to 270 in 1971(Kraitzer 1972). About 80 per cent of the electrical goods such as television receivers and other television components, transistor radios and computer components went to the US. Furthermore, as Hong Kong's trade patterns started to shift away from Great Britain and towards the US and the rest of Asia, the percentage of Hong Kong's total external trade destined for the US rose from 34 per cent in 1965 to 42 per cent in 1970 (Burgess 1972; Lin and Mok 1985: 228). Overall, the annual rate of increase of total exports rose by close to 20 per cent during the late 1960s (Fan 1975).

The general prosperity brought on by the Vietnam War and the expansion of trade produced windfall revenues for the colonial administration (Youngson 1982: 60–1). These revenues allowed for an increase in the size of the bureaucracy which grew by over 50 per cent from 60,000 in 1961 to 94,000 in 1971. Money continued to be put into subsidized housing with approximately 1.5 million, or over 40 per cent of the population, living in government flats (*The Times*, 5 May 1975). In 1971 compulsory free primary education was introduced and the necessary steps to introduce universal secondary education were being made (Goodstadt 1972).

Hong Kong was, therefore, a beneficiary of US spending on the Vietnam War. The war acted as a catalyst for Hong Kong's rapid economic development during the second half of the 1960s and into the 1970s. Indeed, by early 1970 the boom years in manufacturing had caused labour to become increasingly scarce and costly. Hong Kong was forced to contemplate becoming a financial centre in order to offset the high cost of labour in its manufacturing sector.

Taiwan, South Korea and Singapore

For the three future 'miracle' economies that were turning to export-led economic growth in the mid-1960s, the timing of the Vietnam War could not have been better. The point that 'As Japan had fattened off the Korean War, so Taiwan's economy received an incalculable boost from Vietnam's agony' (Gold 1986:86) was also true for South Korea and Singapore. Yet relatively little has been written about the economic impact of the war on the three NIEs. Most analysts simply make a passing reference to the importance of the war and then move on to other matters. However, during the late 1960s and early 1970s each of the three NIEs experienced remarkable economic growth rates which were clearly spurred on by the considerable resources committed to the war.

Taiwan was a major beneficiary of the Vietnam War. With US economic aid being phased out and with the shift to an export-led growth strategy well under way, the extra income from US spending on the war was most fortuitous. US dollars were channelled into Taipei's economy as US troops visited the city on R&R (US Senate 1969/70: 964). A more important factor in the long term was that, as the war escalated, American defence spending in Taiwan rose four-fold between 1965 and the height of the fighting in 1969. Especially critical to the economic development of Taiwan was its exports to South Vietnam which amounted to over 13 per cent of all its exports in 1967 (Naya 1971). The key point here was not so much the absolute value of the exports but the products that were shipped. These included a high percentage of Taiwan's exports of cement, iron and steel, aluminium products, machinery and transportation equipment (Naya 1971: 43–5; EIU 1968: 17, 22). In other words, just as Taiwan's industrialization was getting off the ground and its infant export-manufacturing sector needed a market for its products, the Vietnam War erupted and created a market right on its doorstep.

Taiwan also took full advantage of the explosion in demand within the US market. Taiwan's exports to the US rose from US$120 million in 1966 to a remarkable US$1.7 billion in 1973. Moreover, during the period exports to the US went from 22 per cent of total exports to 38 per cent (IMF 1971: 268; IMF 1978: 100). And, by the early 1970s, Taiwan had a US$600 million trade surplus with the US, which covered the growing deficit with Japan and helped to maintain the island's foreign exchange reserves (IMF 1978: 100). Trade with Japan also expanded markedly. Most notably, Japanese imports provided a substantial portion of the capital goods and other inputs for Taiwan's rapid industrialization during the late 1960s and early 1970s.

The economic stimulus provided by the Vietnam War came on top of other developments which helped to boost the average GNP growth rate between 1965 and 1973 to well over 10 per cent per year (Gold 1986: 85; Liang and Lee 1975: 270). Most importantly, although the Taiwan government kept control over the key levers of the economy, such as bank ownership, state enterprises and protective tariffs, it eliminated most of the barriers to exports and brought in new legislation in 1962 encouraging foreign direct investment (FDI). Helped by the US Agency for International Development (AID), Taiwan aggressively sought out foreign investment. In 1963 the government negotiated a landmark deal with Singer Sewing Company. In 1964 General Instruments, seeking to compete with the increasingly competitive Japanese imports into the US, built a bonded factory making products for the American market (Gold 1986). By the end of 1965 twenty-four more American firms had followed suit. For their part Japanese companies, such as Matsushita and Sony, established joint ventures in Taiwan manufacturing electrical goods. In addition, the Taiwanese government set up the publicly owned China Data Processing Center to promote the use of computers in local industries. Added impetus was given to the export manufacturing strategy by the launching, in 1966, of the Kaohsiung Export Processing Zone (KEPZ). The KEPZ, which was a major factor in growth of electrical exports at a rate of 58 per cent per year from 1966 to 1971, was so successful that it quickly spawned two other EPZs (Gold 1986: 86; Wade 1990: 95). Overall, then, foreign investment moved into Taiwan just as capital and markets were being made available as a result of the Vietnam War. While US spending on the Vietnam War was not the sole reason for Taiwan's economic boom, it was clearly a major contributory factor to Taiwan's strong economic performance from 1965 to 1973.

Like Taiwan, South Korea's remarkable record of economic growth during the last half of the 1960s and the early 1970s owes a great deal to US spending on the Vietnam War. Key to the country's surge in dollar earnings was the government's decision to dispatch South Korean troops to Vietnam. And after these troops showed that they were capable of making a contribution to the fighting, the US put in a request for a second contingent. However, the South Korean public opposed the deployment feeling that their troops were being underpaid and poorly treated. The government used domestic discontent to wrestle a series of concessions from the US government that were laid out in a letter from US Ambassador Brown to South Korea's foreign minister. The new agreement dramatically increased South Korea's dollar earnings from its participation in the war (Han 1978: 899). At their peak strength, between 1967 and 1972, the South Korean government kept 50,000 troops in Vietnam. The full cost of the South Korean forces was covered by the US and their remittances home became a major source of valuable foreign exchange. The Brown letter also provided for South Korean participation in construction projects in Vietnam, paving the way for the development of South Korea's much-heralded construction industry; procurements of supplies, services and equipment in South Korea for Korean, US and Vietnamese forces; procurements destined for Vietnam funded by US AID; and increased loans from AID as well as US technical assistance in order to support exports to Vietnam and other developmental needs. Between 1965 and 1970, roughly US$1 billion was channelled by the US into South Korea as a result of the provisions set out in the Brown letter (Woo 1991: 94).

In addition, although US military aid had been reduced to US$124 million in 1964 it was substantially increased once the US went into Vietnam in 1965. From this base of US$124 million, the Vietnam War added more than US$2 billion in US military aid to South Korea between 1965 and 1973 (Han 1978: 908). While a portion of this amount was spent on the delivery of US weapons and training in the US, enough additional US dollars went into South Korea to make a marked impact on the country's foreign exchange earnings.

Capital also flowed into South Korea as a result of other US policies. The US pushed both Japan and South Korea to agree to a treaty that would normalize their relations. When it was signed in 1965, Japan agreed to provide South Korea with US$800 million in grants, government loans and commercial credit over ten years as reparations. At the same time, the South Korean government's decision to send troops to Vietnam strengthened confidence among US and European firms that the US would be willing to defend South Korea against invasion from the North. As a result, between 1965 and 1967 South Korea received commercial loans from the US, West Germany, Italy and Great Britain. Along with those from Japan these loans totalled US$265 million (Kim 1976: 264). Finally, the Asia Development Bank, which was seen by the US as a key instrument of its policy in a turbulent region, directed 18 per cent of its loans to South Korea between 1968 and 1973 (Woo 1991: 91–2). The Vietnam War and the wider Cold War provided South Korea with a flood of capital with which to pursue its goal of rapid economic growth.

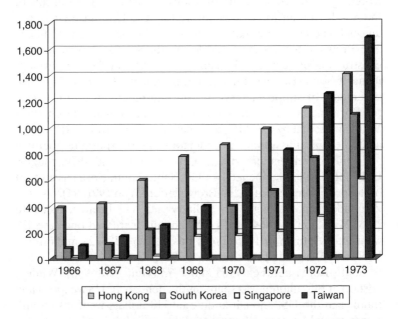

Figure 5.1   Exports to the US during the Vietnam War years (US$ million)
Source: Data from IMF various years.

For South Korea, like Taiwan, exports to Vietnam and to the US were a major boost to the fledgling export manufacturing strategy initiated in 1963 by the Park regime. With the country's industry only beginning to gear up to deliver exports the absolute amounts were far short of the volume of exports into Vietnam from Japan and Taiwan. However, as for Taiwan, a critical effect of the war was that the Vietnam market gave a unique opportunity for emerging state-sponsored business conglomerates, or *chaebol*s, to sell their products internationally. For example, in 1966–7 Vietnam took significant quantities of South Korea's steel products, transport equipment and chemical products (Naya 1971: 43, 45). And Hyundai's first international contracts were for work associated with the Vietnam War, including dredging in Vietnam and highway building in Thailand (Woo 1991: 96). At the same time South Korea's exports to the war-fuelled US economy – which constituted 50 per cent of its total exports – rose ten-fold from 1966 to 1973 (Curtis and Han 1983: 142). Although the Vietnam War was not the only factor at work in promoting exports, it certainly made a significant contribution in the increasing volume and types of goods exported.

The prosperity associated with the Vietnam War years consolidated the hold on power of both the KMT in Taiwan and the new Park regime in South Korea. In Taiwan it helped to propel Chiang Ching-kuo towards the top of the state hierarchy. It allowed him to take over key economic agencies after securing his position at the head of the security apparatus. Chiang reorganized the economic policy machinery, replacing the CIECD with a much weaker Economic Planning Council and gave more policy-making power to the Finance and Economic Small Group of the Executive Yuan which reported directly to him. He also brought younger, better-educated recruits into the KMT and the bureaucracy, including a cohort of young technocrats who moved into the main economic and financial agencies. Furthermore, he introduced new rules to curb corruption. At the same time the KMT leadership had to confront external shocks including China's explosion of an atomic device in 1964, Henry Kissinger's secret visit to China and then President Nixon's visit in 1972, and the loss of Taiwan's seat in the UN to the People's Republic of China in 1971. On top of this, new ideas were entering the island's political debates and questions were being raised about the best way to structure the relationship between the state and the various emerging business groups (Gold 1986). Despite these strains, the obvious success of the economy, significantly helped along by the Vietnam War boom, underpinned a level of social stability that would otherwise have been difficult to sustain.

Initially at least, General Park's hold on power in South Korea was precarious. Elected president in October 1963 after two-and-a-half years of military rule, he received only 36 per cent of the total votes to his major opponent's 35 per cent. For the next two years he faced opposition and criticism from all sides. However, with the advent of the Vietnam War, Park's fortunes began to change. The massive increase in government funds helped Park in a variety of ways (Kim 1976: 264–9). First, the political control exercised through the Korean Central Intelligence Agency expanded appreciably as its numbers and activities were quickly augmented. Second, highly advantageous loans were made to favoured industries and companies which could be called in if government policy was not followed. In the case of the press, the Park government used its control over loans to stifle criticism. Third, a portion of the funds coming into South Korea found its way into Park's party, the Democratic Republican Party, and underwrote its political activities. Moreover, Park's Vietnam policy, aided by the rapid economic growth induced in good part by the Vietnam War, encouraged 'a common sense of purpose and national patriotism' to grow within the South Korean population and Park went on to win the 1967 election handily (Kim 1970: 526). His position, buttressed by the army, enabled him to engineer a period of highly personalized authoritarian rule under the Yushin Constitution adopted by a national referendum in November 1972.

Singapore differed from Taiwan and South Korea in that it received neither US military nor economic aid. However, like Taiwan and South Korea, it did embark on an export-oriented manufacturing strategy which coincided with the US government's military buildup in Vietnam. As a consequence, Singapore also benefited from the war-induced regional economic boom. The increased economic activity from US spending on the Vietnam War was especially opportune in that it compensated for the gradual withdrawal of the British military presence over the period from 1967 to 1971. British expenditures made up nearly 13 per cent of GDP in 1967 and the British employed about 20 per cent of the workforce, mostly in the naval dockyards.

The most dramatic aspect of Singapore's link to the Vietnam War was the rise in its exports to South Vietnam from US$22 million in 1964 to US$146 million in 1969 (UN 1970). About 88 per cent of the value of these exports was in petroleum products which provided fuel for aircraft, helicopters, tanks, military vehicles and naval vessels. A three-fold increase in exports to Thailand over the same period was also driven by the fact that Singapore supplied most of the fuel for the US B52 bombers based in Northeast Thailand. However, the impact of this massive increase in exports of petroleum products should not be exaggerated. A good portion was simply transshipped from bulk tankers to smaller vessels that could navigate the shallower waters of South Vietnam's harbours (EIU 1968; Koh 1970; Loh 1970–1). Even so, Singapore's petroleum-refining capacity was expanded, most notably by the addition of a third Shell refinery in the early 1970s. Moreover, Esso, Mobil, British Petroleum and Amoco were all refining petroleum products and shipping them off to Vietnam. Importantly, Singapore's role in supplying fuel to run the war effort confirmed it as the main refining centre for the region. Furthermore, as a consequence of developments during this period, Singapore became a major centre serving the rapidly growing Japanese petroleum market.

The Vietnam War helped Singapore's emerging economy in a number of other ways. First, US spending on the war accelerated regional economic development and helped to raise the levels of Singapore's entrepôt trade to non-communist Southeast Asian countries and, most notably, to Japan and Taiwan. Net earnings from entrepôt trade more than doubled between 1964 and 1970 with the number of vessels clearing the Port of Singapore similarly doubling between 1959 and 1970 (Editorial Research Staff, Asia Research Bulletin 1971; Senkuttuvan 1972). Second, exports to the US also climbed quickly from only US$52 million in 1966 to US$858 million in 1974. Most notably, exports of textiles, electronics and electrical goods, especially semiconductors, became increasingly important in the early 1970s (Editorial Staff 1971; Huff 1994: 322). Third, the Vietnam War promoted Singapore's ship repair industries. The vast complex of what had been the British navy's dockyards on the island was now employed repairing merchant vessels and repairing and bunkering US warships. Moreover, as oil exploration in Southeast Asia took off in the early 1970s, Singapore began to build oil rigs and supply vessels using the expertise developed repairing ships during the Vietnam War (FEER 1975: 10–11; Koh 1970). Fourthly, Singapore was an R&R centre for US servicemen and gained from their spending. Tourism as a whole made dramatic gains in the late 1960s with Americans, including US soldiers on leave, accounting for nearly a quarter of the 400,000 visitors to Singapore in 1969 (Lim and Ow 1971). Finally, this was the time when Americans appeared to 'discover' Southeast Asia and the economic opportunities it offered. The Vietnam War put the spotlight on Southeast Asia. Economies, such as Singapore's that were obviously in good shape, became targets for investors. Foreign direct investment (FDI) increased ten-fold between 1965 and 1971. The US was by far the top foreign investor with 32 per cent of all FDI, while Great Britain was next with 19 per cent (Elliott 1973). Although this flow of capital may seem rather small, especially when compared to the capital that flowed into, say, Japan or even Taiwan in the same period, with a population of only 2 million the influx of FDI had a very positive effect on Singapore's economy.

Between 1965 and 1973 the turnaround in Singapore's fortunes was startling. The tiny island was transformed from a newly inde-pendent country wedded to an untenable import-substitution policy and concerned about internal communist subversion and possible external threats from its neighbours, to a thriving export-oriented economy with growing and generally positive links to all the non-communist countries of Southeast and East Asia as well as to the US and Western Europe. Indeed, of the three 'miracle' economies that turned to an export-oriented economic strategy in the mid-1960s, Singapore had the highest growth rates. During the Vietnam War years, from 1965 to 1973, Singapore's average annual growth rate was 12.7 per cent while the average annual growth rates for Taiwan and South Korea over the same period were 11 per cent and 10.1 per cent respectively (Krause 1988: S46).

Aided by the economic boost from the Vietnam War, Singapore's success was achieved through a combination of policies whose main focus was a switch to an export-oriented industrial strategy and the attraction of foreign direct investment, especially investment by mul-tinational corporations. The government made use of both statutory bodies and state-owned enterprises to develop what has been termed 'state-directed capitalism' (Huff 1994: 336; Lim 1983). Through its ownership of about 75 per cent of the land in Singapore, including some of the most strategically located property that was handed over when the British abandoned the naval base, the government developed its social and economic infrastructure and advanced specific industrial sectors. Some of the land was used for public housing estates, through the Housing and Development Board and industrial estates – for example, the Jurong Town Corporation established in 1968. Other parcels of land were allocated or bought and sold to promote industries like ship repair and shipbuilding.

At the same time, the prosperity generated by the Vietnam War enabled the government to play a role in the capital market through the development and creation of several financial institutions. The Central Provident Fund (CPF), the government's centralized pension fund, had been set up in 1955, but grew rapidly during the Vietnam War years to cover 75 per cent of the labour force. It became crucial to the government's development plans. With an accumulated fund of nearly US$600 million in 1973 the CPF gave the government access to a cheap, non-inflationary source of finance at below market rates (Huff 1994: 336). In addition, in 1972 the Post Office Savings Bank became a statutory board and proved to be another crucial source of capital for the government. The government also operated the Development Bank of Singapore, which was founded in 1968 and provided development financing. And in 1971 the Monetary Authority of Singapore was established as a *de facto* central bank (Hamilton-Hart 2002). Armed with these financial institutions and the investment incentives, it was able to administer through the Economic Development Board, the government shaped the country's development policies in significant ways.

The Singapore government also established control over the labour market. Labour was essentially de-politicized through the Employment Act and the Industrial Relations Act and brought under the control of the PAP-sponsored NTUC. Strikes and other labour actions became almost non-existent. The National Wages Council, which was set up in 1972 as the economy approached full employment, set annual guidelines for wages across the economy. Moreover, the government regulated the flow of foreign workers into the country to ensure a reasonable supply of labour. In addition, the government invested heavily in the education system and initiated manpower training programmes to ensure that the skills that foreign investors required were available in the Singapore workforce (Lim 1983: 756: Senkuttuvan 1972). These initiatives along with the other policies instituted by the government in the late 1960s and early 1970s, made Singapore a very attractive place for foreign investors. And the more that foreign companies were committed to the future of the country, the more confident Singapore could be that its new-found economic friends would come to its rescue if it were under external threat.

Just as in Taiwan and South Korea, the Vietnam War years from 1965 to 1973 saw the successful launch of Singapore's export-oriented, pro-FDI strategy. The economy's transition was remarkable. Although the prosperity generated by the Vietnam War was only one of a number of factors, which included the astute management of the new strategy by Lee Kuan Yew and his political colleagues, it was critical in setting the Singapore economy on the road to 'miracle' status.

Thailand

Of all the seven economies affected by the Vietnam War Thailand was, in relative terms, the main beneficiary. US military and economic assistance had been increased to US$88 million 1962, prior to the introduction of large numbers of American soldiers into Vietnam in 1965, because of concerns that the communist-instigated civil war in Laos might spill across the border into Thailand. Fear of the spread of guerrilla warfare in the region also prompted 10,000 US troops to be sent to Thailand, the Seventh Fleet to patrol the Gulf of Thailand, and USAF squadrons flown into bases in Northeast Thailand (Pasuk and Baker 1995: 276; US Senate 1969: 613). Although the US forces were removed a few months after arriving, the deployment was a sign of things to come. With the Gulf of Tonkin incident in August 1964 and President Johnson's decision to employ bombing as a major means of fighting the Vietnam War, Thailand became a crucially located ally. On top of this, the Communist Party of Thailand launched its 'People's War' in 1964 and established a presence in the northeast, north and south of Thailand. As a consequence of these developments between 1965 and 1972 the US gave nearly US$600 million in military aid and over US$300 million in economic aid to the Thai government (Thompson 1975: 16). The military aid allowed the Thai army and air force and to be expanded and better trained, the police force to be upgraded, and roads built to gain access to remote areas threatened by communist activity.

But the greatest impact on the Thai economy came with the US spending on the various air-bases that were set up by the US military around Thailand. A large base at Udorn became the main Thai nerve-centre of US bombing operations in Vietnam. It housed not just the USAF but also CIA personnel, US military and Air Force intelligence detachments, and training schools for various groups from Laos. The US also built an extensive communications network in the eastern and northeastern provinces. The main communications station, which attempted to intercept communications and monitor troop operations and other military movements, was the second largest and most sophisticated of its kind outside the US. In 1967 a major highway was built that connected the US-built port at Sattahip to the northeast region so that military and other supplies could be efficiently moved to the individual bases. Roads were also built around the bases to help secure the area and to link each base to the main regional centres so that local supplies could be hauled in (Surachat 1988). The US forces needed electricity and water supplies to operate their installations and so money was put into upgrading electricity and water utilities. The building of the bases, power stations, communications centres and the transportation infrastructure provided a large number of jobs for Thais. Estimates suggest that at any one time over 30,000 Thais were employed on the bases, with more than twice that number employed at various times in construction and other jobs created by the US presence (Hatzfeldt 1969: 24). Local participation in the extensive construction projects and the operation of the bases and communications facilities enabled Thais to develop a variety of skills, such as in the field of engineering, that could, along with the vastly improved physical infrastructure, facilitate future economic development.

Apart from building and operating the various bases, the US contributed to the Thai economy in a number of other ways. First, US army and air force personnel stationed in Thailand steadily increased during the Vietnam War years. At the height of US involvement in the Vietnam War, during 1968 and 1969, there were about 45,000 US Army and USAF personnel stationed around the country. They spent roughly US$30 million a year in the local economy (*FEER*, 2 July 1970). Second, Bangkok was one of the main R&R destinations for US soldiers serving in Vietnam. They injected nearly US$20 million a year into the Thai economy (Viksnins 1973: 442). In addition, overall tourism rose by as much as 20 per cent per year (Truong 1990). Third, Thai troops and 'labour battalions', mostly paid for by the US, were sent over to Vietnam and their remittances contributed substantially to the amount of US dollars circulating in Thailand. In all, between 1964 and 1969 US military spending in Thailand amounted to a phenomenal US$1.2 billion and represented, on average, over 26 per cent of annual Thai export earnings (Benoit 1971: 635; Hungchangsith 1974: 35). It was no wonder that an Economist Intelligence Unit report underscored the extent to which US spending contributed to the 'Thai boom' (EIU 1968: 10).

For Thailand, the Vietnam War did not have a major impact on exports to either Vietnam or the United States. However, it was important in terms of bringing in new foreign direct investment. Certainly, the US military presence in Thailand appeared to attract American investors to the country with the number of US firms in Thailand rising from 88 in 1965 to 240 in 1971. Most notably significant investments were made in the import-substitution manufacturing sector. Japanese firms also began to follow the US lead. Japanese trading companies, for example, made manufacturing investments in various industrial sectors such as textiles, chemicals, steel and metals, and automobiles. During the late 1960s Thailand was the recipient of nearly US$50 million a year in foreign investment. The influx of FDI brought with it increased capital resources, more advanced technology and better organizational and management skills (Pasuk and Baker 1995: 129, 137; Suehiro 1985: 4–39; Surachart 1988: 115).

The Vietnam years in Thailand saw an average annual growth rate of approximately 8 per cent. This expansion was achieved with marked diversification in the economy. The new road networks increased the agricultural land that could be cultivated. The amount of land devoted to new crops, such as maize and tapioca as opposed to the traditional rice and natural rubber, increased. Most notably, the contribution of the manufacturing sector to the gross domestic product rose from 12.5 per cent in 1961 to 17.5 per cent in 1971. At the same time the banking sector and wholesale and retail trade sectors also expanded (Hewison 1989: 53). The country's economic success produced one of the highest accumulations of foreign exchange among developing countries, over US$1 billion in 1968, and gave the country a sizeable cushion against recession (Naya 1971: 56). The small group of bankers and industrialists who were intimately linked to senior levels of the Thai military and the government became very rich as they presided over the rapid growth of the economy.

But the economic boom spurred on in good part by the US spending on the Vietnam War also had political implications. When Thanom Kittikachorn took over from Sarit Thanarat, who died in December 1963, he continued his predecessor's economic policies of working with Bangkok's leading bankers and industrialists. Initially, the rapid economic expansion allowed Thanom to gain a majority in the 1969 parliamentary elections. However, by the early 1970s the economy had grown to such an extent that it was starting to create political tensions. Most of the key bureaucratic agencies overseeing the economy gained legitimacy from the economic boom but the political institutions came under fire for being 'corrupt, incompetent and complacent' (Girling 1981: 115). On top of this, the government had to deal with the advances made by the communists in Vietnam, Laos and Cambodia and the continued threat from internal communist guerrillas. The long-standing alliance of the leaders of the military, the bureaucracy, the royalists and business was starting to crack.

Malaysia

Of the seven future 'miracle' economies Malaysia benefited least from US spending on the Vietnam war. Nonetheless, the war did have a direct impact. Both Kuala Lumpur and Penang received an economic boost as R&R centres for US soldiers serving in Vietnam. The increased petroleum consumption in Vietnam and Thailand created an expanding market for oil from Sarawak, which had joined Malaysia in 1963 and which used Singapore as a transshipment point (Loh 1970–1: 36). Malaysia's exports of its primary products to the United States increased from US$177 million in 1966 to US$240 million in 1968 (IMF 1971). But there was no dramatic increase in commodity prices similar to that during the Korean War. Malaysia's replanting schemes of the 1950s and early 1960s had created a sharp rise in the production of natural rubber and the US could call on additional supplies of domestically produced synthetic rubber (Barlow 1978). Nor was there the military and economic assistance available to Malaysia that was pumped into the other economies.

For Malaysians the key domestic political event of this period was the violent racial clash of May 1969. A series of racial riots followed an election, which the ruling Alliance Party won, but by a reduced margin. The opposition parties, mainly the Malayan-Chinese Democratic Action Party (DAP), made considerable gains, especially in the urban areas. Victory marches and counter-marches in the wake of the election results served only to exacerbate the long-standing tensions between the Malayan-Chinese community, which tended to dominate the country's economy, and the Malay community, which controlled the political institutions. Between 200 and 800 died in Kuala Lumpur and the surrounding area (Means 1976: 12 Milne and Mauzy 1978: 77–100; Slimming 1969: 29–48). Given the country's recent history, the government was concerned that the communists might be able to take advantage of the social and political disturbances to regain a foothold in the peninsula. In the wake of the riots a state of emergency was declared and the return of Parliament was delayed until February 1971. New powers were given to the government in an attempt to forestall future clashes. They included restrictions on the freedom to discuss certain racially sensitive issues. At the same time moves to create a greater sense of unity were undertaken. For example, the Alliance Party coalition was expanded to embrace more parties and was eventually renamed the Barisan Nasional or National Front (Mauzy 1983).

One of the main responses to the May 1969 riots was the New Economic Policy (NEP). Introduced in 1970 the NEP was designed to address the perceived causes of the racial clashes. Its two main goals were to reduce and eventually eliminate poverty among all Malaysians and to bring Malays more into the economic life of the country so that economic imbalances between racial groups would be reduced and eventually eliminated. As rural Malays formed the vast majority of the poor, this goal meant modernizing rural life and encouraging the movement of some Malays into the main towns. It also meant making it possible for Malays to become part of the commercial and industrial life of the country at all levels. The long-term goals of the NEP required an ambitious restructuring of society. This restructuring was fully supported by Malays but left the non-Malay communities – mostly the Malaysian-Chinese and the Malaysian-Indians – particularly sceptical.

Fortunately for the government, in the period directly after the introduction of the NEP the economy grew at around 6 per cent and each of Malaysia's main ethnic communities was able to prosper without appearing to take resources from another. Economic growth was linked to the regional prosperity that had been created by the Vietnam War and the generally strong global economy. Malaysia's exports of tin, rubber, timber, palm oil and mineral oil did reasonably well and investments in industry increased production by 9 per cent in 1971 (Davies 1972). Spurred on by the 1969 racial riots, employment creation and industrialization became major goals of the government. Tariff protection and quota restrictions aided the development of import substitution industries while tax incentives were boosted to promote export manufacturing. Following the introduction of the NEP, 'pioneer status' and tax relief were given to export-manufacturing firms with a specific level of *bumiputra* (Malay) equity ownership and a year later special incentives were established for firms manufacturing and exporting electronic goods. These actions paved the way for Free Trade Zones to be set up, with the first being created in Penang in 1971 (Jesudason 1989: 173; Taylor and Ward 1994). In addition, Singapore's rapid economic growth, spurred by the Vietnam War, created 70,000 jobs for guest workers in 'hard-labour-intensive' industries, most of whom were from Malaysia. Together these developments helped unemployment to drop sharply and job vacancies to grow (Davies 1972; Senkuttuvan 1972). The government under Prime Minister Tun Abdul Razak, who succeeded Tunku Abdul Rahman in September 1970, was widely thought to be steering the economy in the right direction.

The Philippines and Indonesia

Obviously, then, US spending on the Vietnam War had a positive impact on the 'miracle' economies. But why did American aid not have the same beneficial impact on the Philippines that it had on the other economies? Most notably, the Philippines appears to be the exception to the rule. It was a war-affected economy that did not prosper. Despite Manila being an R&R centre and the US increasing its military expenditure by 300 per cent during the Vietnam War years (Benoit 1971: 646–7; EIU 1968: 13–15), the Philippines did not get the same economic lift from the influx of US dollars as did, for example, Thailand.

There were a number of reasons why the economy of the Philippines continued to languish. Each highlights the fact that the sequence of events that led to the rapid development of the seven 'miracle' economies did not materialize in the case of the Philippines. First, neither the events of the Second World War nor the Huk rebellion of the late 1940s destroyed, or even weakened, the old social order. Despite the massive destruction and turmoil that accompanied the Japanese occupation of the Philippines, the pre-Second World War landed elite, which had collaborated with the Japanese, were at the helm at independence in 1946. In contrast to the 'miracle' economies, the elite ensured that there was no effective land reform and that the policies they backed perpetuated the impoverishment of the rural sector. Moreover, although President Magsaysay was able to undertake some reforms in the 1950s he died before completing the task. In many ways the regionally based oligarchy that controlled the Philippines was very much akin to the 'regional strongmen' of Migdal's weak states (1988). Indeed, after independence the Philippines was characterized by 'the lack of a strong state leadership and the complementary tendency of the state to respond in preferential, partisan fashion to demands from segments of the bourgeoisie' (Hawes 1987: 32).

Second, although the bureaucracy expanded in the post-Second World War years, it proved to be corrupt and inefficient (De Guzman *et al*. 1988: 184). There was no development of the administrative structure in order to provide services to rural communities and bring the population under control as in Malaya/Malaysia. Nor was there a concerted effort to upgrade the skills and organizational abilities of bureaucrats as there had been in Thailand in the late 1950s and throughout the 1960s. The lack of an effective bureaucracy made the implementation of reform policies impossible even if the political will had been in place to make the changes. Third, the turn to an export strategy was made more difficult because of the political strength of the those who profited from import-substitution industrialization during the 1950s and 1960s. Investment in exports was largely confined to the agricultural sector. Fourth, while the Philippines did receive some military and economic aid from the US, it was not as substantial as most of the capital inflow experienced by seven 'miracle' economies. Aid during the Korean War was more limited and the increase in US military spending during the Vietnam War years, when countries like Singapore, Thailand and Malaysia were using the influx of capital to kick-start the industrialization process, was offset by increasing capital flight from the Philippines (Boyce 1993: 287). At no time was US military or economic aid used to develop the country's economic infrastructure to the same extent as happened in South Korea, Taiwan or Thailand. Finally, the social and political turmoil in the Philippines deterred investors. The inability of the central government to maintain social stability made it difficult to attract new investors, especially when economic policy was not set up to promote the export of manufactured products.

In sum, then, the sequence of events in the Philippines produced a downward spiral of economic activity in marked contrast to the virtuous circle of economic development set in train by the series of geopolitical events that was experienced by the seven successful Asian economies. The political and economic institutions that were established in the Philippines after the Second World War were unable to support the kind of rapid, export-oriented economic growth produced by the political and economic institutions that were developed in Singapore, Malaysia and Thailand.

Similar points can be made about the Indonesian economy. Although Japanese occupation during the Second World War destroyed the old order in the Dutch East Indies, there was no massive post-war influx of capital that might have allowed a strong central state to emerge. Neither the increase in natural rubber prices resulting from the Korean War nor the Vietnam War had any major impact on the Indonesian economy. Indonesia did receive large amounts of foreign aid – amounting to 27 per cent of government income in the late 1960s after Suharto's overthrow of the left-leaning Sukarno (Robison 1986: 171). However, with a population of 105 million this aid on a per capita basis was very limited. Indeed, it simply served to keep the country on a relatively even keel as the new government sought to deal with economic chaos left behind by the Sukarno regime. Although greater emphasis was eventually put on promoting rural production there was no concerted policy to expand the country's economic infrastructure to the extent achieved in 'miracle' economies. Limited government income also meant that the bureaucracy lacked training and was inefficient and corrupt.

Industrialization was very slow to emerge in Indonesia. FDI was largely in the capital-intensive petroleum and mining sectors, with relatively little investment in manufacturing. The benefits accruing from the profits and wages flowed to a small group of people compared to the labour-intensive economic development in the 'miracle' economies. Moreover, the ineffective bureaucracy was given the task of implementing plans to promote import-substitution industrialization. Only those businessmen with close links to the president – first Sukarno and, then, after the 1965 coup, Suharto – were given the opportunity to develop the economy (MacIntyre 1994b: 253). Receiving few of the benefits that the sequence of regional geopolitical events conferred on the seven successful economies, Indonesia's economy struggled along. It was not until the advent of the oil price rise in the 1970s that Indonesia acquired the capital influx that could have prompted rapid industrialization. However, even then, the lack of an effective bureaucracy and an unwillingness to open up the economy severely hampered Indonesia's attainment of sustained rapid economic development (Karl 1997: 208–13).

Conclusion

The Vietnam War, and especially the American government's spending on fighting the war from 1965 to 1973, had a profound impact on the economies of the seven East and Southeast Asian 'miracle' economies and generated a prosperous regional economy. American military aid and procurement, as well as economic aid, injected huge amounts of capital into the region, especially into Japan, South Korea, Taiwan and Thailand. In addition, Vietnam became a significant market for the emerging export-sectors of Taiwan and South Korea. The expansion of the US domestic market, fuelled by the spending induced by the Vietnam War was a boon to the development of export-manufacturing in Japan and Hong Kong, and especially to the newly created export manufacturing industries of Taiwan, South Korea and Singapore. A study for the Asian Development Bank indicates that approximately one third of the increase in US imports between 1964 and 1968 can be attributed to Vietnam War-related expenditures (Benoit 1971: 632). The key, of course, was that the US allowed unimpeded access to its market for goods from the seven 'miracle' economies for political reasons. Certainly, for the market-hungry economies of East and Southeast Asia, the timing could not have been better. And the Vietnam War also prompted US companies to look beyond Japan, Taiwan and South

Korea for places to invest in Asia. Hong Kong, Singapore and to a lesser extent Malaysia and Thailand also became attractive sites for US companies seeking low-cost, export-manufacturing as well as import-substitution manufacturing opportunities.

Government administrations were generally able to deploy the influx of capital to good effect. All seven governments built on the economic and political institutional foundations established during the Korean War and Cold War years. Infrastructure was further developed, often as a consequence of the need to build roads, railways, airports, port facilities and electricity generation in order to facilitate military deployment. Certainly, American military aid was frequently used in this way. The British administration in Malaysia also built up the infrastructure in order to defeat the communist insurgency and the British navy left behind a major port and support facilities when it withdrew from Singapore. Increased revenues were used by governments to expand the banking systems so that they could serve the goals that had been set for their economies. Rural development was promoted in the larger economies, while in Hong Kong and Singapore subsidized housing produced the urban equivalent of land reform. Both policies created a pool of low-cost labour that facilitated the heavy promotion of industrialization. Particular emphasis was placed on the development of export-oriented manufacturing. Textiles, clothing, electrical goods and electronic components firms flourished during this period while Japan, Taiwan and South Korea also developed a heavy industry capacity. As a result of the rapid industrialization the seven economies quickly absorbed the available labour and by the early 1970s most of the 'miracle' economies were experiencing full employment. The major benefit of this development was a marked reduction in poverty levels and a relatively even distribution of the economic wealth that was being created.

This raises the all-important issue of motivation. Why did the governments and their leaders promote rapid economic growth rather than simply exploiting their positions for personal, predatory gain (Haggard: 1994: 273)? There was, of course, considerable personal accumulation of wealth by some individual leaders. And some analysts have noted the tendency of leaders in Confucian societies to 'act so as to enhance the public good' (Tu 1996: 8) However, the emphasis on rapid development in each of the miracle economies was clearly driven in good part by need to achieve a measure of security and was, therefore, a consequence of the Cold War environ-ment. Nationalism, invariably the product of war, allied to the need to resist both the external and internal threat from communism, drove individual governments and their leaders to push for economic growth as a means of making their societies stronger, more stable and more independent (Zhu 2002: 18–20). And it was around the hegemonic project of strength through economic development that leaders could rally the support of relatively weak societal interests.

Each society, of course, had its own variant of this theme. Japan sought to ensure its security in a threatening world and to regain its national self-respect after the military humiliation of the Second World War. A strong economy was its redemption. South Korea and Taiwan experienced major security threats right on their borders and needed a rapidly growing economy so as to ensure a military strong enough to face down the communists. Hong Kong's security lay in its ability to deliver foreign exchange to both London and Beijing. Only with a strong, growing economy could this be done. Predominantly Chinese Singapore faced the double threat from communism and its ethnic Malay Muslim neighbours, and addressed these threats by building up its economy as quickly as possible. It also reached out and involved US and European companies in its economic development to give them a stake in its continued inde-pendence and prosperity. Malaysia needed a dynamic economy both to undermine the appeal of communism and to allow for greater participation of Malays while not alienating the economically indis-pensable Malaysian-Chinese population. All of the governments of the miracle economies, then, were vehemently anti-communist, strongly pro-business, increasingly nationalist, and willing to inter-vene in the economy in order to promote industrialization and rapid growth.

The period of the Vietnam War also underscored the extent to which government and business in the seven economies, faced with the Cold War threat from communism, worked together. In times of war business often becomes closer to government as a society unites to defend itself against a common enemy. In the seven miracle econ-omies the bureaucracy expanded as each government mobilized and directed resources to face down the communist threat and deal with the uncertain international environment. The increased size and capacity of the seven bureaucracies allowed each government to nurture and direct the transformation of their economies. As the rural economy was modernized and industrialization promoted, so government links into the business community increasingly provided the institutional channels for the continual negotiation and renegotiation of the economic goals and policies that drove the economy forward (Evans 1992: 164). This 'embedded autonomy' of the state (Evans 1995) was in many ways a product of the common perception within each of the seven societies of the need to combine forces so as to rapidly develop the economy and confront the internal and external threats. As a result, then, the state played a crucial role in the industrialization process in each of the seven economies, intervening through the control of capital, or land, or labour, or some combination of all three.

East and Southeast Asia's economic development also occurred in a wider context. At the same time that the 'miracle' economies were seeking to attract FDI, other parts of the developing world, most notably Latin America, were increasingly regulating FDI. The Latin American experience, of course, was very different from the East Asian experience. Weak states had been manipulated by – mostly American – multinational corporations (MNCs) which had exploited the region's raw materials and developed import-substitution industries. Populist uprisings quickly multiplied and the economic strategy most often adopted was one of deepening import-substitution. As a consequence, American and other MNCs seeking a low-cost base for export-manufacturing looked elsewhere. In East and Southeast Asian economies like Hong Kong, Taiwan and Singapore they found the tax holidays, low wages, promise of labour stability and efficient bureaucracies that they sought. Hence, the more FDI-friendly 'miracle' economies of Asia proved to be the major beneficiaries of the turn against MNCs in Latin America.

Of course, although US spending on the Vietnam War was clearly a major catalyst to economic growth in the seven successful Asian economies, there was a dark side to some of the developments during this period. For example, the authoritarian regimes in South Korea, Taiwan and Thailand continued to inflict considerable hardships on political opponents. Labour organizations throughout the region were effectively neutered, often violently (Deyo 1989). Political rights were also curtailed in Hong Kong, Malaysia and Singapore. In none of the seven economies was a vibrant civil society allowed to emerge. Moreover, prostitution in a number of the R&R cities became a very real problem and eventually led to the sex tourism and AIDS epidemic that so bedevils parts of Southeast Asia today.

Yet by the time the US withdrew from Vietnam in 1973, the seven 'miracle' economies had undergone a major transformation as a result of rapid industrialization and economic expansion. Each of the seven economies benefited immensely from the formative and reformative effects of the Vietnam War. The economic and political institutions established in the years prior to the war were given a major boost. The positive feedback produced by the economic success of the late 1960s and the early 1970s cemented in place those political and economic institutions seen to be responsible for the prosperity. And in turn these institutions continued to pursue the economic policies that were proving to be so successful. Ironically, just when the US was having to endure the humiliation of the hasty evacuation by helicopter of its embassy in Saigon in April 1975, its main allies in the region were enjoying a prosperity that few could have imagined ten years earlier.

6
Re-enter Japan

In 1976, in a move that symbolized America's waning influence in Southeast Asia, the US government was asked to close its bases in Thailand. The US agreed to the Thai government's request. Coming close on the heels of the official end of the Vietnam War in 1975, it appeared that America was interested in turning its back on a particularly divisive and dispiriting period in its history. The US did retain its bases in Japan, South Korea and the Philippines and continued to provide a nuclear 'shield' in the face of the communist threat. However, troop withdrawals, which followed the announcement in 1969 of the Nixon Doctrine and the new US policy of promoting greater regional self-help in defence, continued through the 1970s (Weintraub 1976; Woo 1991: 123–5). From 1976 onwards, military aid to East and Southeast Asia was reduced. Loans replaced grants as the main vehicle for supporting military development in the region. US economic aid to Asia dropped from an annual average of US$1.25 billion in the early 1970s to average US$500 million per year during the late 1970s and early 1980s (Inada 1989). That US firms continued to invest in the region and the US market remained open was crucial to the rapid development of Asia's seven 'miracle' economies of Japan, South Korea, Taiwan, Hong Kong, Singapore, Malaysia and Thailand. But, despite President Reagan arresting the decline in America's military interest in the region during the early 1980s, the US was not the dominant military or economic force in East and Southeast Asia that it had been up to the early 1970s.

Gradually, over the ten years following the end of the Vietnam War, Japan came to play an ever greater economic role in the development of East and Southeast Asia. Japanese aid increased markedly towards the end of the 1970s, Japanese foreign direct investment (FDI) rose steadily into the 1980s and a number of countries used aspects of the Japanese 'model' of economic success as a blueprint for their own economic policies. The signing of the Plaza Accord in 1985, which doubled the value of the yen against the US dollar, was a crucial turning point. From then on Japan poured vast amounts of capital into East and Southeast Asia in an effort to find low-cost export platforms for its manufacturing sector.

It is at this point that the Japan-centred explanations for the rise of Asia's 'miracle' economies come into their own. From the late 1970s onwards Japan became a major engine of growth for the region, especially Singapore, Malaysia and Thailand, as well as a model of successful economic development for others to emulate. Yet the Japan-centred explanations tend to underestimate the extent to which Japan was able to build on the economic foundations laid during the height of the Cold War. The major recipients of Japanese aid and FDI were the same economies that had benefited from influx of resources drawn into the region to fight the Korean and Vietnam Wars and the overarching Cold War. The institutional foundations for the region's economic success were already in place and the industrializing, development trajectory well established by the time the Japanese started to move into the region in a concerted fashion. Indeed, Japan's economic 'embrace' of East and Southeast Asia in the years after the Vietnam War could not have gone so smoothly or so successfully had it not been for the commitment by successive US governments of men, money and material, in a massive effort to contain the spread of communism and defend what were seen as America's vital interests.

The proponents of the other explanations for Asia's success from the end of the Vietnam War to the Asian economic crisis also use the rapid economic growth of the Asian 'miracle' economies to reinforce their arguments. Certainly, for those advancing a cultural explanation the region's economic rise from the 1970s onwards has been interpreted as supporting their claims. The greater role for Japan, the increasing success of Taiwan, Hong Kong and Singapore, and the emergence of distinctive business practices within the successful economies have all been attributed to the influence of Confucianism. Similarly, the advocates of the statist, neoclassical economic and American-hegemony explanations all see the events of the late

1970s through to the mid-1990s as supporting their accounts of East and Southeast Asia's economic success. However, all three approaches undervalue the economic stimulus provided by Japanese aid and investment and focus too narrowly on their own limited set of factors in accounting for the region's unprecedented economic growth.

While Japan had a crucial role to play in the region's economic development, its influence has to be placed in historical context. Like many other aspects of Japan's economic development, the Japanese move into East and Southeast Asia was shaped by the Cold War and orchestrated in good part by the American government. With the advent of the Cold War, Japan found its old trading relations with China and North Korea cut off and essentially had to reorient itself towards non-communist Southeast Asia. Having decided that Japan's economy needed to be restored to its former vitality, the US actively promoted increased trade among the non-communist countries of East and Southeast Asia. A major plan for East Asia, NSC 48/1, was adopted by the US government in 1949. It envisaged a triangular trading relationship in which the US would provide the capital and advanced technology, Japan the intermediate goods and Southeast Asia the raw materials and eventually the market (Cumings 1984a:19). To encourage this arrangement, American officials worked actively to overcome resistance stemming from memories of Japan's brutal actions during the Second World War and to help Japan re-establish its links to Southeast Asia (Schaller 1997: 96–112). During the 1960s the US also worked to restore relations between Japan and its former colonies of South Korea and Taiwan. The pattern of trade relations that Japan gradually established within the Cold War context of the 1960s and 1970s began to blossom in the 1980s as Japanese businesses reached out to the region.

The purpose of this chapter, then, is to show how Japan's Cold War-directed economic push into East and Southeast Asia built on the foundations laid by the US so as to promote the rapid economic growth of the other six 'miracle' economies. In turn, this rapid economic growth provided positive feedback for the political and economic institutions in the 'miracle' economies that fostered their economic success. At the same time, however, tensions emerged that led to policy reforms. Nonetheless, despite some institutional and policy changes, the general industrializing trajectory of the seven successful Asian economies, established during the Cold War years, was reinforced.

Cautious Expansion: The Early 1970s to the mid-1980s

In the early 1970s Japanese economic activity in East and Southeast Asia took a significant turn. During the twenty-five years following the end of the Second World War severe restrictions on yen exports had limited overseas investments. However, as the Japanese government removed capital export restrictions in stages between 1969 and 1972, Japanese investment began to move into Asia. Then the decision, in February 1973, to allow the exchange rate to be determined by the market led to a rate of around 280 yen to the dollar and gave an additional boosts to the flow of capital into the region (Yoshihara 1978: 5). The new policy was sparked not only by the rapid rise in Japan's international reserves as the trade surplus rose but also by a number of other pressures that were crowding in on Japanese businesses. These pressures included the need to reduce costs, especially of labour and land, so as to compete effectively with the newly emerging manufacturing economies of South Korea and Taiwan; concerns over the need for assured supplies and greater quantities of raw materials to fuel Japan's economic growth in the wake of the oil price shock of 1973; and calls to solve the growing pollution problem in Japan. This heightened Japanese interest in investing in resource extraction, import-substitution and export-oriented industries was generally welcomed by Asian governments anxious to acquire new investments.

Japan's investments in Hong Kong, Taiwan and South Korea had started in a very limited way in the 1960s and continued into the 1970s and 1980s. However, whereas Taiwan was the major recipient of Japanese investment in the 1960s, Japan's 1972 decision to restore diplomatic relations with the People's Republic of China and to cut official ties with Taiwan temporarily reduced Japanese business's willingness to invest in the Taiwanese economy. By the mid-1970s investment in South Korea was on the increase. It averaged US$150 million per year in the early 1980s, about the same level as Japanese investment in Taiwan (Lucas 1993: 395). Japanese FDI in Hong Kong at this time was higher, hovering between US$300 million and US$400 million per year (OECD various years). A significant, although gradually decreasing, portion of the capital equipment for industrial development in each of the three economies continued to come from Japan. However, by the early 1980s a shift in Japanese investment patterns towards a greater emphasis on Southeast Asia was discernible. As a result, by 1985 the total stock of Japanese investments in the ASEAN (Association of Southeast Asian Nations) economies was US$12.5 billion as opposed to only US$5.4 billion for the NIEs (Pasuk 1990: 30).

Although there was a growing interest in relocating some labour-intensive manufacturing overseas, much of Japan's FDI in Southeast Asia from 1975 to 1985 was geared towards acquiring the raw materials needed to fuel its growing economy. By 1985 almost 50 per cent of the total stock of Japanese investment in ASEAN was in resource-related projects (Pasuk 1990: 30). Most of this resource-related FDI went to Indonesia, especially into the mining, petroleum, timber, pulp and agricultural commodity sectors and was in large part geared to capital-intensive projects rather than labour-intensive sectors (Lindblad 1998: 126–8). While Japan's investment clearly helped boost the Indonesian economy it did not significantly increase Indonesia's employment opportunities and was generally confined to the resource-extraction enclave. A substantial percentage of Japan's export-manufacturing FDI went into Singapore, by far the most investment-friendly of the Southeast Asian economies, with a portion also going to Malaysia and Thailand. Most export-oriented investments went into light manufacturing including watchmaking, toys, electrical machinery, and electrical parts and components (Pasuk 1990: 30). What was extraordinary was the disproportionate boost that Japanese FDI gave to the Singapore economy. As of 1985, Singapore's accumulated direct investment from Japan amounted, on a per capita basis, to US$873 compared to US$71 for Malaysia, US$50 for Indonesia, US$15.5 for the Philippines and US$14.5 for Thailand (ASEAN Centre 1987: 43; FEER 1987).

In deciding which economies and manufacturing sectors in Southeast Asia to invest in, Japanese companies considered a number of factors. Among the most important were the availability of low-cost but relatively skilled labour, political stability, good economic management, tax and other incentives, limited foreign exchange regulations, good infrastructure facilities and appropriate local partners for joint ventures (Chee and Lee 1979: 9; Pasuk 1987: 16–19). Singapore, Malaysia and to a lesser extent Thailand had a distinct advantage in terms of these criteria; many had been developed as a consequence of the Korean War and Vietnam War booms. In addition, these three countries had minimal labour union problems: organized labour had been emasculated as part of the effort to quash any hint of communism. These factors led Japanese manufacturing companies to gravitate towards the three Southeast Asian 'miracle' economies.

The increased flow of Japanese investment to the non-communist Southeast Asian countries was not without incident. In 1972 a Thai boycott of Japanese goods began and Japanese businessmen were accused of unfair trading practices and a lack of concern for the natural environment. Other criticisms were that Japanese firms exploited workers, failed to share technology and devoured resources. In January 1974, while on a tour of Southeast Asia, Prime Minister Tanaka was greeted by anti-Japanese demonstrations and riots in both Bangkok and Jakarta. Concerns about Japanese investment lingered through the 1970s.

One way to assuage the general unease at the increasing penetration of Japanese capital into Southeast Asia was thought to be a better use of aid. Japanese aid, or official development assistance (ODA), had its origins in the reparations that the American government pushed Japan to pay to a number of the countries it had damaged so badly during the Second World War. These countries included Burma, Indonesia and the Philippines. In addition, Japan contributed economic and technical assistance, sometimes through the Colombo Plan, to countries such as Cambodia, Laos, Malaysia, Singapore, Thailand and South Korea. Indeed, with most reparations focused on Southeast Asia, the region became a natural target for Japan's aid programmes (Orr 1990: 53). Yet the fact that the anti-Japanese riots of the early 1970s took place suggested that Japanese aid was not being used effectively nor was it enough. Hence, the Japanese government took the decision to pave the way for Japanese businesses to expand into the region by increasing the amount of aid to Southeast Asia.

This decision to increase Japanese aid was reinforced by a number of events. First, the 1973 oil shock raised concerns about the security of future supplies of oil and other raw materials. With 70 per cent of Japan's oil flowing through the Strait of Malacca, and Japan so dependent on Southeast Asia as a source of raw materials, the region was clearly crucial to the security of the Japanese economy.

Second, the end of the Vietnam War and the reduction of the US role in Southeast Asia meant more pressure from all quarters for Japan to play a greater role in the region. In particular, the US was keen to gear Japanese aid to US strategy. From 1978 onwards, Japan and the US held regular policy-planning talks on how to deploy Japanese aid (Inada 1989: 7). Third, as a result of Vietnam's invasion of Cambodia in December 1978 and the uncertainties that Vietnam's installation of a new, friendly government created, US and regional governments continued to pressure Japan for increased amounts of aid to be distributed to Southeast Asia. The political stability of Southeast Asia was put in jeopardy by Vietnam's actions. By the late 1970s it was clear that the geopolitics that underpinned Japan's economic relationship with Southeast Asia dictated that it was in Japan's interest to boost the amount of aid it funnelled into the region. This approach of stability through aid was embedded in Japan's doctrine of 'comprehensive security' set out in the late 1970s. Aid would be used to ensure that a stable and cordial regional environment was maintained in which Japan was welcomed and Japan's interests safeguarded (Rudner 1989: 114).

Beginning in 1977, Japan substantially increased its aid to non-communist Southeast Asia. In August of that year Prime Minister Fukuda announced that Japan intended to develop a special relationship with Southeast Asia and, to mark the inception of the policy, he set up a US$1 billion-fund for ASEAN industrial projects. During the first half of the 1980s aid became a major dimension in Japan's relations with countries such as Thailand, Malaysia, Indonesia and the Philippines. Between 1976 and 1986 Japan's total ODA increased five-fold, with the four ASEAN members receiving roughly one third of all of Japan's bilateral disbursements. Significantly, on a per capita basis over the period 1982 to 1986 Malaysia received by far the most ODA (US$36.5), followed by Singapore ((US$24.2) and then Thailand (US$22.2). In contrast, the Philippines received US$19.3 per person and Indonesia US$6.0 person (Stubbs 1992: 62). This allocation of aid reflected Japan's interest in building on the economic success of the three Southeast Asian 'miracle' economies during the Cold War years. In addition, Malaysia and Singapore were key to Japanese security because of their control of the Strait of Malacca. Thailand received substantial amounts of aid because of its status as a frontline state in the Cambodian crisis.

Just as importantly, Japan's ODA to the three Southeast Asian 'miracle' economies was geared to the further development of their economic infrastructure so as to help expand their export-manufacturing sectors (Rudner 1989: 115). At the same time, individual Japanese firms which relocated to the ASEAN states were involved in the development of specific aid projects. The bulk of Japan's aid, then, was geared to helping target countries expand their export-manufacturing capacity and increase the efficiency of Japanese export manufacturers which were gradually beginning to relocate to countries such as Singapore, Malaysia and Thailand (International Development Study Group 1989).

As in Southeast Asia, security was a significant factor in South Korea's appeals to Japan in the early 1980s for increased economic assistance. Plunged into recession by the escalating price of oil in 1979–80, South Korea quickly became Asia's largest borrower. The new president, Chun Doo Hwan, who had taken over in a coup after Park Chung Hee's assassination in 1979, needed to revive the economy immediately. After gaining US support he turned to Japan for a US$10 billion aid and loans package that would be disbursed over five years starting in 1982. Chun's administration emphasized South Korea's weakness and its consequent vulnerability in the face of the threat from communist North Korea. South Korea was viewed as a fortress protecting Japan from the scourge of communism and its threat to the stability of the region. Despite the massive increases in its aid budget, Japan was reluctant to raise its economic assistance to South Korea from the roughly US$80 million annually to the inflated figure proposed by Seoul. Nor was Japan willing to acknowledge South Korea as its regional protector. However, after some tense negotiations it was finally agreed that Japan would provide US$4 billion in loans and credits over a seven-year period beginning in 1983. With American and Japanese backing, Chun was able to gain the necessary international financial support to get South Korea's economy back on track and, in the process, save his authoritarian and extremely repressive presidency (Woo 1991: 186–7).

Japan also played a regional role as a model from which other economies could learn. Taiwan and South Korea, in particular, sensed that they were following in Japan's footsteps. Indeed, Japan's industrialization process and technological development provided a real-life 'textbook' case that Taiwan and South Korea could follow (Wade 1990: 334). In addition, in 1981, Malaysia's new prime minister, Mahathir Mohamad, announced a 'Look East' policy that emphasized emulating the best of Japan's qualities and practices. These practices included good business management, discipline and diligence in the workplace, and the idea of developing 'Malaysia Inc.'. The policy, however, was rather vague in its application, although it was part of the rationale for the turn towards a policy of heavy industrialization that included the development of Malaysia's contentious steel and automotive industries. After a few years the idea of modelling Malaysia after Japan faded. It became obvious that it was difficult for a developing economy such as Malaysia's to pursue the policies and practices of Japan's much more advanced economy. Moreover, it became clear that Malaysia's diverse society fitted somewhat uneasily with a model of development that was embedded in a very different, relatively homogeneous society (Milne and Mauzy 1999: 55–6). Yet Mahathir's 'Look East' policy did bring some benefits: an increasing number of Japanese companies showed an interest in Malaysia as a manufacturing centre (Lindblad 1998: 134).

During the decade following the end of the Vietnam War, Japan began to pick up the slack in promoting economic development among the other six 'miracle' economies that America's reduced interest in the region created. Japan's investment and aid to South-east Asia in particular began to have an increasingly significant impact on the region's economies. However, Japan's role as a catalyst for economic development took a quantum leap in 1985 as a result of the US government's search for a long-term solution to the increasingly vexing problem of America's rapidly growing trade imbalance with Japan.

Plaza Accord and After

By the mid-1980s US economic relations with Japan had reached a crisis point. The main reason was the growing US trade deficit with Japan. It had jumped from US$18 billion in 1983 to US$33 billion in 1984 and was threatening to go much higher. American officials sought to deal with the growing trade deficit by signing, in September 1985, the Plaza Accord. It committed the G-5 finance ministers and the governors of their central banks to work towards raising the value of the yen and lowering the value of the US dollar. As a result the yen appreciated sharply in value from 238 yen to the dollar in 1985 to 160 yen to the dollar in late 1986. It then rose more slowly until it reached 128 yen to the dollar in 1988. During the next few years the value of the yen hovered around 140 to the US dollar. The rapid appreciation of the yen, allied to several structural changes that were taking place in the Japanese economy, including the increasing cost of land and labour, forced a number of manufacturing companies to look beyond Japan for low-cost countries that would allow them to continue to produce competitively for the global marketplace (Hatch and Yamamura 1996: 20–1).

Initially, Japanese companies targeted South Korea and Taiwan as the most attractive places in which to relocate. Historical and cultural links made them the obvious, initial choice. However, with pressure from the US Treasury, the currencies of these two economies also began to appreciate. The South Korean won went from 881 won to the US dollar in 1986 to 671 won to the US dollar in 1989 and the new Taiwanese dollar went from 37.84 to the US dollar in 1986 to 26.4 to the US dollar in 1989 (Stubbs 1992: 67, fn.14). At the same time South Korean and Taiwanese global competitiveness suffered from rising wages, labour shortages and the threat of the removal of the US Generalized System of Preferences, which allowed certain goods from specific countries into the US free of tariffs. As a result of these developments, Japanese companies began to look to the non-communist Southeast Asian countries as alternative sites for their new overseas factories.

Fortuitously, a number of ASEAN countries were seeking to attract increased levels of FDI. In 1985–6 a region-wide recession, prompted by low commodity prices and a resulting balance of payments problem, persuaded the governments of Malaysia and Thailand to open up to greater inflows of foreign investment in export manufacturing as a way of diversifying their economies and earning greater amounts of foreign exchange. Slowly, Indonesia and the Philippines followed suit. Moreover, as a result of the crisis induced by the recession, the currencies in Malaysia, Thailand, Indonesia and the Philippines had depreciated. Even the Singapore dollar had appreciated only marginally. Hence, by happy coincidence, just when Japanese companies were looking for low-cost sites for their export-manufacturing plants, key ASEAN states were seeking to attract increased foreign investment. The match proved to be especially advantageous to the three 'miracle' economies of Southeast

Asia. The infrastructure, relatively well-educated labour force, political stability and reasonably strong central governments, all of which were legacies of the Cold War, gave them a distinct advantage as Japanese companies hunted for new low-cost export-manufacturing centres. Hence, while some Japanese investment went into Indonesia and the Philippines, it was the economies of Singapore, Malaysia and Thailand that, in relative terms, benefited the most.

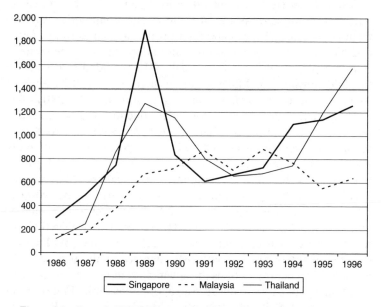

Figure 6.1   Japan's FDI in Singapore, Malaysia and Thailand, 1986–96
(US$ million)
Source: Data from ASEAN Centre various years.

The increase in Japan's direct investments overseas from 1986 onwards is truly remarkable. In the four years from 1982 to 1985 Japan's total FDI was US$20.5 billion. This figure ballooned to US$157 billion between 1988 and 1991 (OECD various dates). Particularly striking was the initial flow of Japanese FDI into Thailand and Singapore. Japanese FDI channelled into Thailand grew from US$48 million in 1984 to US$1.27 billion in 1989. In Singapore it rose from $US302 million in 1986 to US$1.9 billion in 1989 (ASEAN Centre various dates). From 1989 onwards Malaysia and Indonesia also received increasing amounts of Japanese FDI. There was a slight lull in Japan's export of capital in the early 1990s but a further appreciation of the yen in 1993 and 1994 sparked a renewed round of export-manufacturing investment in Singapore, Malaysia, Thailand and Indonesia. Overall, between 1987 and 1995 Singapore received US$8.25 billion in Japanese FDI, Thailand US$7.63 billion, Malaysia US$5.75 billion, Indonesia US$10 billion and the Philippines US$2.64 billion (ASEAN Centre various dates).

Just as Japanese export-manufacturing companies were forced to move into Southeast Asia in order to remain competitive, so firms from Hong Kong, Taiwan and South Korea as well as from Europe and North America were pressed into adopting the same strategy. For example, in 1989 the East Asian NIEs provided nearly half of the FDI flowing into Malaysia and a quarter of the FDI entering Thailand (Webber 1995: 41 quoting Kim 1993; Ma 2001: 245). Indeed, in the global relocation of production and services that began in earnest in the first half of the 1990s, Southeast Asia fared remarkably well, capturing by far the largest portion of FDI of any of the regions of the developing world. The factors that led Japanese businesses to the 'miracle' economies of Singapore, Malaysia and Thailand also led businessmen from other parts of the world to invest in these economies. The legacy of the American-prompted booms of the 1950s and 1960s served these countries well in their bid to attract foreign investment. In terms of the total stock of FDI accumulated by the five main Southeast Asian economies between 1980 and 1995 on a per capita basis the advantage enjoyed by the 'miracle' economies is most pronounced. Singapore's per capita FDI over this period was US$20,760, Malaysia's US$1,512, and Thailand's US$301 while the figures for Indonesia were US$266 and for the Philippines US$93 (ASEAN Centre various years).

Although foreign investment was a major factor in the boom times of the late 1980s and early 1990s, the role of domestic savings should not be ignored. Indeed, during much of the 1980 through to the mid-1990s, domestic savings as a percentage of GDP were high in each of the seven successful economies. Singapore was exceptional. Its gross domestic savings rose from 42.7 per cent of GDP in 1980–4 to a remarkable 50.8 per cent in 1995 (Rao 2001: 14–15). Part of this increase resulted from the mandatory savings required through the Central Provident Fund to which employees and employers contributed. But it also was a consequence of the high growth rates and low inflation which encouraged Singaporeans to save. The savings rates

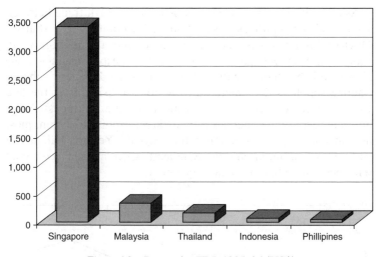

Figure 6.2   Per capita FDI, 1985–96 (US$)
Source: Data from OECD various dates; and ASEAN 2002.

for the other economies generally rose steadily during the period from 1980 to 1995. For example, from 1984 to 1995 Thailand's saving as a percentage of GDP went from 21 per cent to 35 per cent, Malaysia's went from 27 per cent to 36 per cent and South Korea's went from 27 per cent to 34 per cent (Rao 2001: 15). These high rates were a key factor in fuelling the extraordinary economic growth of the post-Plaza period. As one analysis puts it with reference to Thailand, 'Foreign inflows may have sparked the boom. Thai investment made it a big boom' (Pasuk and Baker 1998: 39).

Japan's aid to the 'miracle' economies kept pace with its rapidly increasing levels of FDI. In 1987 Japanese ODA to Malaysia, Thailand, Indonesia and the Philippines rose to US$1.7 billion from the US$1 billion per year over the previous four years. It reached US$2.3 billion in 1990 and US$3.25 billion in 1992 (Japanese Government 1993). A high percentage of this aid was in the form of loans and was for the most part geared to helping the ASEAN states expand their manufacturing base. Emphasis continued to be placed on developing the economic infrastructure – electricity supply and electrification, highways, railways, ports and airports – and on providing bilateral structural adjustment loans so as to ease policy reforms (Kohama 2003: 44).

As a result of the massive influx of Japanese FDI, trade between Japan and the Southeast Asian 'miracle' economies rose sharply. Much of this increase in trade is accounted for by the machinery and equipment that was required to set up the major export-manufacturing plants and the many small-and medium-sized Japanese subcontracting suppliers that migrated to Southeast Asia during the late 1980s and early 1990s. At the same time, the Southeast Asian 'miracle' economies increased their direct exports to Japan, most notably their exports of manufactured goods. Yet, the balance of trade between Japan and the Southeast Asian 'miracle' economies remained substantially in Japan's favour.

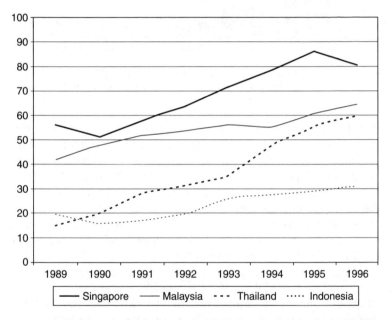

Figure 6.3   Percentage of manufactured goods in exports to Japan, 1989–96 (%)
Source: Data from ASEAN Centre various years.

For these three Southeast Asian economies much of this trade deficit with Japan was offset by increased trade with their traditional Cold War trading partner, the US, as well as by increased exports to the EU and to Hong Kong, South Korea and Taiwan. The rise in exports to the US was particularly pronounced in the cases of Malaysia and Thailand. Malaysian exports to the US increased nearly seven-fold between 1986 and 1995 and Thailand's increased eight -fold (ASEAN Centre 1988; 1996). In many ways the American post-Second World War regional economic plan, which saw the US provide capital and advanced technology, the Japanese the intermediate goods and the Southeast Asians the raw materials and markets, had been stood on its head. The Japanese and the other advanced Asian economies were providing the capital and technology for the Southeast Asians to produce manufactured goods and the Americans were supplying the market. As a consequence, the ultimate impact of the Plaza Accord was not so much to reduce the US trade deficit as it was to encourage the Japanese to export their trade surplus with the US, first to South Korea and Taiwan and then on to Singapore, Malaysia and Thailand.

Spurred on by the massive amounts of Japanese FDI in the region and later by the flood of FDI from the NIEs as well as from the US and the EU, the three Southeast Asian 'miracle' economies prospered. With labour-intensive export manufacturing in sectors such as electronics, appliances, autos and auto parts, powering Thai and Malaysian development, and high-tech, knowledge-intensive industries, such as high-end electronics and computer components, leading Singapore's rapid industrial expansion, the three 'miracle' economies produced phenomenal rates of growth. Once the FDI had started to kick in, for the eight years from 1988 to 1995, Thailand, Singapore and Malaysia had annual average rates of real growth of 9.9 per cent, 9 per cent, and 8.9 per cent, respectively (ASEAN Centre 1997: 8). Indonesia fared nearly as well with a 7 per cent annual rate of growth over the same period. The Philippines continued its painfully slow progress with an annual growth rate of only 2.6 per cent.

The post-Plaza infusion of capital into Singapore, Malaysia and Thailand is very reminiscent of the capital influx that many of the 'miracle' economies experienced during the Korean and Vietnam Wars. Obviously the flood of FDI acted as a catalyst to rapid economic growth. But it also provided more revenues to the respective governments of each of the Southeast Asian 'miracle' economies. Indeed, perhaps somewhat ironically given the tumult that followed the onset of the Asian economic crisis in 1997, between 1986 and 1996 revenues doubled. Each government was, therefore, in a reasonably good position with regard to effective government debt management (IMF 1997). The flood of capital served to both secure in place the economic and political institutions that were associated with the increase in prosperity and, at the same time, to create tensions that pointed towards the necessity of reforming some of these institutions. The end of the Cold War reinforced this sense of a need for reforms.

Restructuring Strategies

The economic success of the seven Asian economies strengthened the economic, political and social institutions out of which the 'miracle' of rapid economic growth had emerged. While each economy had experience periods of slow growth or even recession, these were relatively quickly overcome. The general trend from the Korean War – the late 1950s for South Korea and the 1960s for Singapore – until the mid-1990s was overwhelmingly one of rapid and sustained economic growth. For the economic and political institutions that guided this growth, economic success produced a positive feedback that reinforced their centrality in the policy-making process and their integral role in economic development. The war-driven sequence of events had first weakened the societal forces then prompted the growth of a strong central state. The state then captured and directed the waves of capital that were pumped into the region as well as the domestic savings produced by the societies themselves. This process of development generated a pattern of institutions that were sustained by successive waves of prosperity. Moreover, those actors in the political and economic systems that adapted to the regulatory and incentive structures set out by the institutions prospered and their dominant role in the society's political economy confirmed. Hence, by the late 1970s and through the 1980s the general pattern of economic development in the seven successful economies was firmly established.

Yet tensions emerged in each of the 'miracle' economies. The resulting strains led to modifications, some larger than others, to the institutional patterns that had developed. Internally, the economies of Japan, South Korea, Taiwan, Hong Kong and Singapore faced increasing costs as the rapid industrial expansion ran up against shortages of labour and the rising prise of land. Externally, the dramatic rise in the price of oil during the 1970s, the intensifying competition from low-cost countries such as those in Southeast Asia, and the rising tide of protectionism in North America and Western

Europe all put considerable pressure on the governments to look for ways to restructure their economies so as to effectively surmount these new challenges.

Japan

Japan, which imported all its oil and over 90 per cent of its energy, was especially hard hit by the oil crisis. In particular, the industrial materials sector, notably the steel industry which used large amounts of energy, was greatly affected. The resulting shift in Japan's industrial strategy led to a greater emphasis on high value-added industries and production processes that involved more efficient use of energy and raw materials. Using the policy instruments developed during the early Cold War period and relying on its administrative links to business, the Japanese government oversaw a modification in strategy whereby the production of industrial materials was fairly quickly replaced by the production of machinery and equipment as Japan's main industrial sector. The auto industry and electronics and electrical machinery led the way. One of the key factors in this transition was the introduction of robots in manufacturing processes. Indeed, robots, which not only cut labour costs but reduced energy costs by making the manufacturing process itself more efficient, became an integral part of Japan's industrial capacity. By the early 1990s Japan was by far the largest producer and user of computerized numerical controllers and robots. For example, Japanese manufacturers used over five times the number of robots used by US manufacturers (Bernard 2000: 156: Thurow 1992: 127). In the electronics and electrical machinery sector Japan's development of semiconductors, integrated circuits, computers, VCRs and colour televisions led the way through the early 1980s.

The steadily growing competition from low-cost economies combined with the appreciation of the yen in the post-Plaza Accord years forced Japan to adopt a strategy of government-guided regionalization of its industrial development. Japanese companies extended the approach they had adopted in the 1970s and began to move the production of labour-intensive goods to other parts of Asia, notably Southeast Asia, where land and labour were much less costly and environmental and other regulations much less onerous. At the same time Japanese companies retained the production of the highest technology and high-value goods. For example, they concentrated on 'the production of the most powerful semiconductors, the highest quality televisions, and the most sophisticated appliances, leaving other firms in Asia to manufacture more standardized products' (Hatch and Yamamura 1996: 184). The same developments took place in the auto industry, with places like Taiwan and Thailand increasingly acting as manufacturing or assembling sites for low-priced compact cars in which there was a high percentage of labour-intensive parts (Abbott 2003).

Some analysts have seen this process as part of the 'product cycle' or 'flying geese wing' approach to regional industrialization. According to this view, products have life-cycles in which they are first imported, then manufactured domestically as part of an import-substitution strategy, and then manufactured for export. At some point in time the product will become too expensive to produce for export and so it becomes best to let others make it (Cumings 1984a, Vernon 1971). For example, in the past Japan has passed on major parts of its declining textile, steel, automobile and light electronic industries to Taiwan and South Korea (Cumings 1984a: 3). However, as Bernard and Ravenhill (1995) point out, the process of handing off Japanese industries to the other six 'miracle' economies is more complex than the flying geese approach would suggest. In many cases Japanese companies continue to produce domestically the most profitable high-technology, value-added parts of a product, such as a car or colour television. These products are then shipped to a low-cost country where the labour-intensive parts, such as the door trim, and steering wheels or cabinets, are made and where the whole product is assembled using imported Japanese equipment (see also Abbott 2003: 142; Hatch and Yamamura 1996).

By the early 1990s the doubling of the value of the yen against the American dollar began to create huge problems for the Japanese economy. Costs of electricity, transportation and warehouse space relative to the US and Britain were prohibitive (Ono 2001: 336). Not only was the cost of production so high as to make exports generally uncompetitive, the high value of the yen compounded the problem. In terms of consumption, however, Japan's large domestic market and relatively stable import-substitution sector survived. Moreover, the institutions that had created Japan's economic 'miracle', and enabled the country's economy to outperform its Western rivals for so long, showed a reluctance to be moved aside or adjust to the new circumstance, even in the face of the deepening recession. The economic structure created in the early Cold War years proved to have considerable staying power.

South Korea and Taiwan

South Korea and Taiwan suffered the same pressures as Japan. Both economies had been highly successful using cheap and abundant labour. But they now found labour increasingly scarce and expensive. At the same time cheap labour in Southeast Asia threatened to undercut the competitive advantage that South Korea and Taiwan once held. Moreover, Western states were seeking ways to protect their own markets, for example, through multi-fibre agreements which limited imports of textiles. As a result, both South Korea and Taiwan followed in the footsteps of the Japanese and embarked on a concerted strategy to deepen their export-manufacturing capability by cultivating more capital-intensive and high-technology sectors. In order to support this restructuring of their industrial sectors, both governments turned to secondary import-substitution industries (Schive 1990). The aim was to replace imported iron and steel, chemicals, artificial fibres and other similar goods with domestically produced intermediate goods. In the long term this would enable the economy to make the capital goods needed to produce the new generation of exports such as machine tools, electronic goods and transportation equipment.

Although they had roughly the same goal, South Korea and Taiwan approached the task of industrial restructuring in different ways. Faced in the early 1970s with a military buildup in North Korea and a reduction of US forces on the peninsula, the South Korean military-based government decided to 'augment its defence capability through an accelerated industrial transformation' (Cheng 1990: 164). The Park government used its centralized power to allocate both domestic and foreign credit and to direct the *chaebol* to make the 'big push' towards heavy and chemical industrialization (HCI). It applied intense political pressure to the steel, chemical, metal, machine-building, shipbuilding and electronics industries to ensure that the strategy was carried through effectively (Amsden 1989; Woo 1991: 128–47). The HCI strategy in South Korea proved to be a success. By '1980 heavy industry's share of total output surpassed the share of light industry' (Woo 2001: 259). It also provided the basis for continued rapid economic growth through the 1980s and into the 1990s; average annual growth rates in the 1975 to 1990 period were mostly in the 8–9 per cent range. Technology and skill-intensive industries were given priority and there was a limited, but noticeable, liberalization of the economy, prompted in part by US pressure. However, the government continued to play an active interventionist role in the economy, which was dominated by the large, government-linked conglomerates. Like Japan the institutional structure that had promoted such rapid economic growth in the 1960s, 1970s and 1980s was difficult to change.

Taiwan opted for a more decentralized and gradual shift to secondary import-substitution as the basis for upgrading exports. Taking note of Japan's experience, the Taiwanese government emphasized strengthening existing import-substitution industries while maintaining the continuing competitiveness of the economy's export-manufacturing capacity (Cheng 1990: 165). The government also felt that it was necessary to put considerable resources into research and development and to provide incentives for Taiwan's predominantly small-scale firms to upgrade their technological capacity. Strategic areas, such as automation, information technology, materials, biotechnology and electro-optics, received government support and government-sponsored programmes encouraged the diffusion of labour-saving automation equipment, the attainment of Japanese standards in quality control, and the improvement of access to venture capital for high-tech enterprises (Wade 1990: 99). Specific industries such as steel, machine tools, and electronics and information technology were also targeted for development. The Taiwanese economy moved forward at a rapid rate during the 1970s and 1980s and was in a position by the early 1990s to follow Japan's lead and invest in Southeast Asia and China. As in South Korea, liberalization of the economy did take place during the 1990s, but the overall export-oriented manufacturing trajectory, established during the Cold War/Vietnam War years remained.

Hong Kong and Singapore

Hong Kong and Singapore confronted the same challenges that led South Korea and Taiwan to restructure their economies. However, there were some important similarities and differences in the way each dealt with their rising labour costs and the competition from low-cost neighbours. Hong Kong's manufacturing enterprises, which were dominated by the production of labour-intensive, light consumer goods, relocated much of their production facilities to neighbouring parts of China, especially Guangdong province, where land and labour were more plentiful and considerably cheaper. This transplantation of manufacturing capacity intensified during the 1980s and early 1990s. As a result there was a dramatic increase in Hong Kong's re-export and out-processing activities and a rising demand for banking, transportation, managerial and other trade-related services (Chen and Ng 2001: 216; Kim 1995: 224). Overall domestic exports dropped from 53.5 per cent of all exports in 1980 to 14.4 per cent in 1995. In contrast, re-exports climbed from 23.6 per cent in 1980 to 69 per cent in 1995 (Chen and Ng 2001: 212–14).

Two factors significantly shaped the approach of Hong Kong's business community to restructuring the colony's economy. First, the British colonial government did not provide technological help to Hong Kong's manufacturers, the vast majority of whom were small in size and quite incapable of generating their own research and development capacity. As a consequence, the technological composition of Hong Kong's manufactured exports was well below that of Taiwan and South Korea and only just above that of Indonesia (Chen and Ng 2001: 227–8; Masuyama and Vandenbrink 2001: 10–11). Second, the rate at which Hong Kong's businesses were able to relocate into China was dependent on the willingness of the Chinese government to open up its economy. It was not until the late 1970s, when Deng Xiaoping rose to power, that China came up with its 'Open Door Policy' and reversed its essentially autarkic approach to economic development. During the 1980s Hong Kong businesses expanded their operations in neighbouring parts of China and from the early 1990s onwards China's economic development was truly spectacular. Hong Kong became a transshipment point for both goods and capital (Breslin 2000: 395). It was a regional hub, coordinating manufacturing activities in nearby mainland China and other parts of Asia and, most importantly, a financial centre through which many who wished to invest in China channelled their capital. In this fashion Hong Kong combined its past experience as a manufacturing centre with its long history as an entrepôt.

Like Hong Kong, Singapore sought to restructure its economy by linking up with the surplus labour and cheap land in neighbouring countries and becoming a service hub for manufacturing in the region. It developed what came to be called the 'Growth Triangle', combining Singaporean capital with the cheap land and abundant labour in the nearby Riau Islands of Indonesia and the state of Johore across the causeway in Malaysia. Singapore also created industrial enclaves in other labour-rich areas of Asia as a way of promoting its 'external economy' (Rodan 2001: 152). Moreover, as Singapore's neighbours grew and prospered, so the island became the regional business centre providing a wide range of services. By the mid-1990s Singapore had become host to over 4,000 multinational corporations, many of which had divisions that performed regional headquarters functions (Chia 2001: 183).

However, unlike Hong Kong, Singapore also emphasized upgrading the technological base of its economy. From the early 1970s, the electronics industry was central to Singapore's export-manufacturing success. The electronics sector grew from producing labour-intensive, relatively low-tech electronic parts and products to manufacturing computers, computer peripherals and components, and later semiconductors. The government helped this evolution with funds for research and development, often as a shared enterprise with major corporations such as Texas Instruments, Hewlett Packard or Canon. In addition, the government promoted skills-development programmes and tertiary education in science and technology (Chia 2001). Singapore's intent was to maintain a substantial export-manufacturing base within the country rather than follow Hong Kong's example and see its industrial sector hollowed out. Foreign direct investment continued to be encouraged with MNCs and government-linked companies leading the restructuring process (Low 2001). As with the other 'miracle' economies, Singapore's economic trajectory followed the basic outline developed in the Cold War/Vietnam War years of the late 1960s and early 1970s.

Malaysia and Thailand

Malaysia's development strategy went through three distinct phases between the early 1970s and the mid-1990s. First, during the 1970s, export-oriented industrialization was actively promoted through the introduction of export-processing zones (EPZ). Electronic goods and textiles and garments constituted the majority of Malaysia's manufactured exports, with electrical goods and electrical machinery contributing 48 per cent of gross manufacturing exports by 1980

(Kanapathy 2001: 145). By 1982 over 100 of the world's leading electronic companies had factories in Malaysia and it had become the largest producer of semiconductors in the world (Jesudason 1989: 174). This strategy substantially increased employment; however, high import content of the finished goods restricted the overall benefit to the Malaysian economy.

Second, in the early 1980s the Malaysian government attempted to emulate Japan and South Korea by embarking on a publicly funded heavy industry programme. Led by the Heavy Industry Corporation of Malaysia (HICOM), Malaysia's 'big push' into the production of cement, iron and steel, chemicals, pulp and paper, refined petroleum and a national car was implemented using government funds, tax incentives, tariff protection and import quotas and licensing requirements (Kanapathy 2001: 144–6). This attempt at secondary import-substitution was undertaken in order to link the growing export-manufacturing sector more closely into the national economy. This new strategy, championed by the Prime Minister Dr Mahathir Mohamad took effect as the government was implementing the NEP which sought to alleviate poverty and ensure that Malays played a greater role in the economy. The NEP and the heavy industry progamme could be pursued concurrently because of the windfall revenues received by the government from the discovery and exploitation during the 1970s of new oilfields off Sarawak, Sabah and the peninsula's east cost. Natural gas was also discovered off Sarawak and developed for both export as LNG and for domestic use in major industrial plants. During the second half of the 1970s, the value of crude oil exports rose by over 40 per cent per year and by the height of the oil boom, in the early 1980s, oil and LNG accounted for 29 per cent of Malaysia's export earnings (Drabble 2000: 231; Jomo 1987: 119–20; Malaysia 1979: 9). However, with the collapse in the price of oil as well as the prices of Malaysia's other commodities – natural rubber, palm oil and tin – the heavy industry programme, along with the rest of the economy, ran into trouble.

The third phase of Malaysia's development strategy occurred following the regional economic recession of 1985–6. The recession, brought on by the collapsing prices for Malaysia's raw materials, prompted the government to introduce policies that would make the country a major export-manufacturing centre. In 1986 the government promulgated the Promotion of Investments Act. It liberalized the investment process in place under the NEP to ensure Malay participation in FDI projects, and made provision for special incentives for investing in particular sectors associated with export-manufacturing. Special emphasis was also placed on continuing Malaysia's long-standing commitment to free public education at all levels and the development of skills training and support for scient-ific education. This was done to provide overseas investors with the skilled workforce that they were looking for. In addition, foreign labour was allowed into the country to help keep labour costs down. Fortuitously, this new strategy coincided with the search for low-cost platforms for its export-manufacturing industries by Japan and other countries. The resulting flood of FDI into Malaysia created an eco-nomic boom that continued until the financial crisis of 1997.

In Thailand the restructuring of the economy centred on a switch in the first half of the 1980s from an emphasis on the export of resource-based, primarily agricultural, products combined with an import-substitution industrializing strategy, to the export of manu-factured goods. A series of external events prompted this change in economic policy. Most importantly, with the Thai baht tied to the US dollar from the late 1970s onwards, Thai exports became more expensive as the dollar appreciated during the early years of the 1980s. In addition, the worldwide decline in commodity prices, which started in the late 1970s, made agricultural exports sluggish. Moreover, public borrowing abroad, which was increased as the government tried to cope with the second oil-price hike of 1979–81, reached a dangerously high level by the mid-1980s. In 1984 it was clear that the economy was in trouble. There was an increasingly obvious balance of payments problem and a growing number of bankruptcies. A change in strategy was required (Bowie and Unger 1997: 142–50; Hewison 2001: 83).

The new economic strategy encouraged the export of manufac-tured goods. In November 1984 the baht was devalued by nearly 15 per cent. In 1985 the baht was allowed to float and depreciated in value by a further 20 per cent by the end of 1987. Complementing this move the government reduced tariffs on imported goods used in the manufacture of exports and removed key export taxes. The Bank of Thailand also accorded exporters access to special credit facilities. Fortunately, the flood of Japanese FDI, quickly followed by invest-ments from other parts of Asia, the US and Western Europe, rapidly turned the Thai economy around and set the stage for a period of remarkable economic growth. Importantly, Japanese companies were able to take advantage of the extensive economic infrastructure that had been built by the Americans during the 1960s and early 1970s and to deal with a bureaucracy that had developed and matured under America's tutelage and that was able to plan an economic strategy and implement government policies. Thailand's main export-industries included textiles, clothing and toys during the late 1980s and computer components, integrated circuits, electrical appliances, and auto and auto parts from 1990 onwards (Masuyama and Vandenbrink 2001: 10–11; Pasuk and Baker 1995: 161). The strong economic growth lasted until 1995–6 when the economy began to falter as a prelude to the 1997 currency crisis.

The Philippines and Indonesia

Obviously, then, it was in Southeast Asia that Japan's policy of regionalizing its economy had the most impact. Especially after the Plaza Accord of 1985, Japanese investment flooded the region. Yet not all Southeast Asian countries benefited equally from the search by Japanese business to find low-cost platforms for their export-manufacturing ventures. The key to success in attracting Japanese FDI was what may best be termed 'absorptive capacity' (Stubbs 1989a: 520; see also Caldwell 1974: 9, 155; Deyo 1987: 237–8; Orr 1987: 49, 52). Absorptive capacity refers to the ability of the state to manage effectively and, where necessary, to direct domestic and foreign capital and the capacity of the economic and social infrastructure, especially educational facilities, to support rapid economic expansion. Critically, it was the experience of Singapore, Malaysia and Thailand in developing their administrative institutions as well as their economic and social infrastructures during the Korean and Vietnam Wars that made them the targets of Japanese investments. They could also make effective use of the Japanese aid that poured into the region. The Japanese were able to build on the foundations laid as a result of America's commitment of funds and troops to the region.

By contrast, the lack of absorptive capacity in the Philippines and Indonesia meant that they had a more difficult time ensuring that Japanese investments and aid were put to productive use. Notably, at the behest of the Americans, the Philippines was one of Japan's major recipients of aid throughout the 1980s (Orr 1987: 53). But, rather like the large amounts of American aid that had been made available to the Philippines in the 1960s, Japanese aid was dissipated through pork-barrelling and provincial-level patronage. Family clans and provincial land barons with regional power bases used the US-modelled political system to battle with Manila and all but paralysed the government's ability to set the country on a course for economic development (McBeth 1989; Tiglao 1994). As a result, the central government was so besieged, inefficient and corrupt and the economic infrastructure so ill-developed that effective use could not be made of the aid that was delivered. The overall economic and political malaise scared away Japanese FDI and few others chose to invest in the Philippines.

Indonesia fared a little better than the Philippines. When Suharto assumed power in 1966, he followed the advice of a group of Western-trained economists at the University of Indonesia to open up the economy. He put windfall revenues from the first petroleum price rise of 1973–4 into economic infrastructure projects in the rural areas so as to raise agricultural productivity. However, once oil revenues began to dominate the economy later in the 1970s, these developments were offset by a return to large-scale government intervention to develop an import-substitution industrializing strategy. Accompanying this turn of events was a renewed intensity in the level of corruption. Indeed, political and administrative corruption of all types became was so pervasive that it discouraged potential traders and investors from doing business with Indonesia (Bowie and Unger 1997: 52; Kang 2002: 189; Robison 1986: 391–5). Moreover, as Terry Karl (1997: 212–13) points out, Indonesia used its petrodollars to promote a particular set of political and economic institutions, which were in may ways similar to other weak 'petro-states' and which were particularly vulnerable to an acute economic downturn. This quickly became evident in the 1997–8 economic crisis. Indonesia experienced a massive exodus of investment capital which continued through to 2001 and left the economy foundering. While there are some similarities between the three Southeast Asian 'miracle' economies and Indonesia, these should not be exaggerated. The US did support the Suharto regime once it came to power but Indonesia was not as central to US anti-communist strategy as was Thailand, for example. Furthermore, it did not have the strong state apparatus to direct foreign capital into productive uses. Certainly, Indonesia did not benefit in the same way from the geopolitically driven sequence of events that so influenced Singapore, Malaysia and

Thailand and allowed them to build a relatively robust manufacturing economy.

China

By the early 1990s Japan was returning to the kind of relationship with China about which many of its post-Second World War leaders had dreamed. Japan was China's biggest aid donor, Japanese companies were investing heavily in China's rapidly expanding industrial base and trade between the countries was growing exponentially. In order to reach this point both countries had travelled down very different roads. China had gone through a period of major upheaval and it was only with the restructuring of the economy that occurred in the late 1980s and early 1990s that it was possible for the Chinese economy to once again fully engage the global economy. In the meantime Japan had become the major engine of growth for the region.

Yet in the broadest of terms China can be seen as having gone through many of the same experiences as its neighbours who were on the other side of the Cold War divide. It too was heavily influenced by the sequence of 'hot' wars and the Cold War that dominated East and Southeast Asia for over thirty years. Clearly, China is unique in its size and the vast numbers who are weighed down by rural poverty and these factors greatly affected the impact that the geopolitical events of the region had on its development. But the similarities with the seven 'miracle' economies should not be overlooked. Once the Chinese Communist Party (CCP) took over the government in 1949, it was able to develop a relatively – at least in terms of China's recent history – strong central government. The civil war had produced a massive social dislocation which left the new government with a comparatively clean slate on which to map out its new political and economic institutions. The immediate outbreak of the Korean War and the continuing encirclement of China by the US and its allies provided the imminent military threat that justified building a strong central administration with political and economic power firmly in the hands of the central leadership (Chen 2001: 87; White 1988: 155). The Soviet Union's government, the CCP government's mentor for the first few, formative years of its existence, 'favoured concentrated social control' (Migdal 1988: 272). It also acted as a model for the creation of a 'vast latticework' of political and economic institutions to ensure the government's full control of the Chinese society and economy and to expedite the push for rapid industrialization (White 1993: 2). Under Mao Zedong, and especially under the skilful administrative leadership of the enigmatic Zhou Enlai, the governmental apparatus was adapted to China's circumstances and its capacity quickly developed. This increased administrative capacity, aided by limited Soviet economic aid and technical resources, slowly developed an import-substitution-oriented industrial strategy.

The essentially self-contained Chinese economy then went through a long period of constant upheaval before Deng Xiaoping took over the CCP in 1978 and started the process of economic reform. The economy was opened up slowly with the initial focus on Special Economic Zones established along the southern coast. This strategy replicated the one followed by several of the 'miracle' economies. It was not until the end of the 1980s and into the 1990s that a strong export-orientation strategy was given priority by the Chinese government. From 1993 onwards FDI started to flood into China and the economy went through a remarkable transformation.

For China, between 1949 and the late 1980s, the missing ingredient in their quest for rapid industrialization and sustained high rates of economic growth was a large wave of capital. The opening up, of the Chinese economy fortuitously coincided with the increasing availability of capital in the region as the more developed of the 'miracle' economies looked to invest their rising profits and to move export manufacturing to lower-cost areas. Japan and the overseas Chinese community have provided by far the largest portion of capital to flood into China. As the Chinese economy opened up, Japanese aid soared. China quickly became the top-ranked recipient of Japanese aid. Between 1992 and 1996 Japan disbursed over US$1.6 billion in grants and US$4.5 billion in loans to China (Lim 2003: 215). Similarly, Japanese FDI shifted from Southeast Asia into China during the same period, rising to nearly US$6 billion by 1997 and giving a major boost to China's economic development. However, most FDI during this period came from overseas Chinese in Taiwan, Hong Kong and the Southeast who contributed over 50 per cent of all FDI to China – or more than US$250 billion – over the four years from 1995 to 1998 (Breslin 2005; IMF 2003).

The Cold War, then, shaped the economic development of China in two important ways. First, it influenced how the political and economic institutions in China emerged from the civil war period. The constant external threat made the CCP's task of centralizing power and building both state capacity and autonomy easier. The threat from the US and its allies in the region also helped to legitimize the CCP's authoritarian rule. Although there has been a considerable debate about the extent to which China may be considered a 'developmental state', there are clear indications that, in very general terms, China's political and economic development and the development of Asia's miracle economies were influenced by the region's 'hot' wars and the Cold War in very similar ways (Deans 2004; and also Breslin 1996; White 1988). Second, The economic dynamism of Japan and the other 'miracle' economies contributed significantly to China's economic restructuring and to its economic engagement with the global economy. The timing of the decision to open up the Chinese economy coincided with the search on the part of regional businesses for new lower-cost, export-manufacturing platforms. And, with Japanese and overseas Chinese companies leading the way, the American and European firms quickly followed. As a result, China's process of economic restructuring was given an enormous boost.

Conclusion

During the two decades following the end of the Vietnam War Japan gradually replaced the US as the main driving force behind rapid economic growth in the Asian 'miracle' economies. Primarily through its diffusion of FDI to South Korea, Taiwan, Hong Kong, Singapore, Malaysia and Thailand, but also by its use of aid and the partial opening up of its market, Japan acted as a catalyst to sustained, high levels of economic development. This is not to argue, of course, that American companies failed to engage the region or that the US was no longer crucial to the seven 'miracle' economies. On the contrary, American FDI was channelled into both resource extraction and export-manufacturing industries and the US market remained significant for all of Asia's most successful economies. However, from the mid-1970s onwards it was the Japanese economy that came to dominate the successful economies of East and Southeast Asia.

It is clear that the US-funded economic development of the 1950 to 1975 period was crucial to the economic links that Japan promoted with South Korea, Taiwan and Hong Kong in subsequent years. Importantly, however, Japan's economic relations with South Korea and Taiwan in particular date back to the 1960s. As each of these economies industrialized they acquired much of their technology, capital equipment and parts from Japan and having embarked on this strategy they had to keep on buying from Japan as they upgraded their industrial capacity. As a consequence, the trade and investment links of the three NIEs were continued, and indeed deepened. This was most noticeable as both Taiwan and South Korea moved up the 'technological ladder' by employing Japanese technology, in the decades following the Vietnam War (Hatch and Yamamura 1996: 178–80). In many ways the investment, trade and technology ties were reinforced by the relationships that had been forged during colonial times. Personal friendships arising from South Koreans or Taiwanese having attended university in Japan or from Japanese officials and businessmen having been stationed in Korea or Taiwan formed the basis of a number of post-Second World War cooperative business ventures. There was also a sense that both sides understood the other, especially in terms of the institutions in which they operated, because of their common experiences — which for many Koreans and Taiwanese included learning Japanese — during the period of Japanese colonialism. These links were crucial as Japanese businesses moved more aggressively into the region after restrictions on yen exports were eased in the early 1970s.

However, it was the economies of Southeast Asia that provided Japanese companies with the low-cost manufacturing bases that they were looking for and, therefore, benefited the most from Japan's region-embracing economic strategy. Significantly, Singapore, Malaysia and Thailand did rather better than their neighbours from Japan's export of capital. The series of wars which drew resources into the region enabled each of these countries to build up their economic infrastructure, produce a relatively skilled and educated workforce, start the industrialization process, and develop a reasonably strong central government that Japanese companies could rely on to maintain a stable and predictable economic environment. The sequence of geopolitical events had generated political and economic institutions in these three 'miracle' economies that attracted substantial amounts of Japanese FDI and made the most use of both Japanese aid and investment. Both Japan and the successful economies of Southeast Asia, then, profited from the chain of events that preceded Japan's economic expansion into the region.

Hence, although a number of the explanations for Asia's economic success help to account for events in the post-Vietnam War period, each has its limitations. In particular, Japan-centred explanations are useful but need to be set alongside the American-hegemony explanations. Spending by the US on the Korean War, the Vietnam War and the Cold War laid the foundations for Japan's successful expansion into East and Southeast Asia. Similarly, the neoclassical economic and the statist explanations point to the need to carefully evaluate specific economic policies. But they too must be employed in conjunction with explanations that indicate how capital became available to develop the export-oriented approach and how and why the capacity of the 'miracle' economies' central governments were strengthened. Certainly no explanation of Japan's role in promoting rapid economic growth within the 'miracle' economies of East and Southeast Asia is complete without acknowledging the way that the various 'hot' wars and the Cold War shaped the economic and political institutions on which Japan's successful economic expansion into the region was based.

7
Liberalization, Economic Crisis and Regionalism

The Cold War came to an end in 1989. In Europe this was symbolized by the fall of the Berlin Wall. In Asia it was marked by the withdrawal of Vietnam from Cambodia and the signing of an agreement between the Communist Party of Malaysia (CPM) and the Malaysian and Thai governments by which the CPM was dismantled. Although vestiges of the Cold War lingered on in the Korean peninsula and the Taiwan Strait, communism was no longer seen as the threat to the region it had once been. Just as the Cold War was a major factor in the rise of the seven Asian 'miracle' economies, so its demise also had a significant effect. The international context within which the seven successful Asian economies had achieved their rapid rates of growth changed in very important ways. And these changes, in turn, had an impact on the domestic dynamics that shaped each Asian country's economic and political life. At the same time, however, while some new institutions were created and others were overhauled in reaction to the newly evolving circumstances, many of the political and economic institutions that had been shaped by the Cold War continued to function. The Cold War still cast a long shadow. Perhaps inevitably, the resulting tensions, between the surviving Cold War-rooted institutions on the one hand, and the newly created institutions and the changing circumstance that had spawned them on the other, generated problems for Asia's seven 'miracle' economies.

While 1989 marked the end of the Cold War, its influence over events in East and Southeast Asia had been on the wane for nearly a decade (Zhu 2002). Although the US maintained its deep distrust of the Soviet Union during the 1980s, its relations with China were much less strained. Following on from the normalization of US–China relations under President Nixon in 1972, China and the US, although still wary of each other, were far less distrustful than at the height of the Cold War. As a result of the more relaxed relations between the US and China, regional affairs took on a new complexion. Japan and China normalized relations. Taiwan became more isolated and remained troubled by the China threat. During the 1980s, however, the US renewed its commitment to Taiwan, China became more conciliatory, and tensions eased to such an extent that Taiwanese capital was allowed into several of China's special economic zones along the coast. Also, during the 1980s, South Korea moved well ahead of North Korea in terms of economic development and, as a consequence, military strength. The threat from the communist North appeared not nearly so immediate or so potent as it had in the past.

An important effect of this ebbing of the Cold War was that the US became less willing to overlook the essentially mercantilist approach – especially the protectionist dimension – of its major allies in the region. American pressure to liberalize the economic institutions that had underpinned the rapid economic growth of seven successful economies, when combined with other changes in the international political economy and the domestic economies of the region, eventually brought about economic and political reforms within the seven 'miracle' economies. These reforms, in turn, produced several changes, especially to the financial sectors of the seven economies, a number of which proved beneficial while others had traumatic repercussions. Another significant effect of the ending of the Cold War was the lessening of the social unity that the threat from communism had created within the seven 'miracle' economies. Societies tended to fragment as the anti-communist hegemonic project became less relevant as a rallying call for collective action and economic cooperation. Similarly, the perception that the external threat was on the wane tended to undermine the rationale governments used in order to intervene to regulate and direct their economies and societies.

Analysts who have sought to account for the success of the post-Cold War period of economic and political liberalization and the traumatic events of the Asian economic crisis have generally used variations of the categories of explanation set out in the introductory chapter. Indeed, most commentators are quick to show how the events of the 1980s and 1990s confirm their analyses of the initial rise of the 'miracle' economies. Those who adhere to the neoclassical economic approach note the liberalization of the region's economies led to strong growth rates and that the economic crisis was brought on by corrupt governments interfering in the economy to further their supporters' business interests. However, they underplay the external factors that contributed to the crisis. Statists see the strong economic performance of the Asian economies as attributable to government guidance and the Asian economic crisis as arising from a weakening of the state's managerial capacity. They tend to ignore the problems created by the expansion of the various economies and the tensions that this created.

Proponents of the American-hegemony explanation argue that US pressure to get Asian governments to bring their economic policies more in line with Western-style capitalism was a significant factor in the lead-up to the crisis. Supporters of the American-hegemony approach also see the US as using the crisis to encourage US corporations to buy up assets in the region at fire sale prices. They miss the internal factors at work in generating the crisis and the fact that relatively few local companies were actually acquired by US corporations (Robertson 2005). Those using the Japan-centred and cultural explanations tend to focus on the successes of the region during the 1980s and 1990s. Apart from noting the destabilizing effects of the influx of short-term capital into the region and the rapid rise in low-priced exports from China, supporters of the Japan-centred and cultural approaches have relatively little to say about the causes of the Asian crisis.

This chapter reviews the major consequences of the ending of the Cold War for East and Southeast Asia's political economy. It builds on a number of the explanations that seek to account for Asia's economic success. America's role in pushing for economic and political reforms is stressed, as is the impact that US pressure had on the various economic and political institutions in each of the 'miracle' economies. However, the chapter departs from most American-hegemony and statist explanations by linking the causes of the economic crisis back to the institutions that were established as a result of the Cold War. The argument is made that the economic and political reforms that accompanied the liberalization process created a dissonance with those Cold War-rooted economic and political institutions that remained at the centre of the economy. The resulting discord was the major cause of the Asian economic crisis of 1997–8. The chapter also explores the rise of East Asian regionalism. Again it underscores the long shadow that the Cold War casts over the region's political economy. The analysis emphasizes the way in which the common experiences of facing the sequence of geopolitical events, that swept through the region from the Second World War onwards serves to produce a collective identity among many of the countries of East and Southeast Asia. These experiences, combined with the similarity of many of the region's domestic economic and political institutions that evolved out of the Cold War years, help to bring the countries of East and Southeast Asia together into one loose, but increasingly coherent, economic region.

Liberalization

As the Cold War eased, successive American administrations put greater and greater pressure on the seven successful Asian economies to liberalize. This pressure coincided with a number of other trends that were pushing the governments of the more advanced economies of East and Southeast Asia in the same direction. Internationally, the forces of globalization encouraged governments to seize the opportunities available as highly mobile capital searched for higher profits (Cox 1997: 23). Moreover, shifts in the international economy, such as the oil-price hikes of 1979–81 and the collapse of commodity prices in the following years, also had their impact on the seven 'miracle' economies. Domestically, governments were coping with the effects of over twenty-five to thirty years of sustained, rapid economic development. The high rates of growth in the successful Asian economies produced an expanded industrial sector, a dynamic business community, and a relatively well-educated middle class. Societies were more diverse, complex and modern. These international and domestic factors forced governments into implementing reforms that led to periods of economic, and in some cases political, liberalization.

By the late 1980s and early 1990s 'the warm, fraternal and dependent relationship with the United States, solidified by the common cold war opposition to the USSR, China and communism, had given way to technonationalist competition in a host of economic sectors'

(Pempel 1998: 137). In its attempt to limit Japan's mercantilist approach and liberalize its trade practices, the US government had pushed the Japanese government to accept the Plaza Accord and increase the value of the yen; abolish formal barriers to inward FDI; and reduce, if not eliminate altogether, tariffs, import-quotas and non-tariff barriers. The Americans were also successful in pressing for voluntary export restraints (VERs) on specific Japanese exports, such as televisions and steel, and forcing on Japan an agreement to 'manage trade' in semiconductors. These measures encouraged Japanese companies to relocate their export-manufacturing plants to places such as Southeast Asia. The appreciation of its currency and the hollowing out of its industry caused Japan's economy to stagnate (Grimes 2001). Indeed, in these circumstance no economy could continue to grow.

Domestically, the boom and bust that followed the Plaza Accord created rifts in Japanese society. The LDP, the dominant political party in Japan since 1955, lost power in 1993 to a non-LDP coalition when it splintered largely because of the deteriorating economic situation. The LDP returned to the governing coalition a year later and in 1966 the prime minister was once again selected from their ranks. However, electoral reform went into effect with the 1996 elections, changing the dynamics of the party system although not necessarily the pivotal position of the conservative LDP. The political reforms allied to changes to the economy, such as the internationalization of Japanese capital, increases in the number of foreign-owned firms, and the weakening of links connecting Japan's *keiretsu*, suggest a possible 'regime shift' (Pempel 1998). Yet, many of the Cold War institutions still linger on. The government still has 'conservative interventionist' tendencies. The bureaucracy retains a great deal of power to regulate the economy and society. Most notably, while the export sector is very competitive and internationally oriented, other sectors including the import-substitution and domestic services industries, like agriculture, textiles, food processing, insurance and construction, are highly regulated and heavily subsidized. Indeed, the 'iron triangle' of politicians, bureaucrats and vested business interests, which was forged into its present configuration during the Cold War years, is still strong (Sakakibara 2001). Hence, American demands for reform, domestic upheavals and the pressures from globalization changed some Japanese institutions but by no means all. And in a number of cases the changes have been relatively superficial.

In South Korea, liberalization, especially in the financial sector, resulted from US pressure and changing domestic political dynamics. During the 1980s and 1990s South Korea was forced to adjust to US demands to reduce tariffs and to liberalize its trade and financial services (Loriaux 1997: 12; Woo 1991: 190, 193–4, 202). At the same time, the government of Chun Doo Hwan, seeking to extricate itself from the debilitating recession of the early 1980s, turned for guidance to the US-trained economists who staffed key economic agencies. Their advice to liberalize echoed that of the US government. The reduction of the government's leverage over the economy, especially its power over the *chaebol*s (business conglomerates), centred primarily on freeing up the system of credit. The government essentially relinquished its capacity to control and direct credit; it privatized the banks it had set up or acquired and through which it allocated financial resources. Reforms allowed foreign banks to operate within the country, a stock market to be developed and state regulation of the financial sector to be curtailed (Euh and Baker 1990: Weiss 2000).

A second wave of liberalization took place in the early 1990s when the government divested itself of many of its monitoring and coordinating powers (Thurbon 2003). The folding of the Economic Planning Board, which had been at the centre of the state direction of the economy during the 1960s, 1970s and 1980s, into the Ministry of Finance in 1993 was symbolic of the extent to which the government's capacity to manage the country's economic development was reduced. The government's overall goal was to meet the criteria laid out for membership in the OECD. Most notably the criteria included the liberalization of capital transfers. The goal of OECD membership was finally achieved in 1996. In addition, the government authorized the creation of 24 new merchant banks and allowed them to make use of short-term overseas loans and to invest outside the country (Lee 2000: 127–8). However, the liberalization of the economy and especially the financial sector was undertaken without instituting regulatory or supervisory systems that would ensure the effectiveness of the liberalization policies (Lee and Kim 2000: 123). Certainly, 'the government failed to develop an effective mechanism of prudential regulation which was a necessity for liberalization' (Lee 1999: 150).

Taiwan's liberalization process took a different route. Faced with the same pressure from the US government to liberalise as South

Korea had experienced and similar domestic demands to reform the economy, the Taiwanese government chose to act in a more cautious and measured way, especially with regard to the liberalization of the financial sector. The government continued as a major shareholder in many of the island's banks, no merchant banks or finance companies were allowed, and foreign participation in the local capital market was strictly controlled. In addition, while limits on both inward and outward FDI movements and long-term capital transactions were reduced, restrictions on short-term borrowing, local firms taking on foreign loans, and overseas operations by banks were generally maintained. And the government kept its supervisory capacity. Taiwan's Central Bank of China and the Monetary Affairs Department of the Finance Ministry were assigned extra staff to fulfil the crucial monitoring function (Zhang 2002).

One of the reasons for Taiwan's caution arose from geopolitical factors, or what may be thought of as a remnant of the Cold War. Whereas the threat from North Korea appeared to be on the decline, China by contrast was gaining in both military and economic strength and was thus perceived to be a continuing menace to Taiwan. With national security and economic security seen as intimately linked, the government clearly felt the need to ensure that the island's credit system, which was pivotal to the success of the whole economy, was not put in jeopardy; hence, the government's interest in moving more circumspectly and more systematically down the road to financial liberalization. Moreover, with Taiwan's international outcast status preventing it from joining the OECD, it was not under the same pressure as South Korea to liberalize in order to gain membership (Weiss 2000: 30–1).

For both South Korea and Taiwan, liberalization was complicated by the parallel process of democratization. As with liberalization, the catalyst for democratization was both pressure from the US and internal developments such as the growth of an educated middle class, the necessity of accommodating an increasingly diverse and powerful business sector, and schisms within the ruling elite. However, while democratization took place at roughly the same time in each society and in response to generally similar internal pressures for greater political participation, the actual process was different in each case. In South Korea democratization occurred in the late 1980s as Chun Doo Whan attempted to engineer a transfer of power to his handpicked successor, a former general, Roh Tae Woo who represented Chun's Democratic Justice Party. Despite a series of divisive moves, including an attempt to install Roh through indirect elections under the old constitution, Roh eventually responded to the large-scale street demonstrations and widely backed calls for a more open political process. He announced, in June 1987, a series of changes to the constitution which included direct presidential elections and the restoration of human rights. Remarkably, with the opposition candidates splitting the vote, Roh won the December 1987 presidential elections with only 36.6 per cent of the total ballots cast. Subsequently, in 1992, the first civilian president, Kim Young Sam, was elected and in 1997 Kim Dae Jung, a long-time critic of the authoritarian regimes of Park and Chun, was elected to the presidency. In 2003 Kim was succeeded by Roh Moo-hyun.

The process of democratization in Korea took place against the backdrop of economic growth. Prosperity helped to dissipate some of the tensions that built up as the new political system was negotiated. However, building a mature democratic system was not easy and some aspects of the opening of the political process had important consequences for the economy (Ahn and Jaung 1999). The state's autonomy was undermined as political parties became dependent on funding from businesses to fight elections. Political corruption, which had been a significant factor in periods of Korea's recent history, once more became endemic. Political parties, which had little experience from the Cold War years to draw on, were in a continuous state of flux as they went through a series of splits and mergers in the post-1987 period. These constant changes in the party system, the heavy reliance on regional support in presidential elections, and the change of president every five years produced inconsistencies in the country's economic policy. Indeed, liberalization was undertaken on an *ad hoc* basis rather than as part of a systematic strategy to reform the economy. As Jaymin Lee argues (1999: 151), 'Korea thus came to have a non-system in industry and finance.' Many of the old Cold War institutions, such as the *chaebol*s and key parts of the bureaucracy, muddled along bereft of the old system that had allowed them to function effectively and with South Korea's volatile democracy seemingly unable to piece together a coherent, new economic system within which they could operate.

Democratization in Taiwan evolved in a less chaotic fashion. In part it was more orderly because the old authoritarian regime had been managed by a Leninist party, the KMT. It could more easily adapt to the new democratic environment than could the military regime of South Korea. Like South Korea, the major shift to a democratic course came in 1987 when martial law ended. The decision to end martial law was the product of steady pressure from opposition groups who were supported by demands from overseas allies, especially groups in the US. As these pressures mounted, the KMT realized that it could retain the political initiative if it led the democratization process rather than be dragged along by it (Cheng and Lin 1999). Among other reforms enacted in 1987 the opposition Democratic Progressive Party (DPP) was officially recognized, controls over the press were lifted, and more generally restrictions on political activities were removed. When Chiang Ching-kuo died in 1988, Lee Teng-hui succeeded him as president and, after solidifying his position, began further democratic reforms. Most notably, in 1991 the original members of the legislature, who had been elected in 1947 to represent all of China, were forced to resign and new elections held. In 1996 Lee was re-elected president in the first direct popular election. Four years later he was succeeded by Chen Shui-bian. Chen represented the DPP and his election brought to an end the KMT's dominance of Taiwan's politics. In general the continuity provided by the KMT and the presidency of Lee Teng-hui worked to ensure that the bureaucracy was able to maintain a coherent economic strategy during much of the 1990s based on a gradual and systematic reform of the old Cold War institutions. However, while the DPP has retained aspects of the KMT approach to economic development, there are signs of a fragmenting of the political system which may create problems down the road (Wong 2003: 256).

Rather like South Korea and Taiwan, Thailand and Malaysia were under pressure from Western powers, primarily the US government, throughout much of the 1980s and 1990s, to liberalize their economies. In addition, balance of payments problems and the region-wide economic recession of the mid-1980s forced both governments to turn to liberal reformers to plot a more export-oriented economic course. These liberal reformers, usually Western-trained technocrats, sought to open up the economy to market forces through deregulation and privatization, and to encourage the free flow of capital and trade so as to exploit the perceived mutual gains from participating in the expanding global economy. In Thailand liberalization was undertaken in two phases. First, directly after the recession, a decision was taken to promote the export sector and devalue the baht. The second phase came in 1991 following a coup which installed as prime minister Anand Panyarachun, a former foreign service official and technocrat. Among other policies, Anand and his reform-minded cabinet cut import taxes, and so removed tariff protection from inefficient sectors that had been established during the period of import-substitution industrialization; drastically reduced tariffs on capital goods to encourage the importation of manufacturing equipment; 'made the baht openly convertible and cleared away various exchange controls'; and expanded the role of the stock market 'as a key institution for further capital development' (Pasuk and Baker 1995: 356).

Just as with the sequence of events in South Korea, during the period of increased economic liberalization the pressure for democratization in Thailand bore fruit. A brief flirtation with democracy between 1973 and 1976 was ended by a coup which suspended Parliament. The 1979 elections ushered in a period of 'quasi-democracy' as first General Kriangsak Chomanan and then, from March 1980 onwards, General Prem Tinsulanon took over as prime minister in a military-dominated Parliament. With the disappearance of the domestic insurgency, the waning of the threat from Vietnam, and the increasing involvement of senior military officers in commercial ventures, the military fragmented and Parliament appeared to get stronger. As prime minister, Prem survived two attempted coups, three elections and five changes in cabinet before giving way, after the 1988 elections, to Chatichai Choonhavan. Chatichai, who, unlike Prem, was a civilian businessman and came from the ranks of the parliamentarians, put together the first fully parliamentary-based government. In 1991 a coup threw Chatichai out and he was replaced by Anand. The subsequent election was indecisive and the military attempted to regain control through the appointment of General Suchinda Kraprayoon as prime minister. In May 1992, after a series of large and bloody Bangkok street demonstrations, which were backed by the business community and which vehemently opposed military rule, King Bhumibol was forced to step in and resolve the *impasse*. In new elections in September 1992 political parties opposing the military won a narrow victory. Thereafter the military's influence over Thai politics, which had been deeply entrenched over many years, and which had been reinforced by the domestic insurgency and other aspects of the Cold War, gradually receded and governments became increasingly rooted in elected parliaments.

Economic liberalization, therefore, went hand-in-hand with political liberalization. Thailand's middle class and business leaders gradually eroded the political power of the military. However, as the new political system was worked out, factionalism and fragmentation proved to be major problems. Each of the relatively large number of political parties tended to revolve around particular personalities, with popular support swinging markedly from election to election. As a result, Thailand had a succession of prime ministers – Chuan Leekpai in 1992, Banharn Silpa-archa in 1995, Chavalit Younchaiyudh in 1996, Chuan Leekpai in 1997 and Thaksin Shinawatra in 2001 – each from a different party. Moreover, with the economy booming from the massive inflow of FDI, the political parties looking for increasing amounts of money to fight elections and underpaid bureaucrats seeking to gain from the rapid expansion of wealth, corruption grew to epidemic proportions. Not surprisingly, devising a coherent economic strategy in these circumstances proved extremely difficult. As in South Korea, a good deal of the liberalization of the economy took place without the necessary regulatory supervision in place to monitor the changes that were occurring. In particular, the opening up of the financial sector was not accompanied by the upgrading of the prudential surveillance and regulatory system. The institutions that survived the ending of the Cold War were not capable of dealing with the transformation of the economy that liberalization ushered in. Nor, in the years preceding the 1997 economic crisis, were new institutions created to fill the void.

Malaysia responded to the mid-1980s recession and the pressure from the industrialized countries to liberalize in several ways. First, faced with the possible failure of his heavy industrialization policy, Prime Minister Dr Mahathir Mohamad turned to joint-venture foreign investment to bail out the various projects. Foreign companies were actively encouraged to coordinate their investments with leading Malay businessmen. Second, the government's interest in privatization, which had begun in 1983, was intensified. Gradually, privatization was extended to a range of activities including airlines, airports, railways, road construction, shipping and telecommunications. Third, labour laws were introduced to weaken existing unions and allow for enterprise unions so favoured by Japanese investors. Fourth, corporate tax rates were lowered. Fifth, the short-term export credit facility was expanded to encourage increased exports. And, finally, in 1990, tariffs were lowered across the board with major cuts made to the import tax on business equipment (Bowie and Unger 1997).

There was some resistance to the push to deregulate the Malaysian economy but in the end the momentum to liberalize was sustained. Resistance to liberalization came from those who argued that government intervention was needed to ensure that Malays gained a role in the expanding economy. The fear was that the balance of economic and political interests that had been achieved by the New Economic Policy (NEP) in the wake of the May 1969 riots would be undermined if the government's ability to carefully manage the economy was eroded. Advocates of government management argued that it had secured a greater economic equality between the Malaysian–Chinese, who had traditionally dominated the economy, on the one hand and the Malays, who had traditionally been economically marginalized on the other. However, with the economic boom created by the tidal wave of Japanese investment and the success of the NEP in redressing the economic imbalance among Malaysia's racial communities, the government felt it could move to further deregulate the economy. Most notably, in 1991, the new finance minister, Anwar Ibrahim, actively promoted a programme of liberalization that parallelled in important ways the policies adopted by Anand in Thailand. He opened up the capital account, set interest rates above US dollar interest rates, essentially pegged the ringgit to the US dollar, and developed the Kuala Lumpur Stock Exchange. The Malaysian central bank, Bank Negara Malaysia (BNM), which was given the responsibility of regulating the financial sector, was generally better positioned to do so than the Thai regulatory institutions. However, with some notable lapses in terms of politically well-connected banks and key politically driven financial transactions, the BNM was not nearly as effective a regulator as the agencies in Singapore (Hamilton-Hart 2002).

Economic liberalization in Hong Kong and Singapore had a very different history to that of other 'miracle' economies. As entrepôts and 'free ports' for long periods of their recent past, Hong Kong and Singapore were essentially tariff free. Hence, there was no need for the US to exert pressure for greater trade liberalization. Both also had fairly well developed and relatively open financial sectors by the mid-1990s. Hong Kong's financial sector had grown around the goal of providing an open, competitive and stable environment with relatively little government intervention. However, reforms to the colony's financial system were undertaken in a piecemeal fashion mostly 'as a result of market pressures and in response to crises' and, therefore, lacked coherence (Chen and Ng 1999: 227). Singapore, on the other hand, encouraged growth in the financial sector and maintained a relatively strong system of prudential surveillance and regulation. The Monetary Authority of Singapore was the lead agency in regulating the financial sector and used its monitoring and supervisory authority to good effect (Chia 2001).

Hong Kong, Malaysia and Singapore failed to follow South Korea, Taiwan and Thailand in liberalizing their political systems. Hong Kong did become more democratic, especially during the 1980s and 1990s. But this process was complicated and ultimately compromised by the transfer of sovereignty in 1997 from the UK to China. The maturing of the Hong Kong economy coincided with the negotiations during the early years of the 1980s to transfer sovereignty over Hong Kong from Britain to China. The Sino-British negotiations, which culminated in 1984 in the signing of an agreement known as the Basic Law, politicized the Hong Kong population. The British responded to local pressure for greater political participation by establishing elections for local and district administrative boards and for some seats in the colony's Legislative Council. The elections proved successful and calls from both inside and outside Hong Kong for a fully elected Legislative Council grew. The 1989 Tiananmen Square crackdown only served to accentuate the interest within the colony for greater political participation. For the 1995 Legislative Council elections Governor Chris Patten opened up the voting process but this was heavily criticised by the Chinese government and their Hong Kong representatives. When it took over Hong Kong in 1997 the Chinese government went back to the original 1984 agreement on the election of the Legislative Council which called for 24 directly elected and 36 indirectly elected members. Only in 2004 was provision made for half of the members to be directly elected. Essentially, this ensured that pro-Beijing parties dominated the Legislative Council in the post-1997 era. The change in regime, however, complicated the economic governance of the Hong Kong Special Administrative Region (SAR). Working with the old colonial bureaucratic structure, while at the same time attempting to balance the rising economic and political expectations of the general population, Beijing's interests, and the concerns of the traditionally influential business community, made it difficult for the Hong Kong

SAR to develop a coherent economic strategy (Luk 2003; Tang 1999: 326).

Singapore and Malaysia present an intriguing puzzle for scholars interested in democratization. Unlike South Korea, Taiwan and Thailand neither Singapore nor Malaysia adopted policies that would have let to greater democratization along Western liberal lines. Much of the literature on democratization (Huntington 1991) predicted that a period of rapid economic growth would produce a period of political change leading to the establishment of a fully fledged liberal democracy. Yet, despite their phenomenal growth rates during the late 1980s and early 1990s, Singaporeans and Malaysians continued to support 'semi-democratic', soft authoritarian regimes. Both countries had a long-standing tradition of regular elections and governments responding to the electoral concerns. Unlike South Korea, Taiwan and Thailand, which had been governed by military-backed dictatorial and highly oppressive rulers, Malaysia and Singapore had been governed by respected political parties which were regularly required to seek electoral mandates from the voters. Moreover, their ruling political parties developed coalitions, or spread their recruiting net fairly widely, so as to accommodate the divergent views within the political life of the country. In addition, the governments of Singapore and Malaysia were sustained by what may best be termed 'performance legitimacy' (Stubbs 2001). Certainly, the PAP government in Singapore and the UMNO-led ruling coalition in Malaysia have engineered a level of shared economic development and social and political stability not thought possible even thirty years ago. Their successes have made them, and the system in which they operate, relatively popular among the people of their respective countries.

The American government's post-Cold War attempts to proselytise its notion of political liberalization or 'good governance', including Western liberal democracy and respect for human and political rights, proved counter-productive in Singapore and Malaysia. As they gained confidence from the performance of their economies in the early 1990s the governments of Singapore and Malaysia hit back at the US. They asserted that 'Asian values' – including the protection of community interests, the emphasis on harmony and the fear of weak states and disorder – were just as valid a basis for good governance as those put forward by the West (Mahathir and Ishihara 1995: 80–6; Mahbubani 1995). The forceful way in which the leaders of Singapore and Malaysia presented their side of the 'Asian values' debate was indicative of the extent to which they were unprepared to move their respective societies further down the road towards Western-style liberal democracy (Mauzy 2001). Of course, each government was all too willing to use its powers to silence its critics. And, while Singapore remained corruption-free, in Malaysia corruption grew as the economy expanded and the parties that made up the ruling coalitions, especially UMNO, increasingly took part in the Malayan economy (Mehmet 1986; Gomez and Jomo 1997). In terms of democratization at least, the political systems in places like South Korea, Taiwan and Thailand moved closer to the 'semi'/Asian-democracy model that had been established in Japan or Malaysia than to the Western liberal democracy proposed by the US.

The end of the Cold War, then, combined with a series of other factors to open the way for greater economic liberalization, and in some cases greater political liberalization, of the seven Asian 'miracle' economies. The US government used the leverage it had built up during the Cold War – access to their market and continued military support – to pressure their Asian allies during the 1980s and early 1990s to open up their economies and democratize their political systems. But the process of liberalization was not always undertaken in a systematic way. The Cold War and the communist threat had provided the rationale for governments to develop a coherent developmental interventionist set of institutions and policies that promoted economic growth. Economic liberalization, especially when it was accompanied by political liberalization that produced piecemeal and inconsistent policies from a variety of leaders, as in Thailand and South Korea, tended to undermine aspects of the old approach to economic development without ensuring that a new, comprehensive strategy was put in its place. The liberalization process, then, left some of the old Cold War institutions and policies intact while dismantling others. The resulting policy disjuncture meant that those societies that had moved to liberalize their economies the most were particularly vulnerable if an economic downturn were to hit the region.

Economic Crisis

On 2 July 1997 the Thai government admitted defeat in its battle to maintain the baht at just over 25 to the US dollar and allowed the currency to float. By the end of trading that day the baht had dropped 16 per cent in value, within weeks it had depreciated by a third of its 2 July value, and by January 1998 it was selling for around 55 to the dollar (Montes 1998). Investors who had flocked into the region to take advantage of the strong growth rates allied to stable currencies turned tail *en masse* as the depth of Thailand's problems became apparent. As confidence in the Thai economy ebbed away, questions arose about the viability of other economies in the region. The crisis quickly spread to Malaysia, Indonesia and eventually to South Korea. The contagion effect saw the Malaysian ringgit, the Indonesian rupiah and the Korean won all drop substantially in value over the next six months (Montes 1998: xv). By January 1998 the Asian currency crisis had turned into a financial crisis and was well on its way to becoming a full-blown, economic, political and social crisis of major proportions.

The origins of the crisis were complex with a number of factors coming together to precipitate the July 1997 collapse of the Thai baht. Key to the concatenation of events was the liberalization of the financial sector without the necessary precautionary oversight. This development made the Thai financial sector susceptible to any slowdown in the economy. With most of Thailand's capital inflow from 1987 to 1992 entering the economy in the form of FDI or long-term investments there were relatively few problems. Going back to the Vietnam War, the bureaucracy had developed the capacity to monitor and supervise these kinds of transactions. However starting in 1992, as FDI shifted to China, Thailand encouraged more short-term capital to fill the expanding needs of the economy and so maintain the high growth rates. And, simultaneously, the rapidly growing US economy was more than willing to provide what Susan Strange (1998: 1) has called 'mad money' or vast amounts of short-term capital sloshing around the global economy looking for high, immediate returns and 'far beyond the control of the state and international authorities'. Importantly, in Thailand an increasing portion of this short-term investment was lost through corrupt business practices or found its way into construction and property, such as golf courses, hotels and commercial office blocks, as well as the stock market, rather than into manufacturing and other directly productive enterprises. The result was a property and share price bubble that bore little relationship to the real health of the economy.

By 1996 the export-manufacturing sector, on which Thailand's rapid economic development of the late 1980s and early 1990s was based, was running into trouble. In 1994 China devalued the renminbi by 35 per cent against the US dollar and starting in April 1995 the Japanese yen also began to depreciate against the US dollar. With the Thai baht essentially pegged to the value of the dollar, Thai exports found it difficult to compete with cheap Chinese manufactured exports and even some Japanese products. At the same time there was a major slowdown in the global market for electronic goods. Overall, Thai exports, which had grown by 22 per cent in 1994 and 25 per cent in 1995, actually contracted in 1996 (Jomo 1998: 31). Total growth for 1996 was down to 5.5 per cent after being over 8 per cent in the previous three years and the current account deficit was 8 per cent of GNP (MacIntyre 2001: 96). In late 1996 the economy slowly began to unravel. Those in the currency market began to speculate that the value of the baht would eventually be driven down. Early in 1997 rumours about the problems facing Thailand's largest finance company began to circulate. The Bank of Thailand, fearing that foreign investors would be discouraged and that Thai companies which had borrowed abroad in US dollars would be exposed, started to use its reserves of dollars to buy baht and shore up its value. With exports still relatively stagnant, the economy becoming more and more sluggish, a widening current account deficit, and the Bank of Thailand's reserves too low to continue to intervene in the currency markets, the unrelenting pressure forced the government to authorize the floating of the baht.

Thailand, like the other 'miracle' economies, had been through economic downturns before. It could reasonably have been expected that another slowdown would overtake the economy at some point. However, it was the severity of the recession and the domino effect as it hit other economies in the region that proved so shocking. The severity of the crisis can be attributed to three factors. First, Thailand did not have the institutional capacity either to anticipate the problems or to manage events as they unfolded (Haggard and MacIntyre 1998: 385). Liberalization had reduced the government's capacity to monitor the financial sector and while the bureaucracy was able to retain an ability to deal with FDI and long-term bank loans, it had no experience with the short-term 'hot money' loans that flooded Thailand from 1994 onwards. Moreover, as Cameron Ortis (1999: 45) points out, this development was compounded by the fact that, as the private sector rapidly expanded, the best and the brightest from the bureaucracy were lured away to well-paid and prestigious positions in Bangkok's businesses. Moreover, the senior officials who were left behind did not always rely solely on their government salaries but often supplemented their incomes from their network of business contacts. This behaviour further complicated the difficulties for politicians who were required to respond to the crisis and who were being pressured by their financial backers and business colleagues to maintain the baht's dollar value (MacIntyre 2001: 96–101).

Second, investor panic was a major cause of the severity of the crisis (Montes 1998: 51–4). Some analysts (e.g. Woo 2000: 115) even list investor panic as the cause of the crisis. There is an argument that increased capital flows have more often than not been followed by 'panics' and 'manias' and, therefore, the sudden, panic-ridden withdrawal of short-term investments from all of Southeast Asia should not have come as a surprise. Compared to the liberalization of trade, the liberalization of capital often has traumatic consequences. This possibility was totally ignored by the US–Wall Street–Treasury Complex that pushed for reform of national banking systems and the deregulation of global capital flows (Bhagwati 1998). However, there is also the argument that those investing in the region should have been much more discriminating, first in placing their investments and then in taking them out. Generally, the data were available to allow for more nuanced judgements about investment strategies in Southeast Asia. It was the herd instinct that drove investors to get out of the region as a whole, not just Thailand, at the first sign of trouble. Their departure was clearly a significant factor in moving the crisis from one involving attacks on regional currencies to one which undermined whole economies.

Third, the US government and the IMF proved to be significant factors in the magnitude of the economic crisis that hit the region. The US Treasury and the IMF worked in tandem to liberalize fully the capital accounts of the major Southeast Asian countries. For Joseph Stiglitz (2002: 99, his emphasis) this process of liberalization was '*the single most important factor leading to the crisis*'. In addition, neither the US nor the IMF gave adequate warning to Thailand or the other affected economies of the impending crisis and, when the crisis hit the region, the US government failed to offer the kind of immediate help it had given Mexico just over two years earlier. It left the IMF to help the Thais and the other crisis-ridden governments out of their dilemma.

However, the IMF, to which Thailand and Indonesia appealed for emergency funding and to prescribe a way out of the crisis, initially misdiagnosed the problem. It assumed that the Asian crisis was similar to the Latin American crises, which were created by government debts and high inflation, and with which they had dealt in the past. The IMF officials imposed higher interest rates, forced banks that could not meet the capital adequacy ratio to shut down, reduced government spending and pushed for further market opening. The idea was to cut demand and liquidity and encourage foreign private investors to deploy their capital so as to kick-start the economy. But foreign capital was frightened off by the economies' downward spiral. And the IMF's policies simply deepened the crisis. The problems plaguing the Asian crisis-ridden economies were not those of Latin America. What was needed was more, carefully regulated liquidity, not less. As a result of the high interest rates and the closing of the weakest banks, those companies that were still producing goods and had weathered the initial storm were put to the sword. Bankruptcies increased exponentially as viable companies lost their domestic markets or found that they were unable to get loans at reasonable prices so as to continue operating. They were forced to renege on the payment of their bills. The knock-on effect of the growing number of bankruptcies was disastrous. The IMF's initial policy prescriptions helped to convert the currency crisis into a deep economic recession and a social tragedy (Kwon 2003; Stiglitz 2002: 98–118).

Table 7.1   Annual GDP growth rates, 1995–2002

	1995–96	1996–97	1997–98	1998–99	1999–00	2000–01	2001–02
Japan	3.9	1.8	−2.7	0.2	2.4	−0.6	0.3
Hong Kong	2.2	5.2	−5.1	2.9	10.9	0.1	2.3
Taiwan*	6.1	6.7	4.6	5.4	5.9	−2.2	3.6
South Korea	6.9	4.9	−6.6	10.7	8.8	3.0	6.3
Singapore	7.6	8.8	1.5	5.4	9.9	−2.0	2.2
Malaysia	8.3	7.5	−5.8	5.8	8.3	0.4	4.1
Thailand	5.4	−1.1	−7.7	4.2	4.3	1.8	5.4
Indonesia	7.5	4.3	−16.7	0.3	4.8	3.3	3.7
Philippines	6.9	5.3	0.1	3.2	4.0	3.4	4.4
China	10.0	8.5	7.4	7.1	7.9	7.3	8.0

Sources: Data from World Bank 2001; Republic of China various years.

The economies of other countries in the region were hit hard as the crisis spread from Thailand. The major casualties were Indonesia, Malaysia and South Korea. By any measure Indonesia suffered the most from the crisis. Following the collapse of the Thai baht, there were enough similarities between the Thai economy and the Indonesian economy for a sustained attack on the Indonesian rupiah to be mounted by currency traders. The economy ran into increasing problems and by January 1998 the rupiah slumped to around 80 per cent of its July 1997 value (Montes 1998: xv; Robison and Rosser 2000: 171). The weakness of Indonesia's financial sector, which had been steadily liberalized during the 1980s so that the total number of banks increased from 124 in 1988 to 244 in 1994, quickly became obvious (Montes and Abdusalamov 1998: 166). The tight credit and higher interest rate policies dictated by the IMF produced bankruptcies and a spiralling downward of the economy as capital fled the country. Companies found they could not pay their debts. A number of banks were forced to close their doors, creating a good deal of panic. By mid-1998 the non-performing loans, or bad debts, within the country's banking system had sky-rocketed from 9 per cent just before the crisis to an estimated 50 per cent in mid-1998, inflation was threatening to go as high as 80 per cent, and the economy was contracting rapidly (Soesastro 2000: 135; Robison and Rosser 2000: 171–2).

The near collapse of the financial sector prompted major social and political repercussions. In turn, these social and political consequences of the financial crisis helped to feed the downward recessionary spiral of the country's economic fortunes. With government revenue markedly reduced by the crisis and the IMF insisting on major cutbacks in food and fuel subsidies, riots broke out. As Joseph Stiglitz (2002: 119) points out, 'Riots do not restore business confidence. They drive capital out of a country.' Open violence, not just in Bangkok but also places such as Aceh, East Timor, Ambon and Central Sulawesi, took many lives. By July 1998 poverty levels had increased dramatically (Robison and Rosser 2000: 172). As a consequence of the economic and social turmoil, Suharto, the autocratic and highly corrupt president of Indonesia, was forced to resign in May 1998. His vice-president, B.J. Habibie took over. Slowly, Indonesia worked its way towards a more democratic political system. However, the political vacuum that Suharto's fall created also highlighted the country's administrative weaknesses. The Indonesian bureaucracy was underfunded, and as a result often corrupt; lacked training and skills; and was incapable of dealing with the economic and social pandemonium that had broken lose. It had a particularly hard time trying to stem the tide of economic recession and putting Indonesia back on an even keel.

The Malaysian ringgit also came under attack, creating major economic problems for the Malaysian government. Assuming that the Malaysian economy was fundamentally sound, the government initially did very little apart from publicly defending the economy as strong and arguing that it should not be side-swiped by the emerging crisis. However, eventually with the ringgit and the stock market both dropping precipitously, and with Prime Minister Mahathir making the situation worse by attacking currency speculators and appearing to be at odds with his finance minister, Anwar Ibrahim, it became clear that something had to be done. In December 1997, Anwar and his advisors at the central bank drew up a set of policies to tackle the crisis. Anwar's prescription appeared to follow the IMF line. Public spending was immediately cut by 18 per cent; major infrastructure projects were postponed indefinitely; interest rates were determined by the market, and, with credit reduced, promptly rose markedly; and the ringgit continued to be allowed to float freely. But this package of policies did not contain the crisis (Athukorala 1999: 34–5; Nesadurai 2000: 93–7). Indeed, by mid-1998, with interest rates up, another round of bankruptcies ensued, putting added pressure on the already vulnerable banking sector. Moreover, government bail-outs of high-profile Malay-run companies were perceived as the government simply trying to help out its friends. The result was further downward pressure on the ringgit and the stock market (Jomo 1998b: 186–8).

The government became concerned that the traumatic social upheaval and riots of May 1969 might return were the downward spiral in the economy not arrested quickly. A personal battle between Mahathir and Anwar also divided the government. Eventually, determined not to allow the delicate political and economic balance between the various races in Malaysia and in particular the gains made by the Malays to be jeopardized, Prime Minister Mahathir ousted his former protégé by having him arrested on highly contentious charges related to corruption and sexual misconduct. At the same time Mahathir introduced a new package of economic policies that essentially reversed Anwar's IMF-style approach. Major infrastructure projects were revived, liquidity was injected into the financial system, thereby reducing interest rates, and, most importantly, in September 1998 restrictions were placed on the movement of short-term capital and the ringgit was pegged at 3.80 to the US dollar (Nesadurai 2000: 97–104). In the wake of the implementation of these policies the economy rebounded. Interest rates came down, the stock market gradually revived and unemployment dropped. Malaysia slowly emerged out of its severest recession since the Second World War.

South Korea was the other economy in the region hard hit by the crisis. Its economy was running into trouble even as the Thai economy was on the verge of collapsing. The inconsistent way in which the economy, especially the financial sector, had been liberalized created major problems for the banks and other financial institutions as well as for the *chaebol*s. Most significantly, the government allowed the banks and the *chaebol*s to borrow overseas in order to finance increased industrial expansion. As a result, the country's external liabilities grew rapidly with short-term debt in particular rising dramatically. Operating on the basis of a high debt load was not new. In the past the South Korean business sector had often relied on loans – usually domestic and government-backed – to finance its investments. The problem this time was that by June 1997 much of the debt was to foreign investors. In addition, the country's 'short term debt was more than three times the size of its reserves, a higher ratio than for any other country in the region' (Smith 1998: 67). As the dependence of the economy on external financing grew, the industrial competitiveness of South Korea's major industrial conglomerates weakened. A depreciating yen after 1995, which made Japanese manufacturing rivals more cost-competitive; increasing labour costs; limited investment in technological innovation during the 1980s and early 1990s; and restrictions placed on specific Korean imports by the US government all contributed to a deterioration in the economic well-being of the *chaebol*s (Bevaqua 1998: 430–3; Smith 1998: 68–70). Indeed, in 1996 bankruptcies began to occur among financial institutions and share prices started to tumble. During the first half of 1997 the Hanbo steel company went bankrupt amid indications of high-level corruption. Eight of the country's

30 *chaebol*s came crashing down. The most serious casualty was the Kia Motor Corporation, the third largest car maker in the country and the eighth largest *chaebol* (Chang 1998: 224–5; Garran 1998: 124–5). By all indications the South Korean economy was on a downward spiral.

South Korea's links to Southeast Asia emphasized its growing economic problems. First, South Korea's exports to Southeast Asia grew rapidly during the early 1990s so that by 1995 they constituted over 30 per cent of all exports. As the crisis struck the region so the Southeast Asian market began to dry up. Second, South Korea's merchant banks had become heavily involved in Southeast Asia's stock and bond markets. Often they had borrowed heavily from foreign sources to fund their ventures. As the Thai, Indonesian and Malaysian economies hit the skids these banks were increasingly vulnerable. Third, the fear arose that the Japanese banks left exposed by the crisis in Southeast Asia would have to call in their extensive loans to Korean banks and *chaebol*s. With investors wary of any sign of weakness in any of the region's economies, it was perhaps inevitable that eventually the high debt load of Korean banks and companies would attract attention and that South Korea would be caught up in the stampede of investors fleeing the region.

As attention shifted to South Korea, the economy began to collapse. The South Korean won came under severe pressure and had to be propped up at considerable cost to the central bank. The fall of the won increased the country's debt burden and bankruptcies became more and more common. Towards the end of November the crisis reached such proportions that the government decided to call in the IMF. In early December a series of new policies was announced along the normal IMF lines. But the credit-tightening approach only increased the number of bankruptcies and failed to stem the tide of economic collapse. Within a few months the IMF began to back off its rigid policy stance. It set aside its insistence on a budgetary surplus and allowed some credit to be channelled to firms whose funding shortages were making it difficulty for them to take advantage of the weak currency to increase exports. (Chang 1998: 229). Slowly, the large short-term debt was restructured and interest rates returned to pre-crisis levels by mid-1998. The currency began to gain ground from the lows of 1,800 won to the US dollar of January 1998 to stabilize at around 1,100 won to the US dollar in the second half of the year. And, with imports drastically reduced, foreign exchange reserves began to build up once again. The GDP fell by 5.8 per cent in 1998 but rebounded strongly in 1999. After the enormous hardships experienced by almost everyone in the country the economy began to get back on track.

Although the initial response to the Asian crisis by those governments affected most was one of confusion and panic, their later attempts at rehabilitating the economy appeared to instinctively fall back on old, tried and tested approaches to economic development. Thailand relied heavily on the IMF, which eventually revised its policies so as to put the US$17.2 bail-out package to use getting the Thai banks and manufacturing industries back on their feet. In January 2001, Thaksin Shinawatra and his Thai Rak Thai party won 365 of the 500 seats in the lower house of the Parliament and proceeded to introduce a number of political and economic reforms in response to the fallout from the crisis. What was widely seen as an outdated and inadequate bureaucracy was overhauled. In a wholesale restructuring, Prime Minister Thaksin created new ministries around what were identified as key areas for future development. Certainly, Thaksin's 'democratic authoritarian' style is reminiscent of past autocratic governments of Thailand's period of rapid economic growth. Moreover, he has picked out 'small and medium enterprises, agribusiness, automobiles, the rural sector, and tourism to spearhead Thailand's longer term growth' and has adopted a 'state-guided "developmental state"' approach which is based not just on the export-manufacturing sector but has a strong domestic orientation to it that is reminiscent of previous Thai economic strategies (Thitinan 2003: 288; see also Pasuk and Baker 2004).

In Malaysia the government's reliance on state intervention to pull it out of the crisis was made possible by the bureaucracy's capacity to draw up and implement the plans for capital controls and a fixed currency peg. The currency peg proved particularly valuable in promoting exports once companies could acquire the necessary capital to gear up their production. Ironically the IMF, which initially strenuously opposed capital controls and the peg, has since recanted and acknowledged the extent to which it paved the way for Malaysia to lift itself out of the crisis (Burton 2004). In addition to the radical currency policies, and perhaps almost as a reflex action, the government created the National Economic Action Council with a control room to monitor daily changes in the economy and with direct access to the prime minister. This set of policies closely mirrored the administrative structure set up during past crises. For example, it clearly reflected aspects of the administrative structure created to fight the communist guerrillas in the emergency years, the administrative infrastructure established by Tun Razak in his national development campaign of the early 1960s, and the National Operations Council that was set up to deal with the aftermath of the 1969 race riots (Milner 2003: 294; Stubbs 1989b: 271). The Malaysian bureaucracy was also able to deal with the problems of the non-performing loans, bank mergers and other issues that arose in the wake of the crisis. Indeed, there is evidence to suggest that the stronger a country's bureaucracy, the more effective it was at rebuilding the economy.

As Linda Weiss (2003) points out, the restoration of economic stability and growth in South Korea was also highlighted by moves to restore some of the state's former capacity to direct and regulate the country's economic development. At the end of 1998, a new reform bureaucracy was installed which centred on the newly created Financial Supervisory Commission (FSC). The FSC has the power to ration credit to the *chaebol*s and guide the economic restructuring process. The state has also overseen the restructuring of the financial sector and especially the process of bank mergers. At the same time the state has become involved in specific development projects, such as creating a software industry. Obviously, although a degree of liberalization has continued to take place, state intervention will remain an important dimension of South Korea's economic development. Indeed, the crisis that hit South Korea clearly demonstrated that liberalization without strong prudential state regulation is a recipe for disaster.

Overall, then, it is not possible to fully understand the Asian economic crisis without factoring in the extent to which the end of the Cold War brought about a dismantling of the relatively coherent set of economic and political institutions in the 'miracle' economies that had been established during the Cold War years. Among the 'miracle' economies the two hardest hit by the crisis were Thailand and South Korea. These two economies had experienced the most extensive and, in many ways, most haphazard process of economic and political liberalization. The new set of liberalized institutions sat uncomfortably with the old Cold War institutions. As Marco Orrù and his colleagues note (1991: 362, quoted in Beeson 2002: 16–17), 'To be "technically efficient", firms must consider and comply with the institutional setting in which they are embedded.' As some aspects of the old Thai, South Korean, and to a lesser extent Malaysian, bureaucracies were made redundant, and as each country's firms were liberalized and became disembedded from the old order, each country's economy became vulnerable to shifts in the international and regional political economy. The result was the Asian economic crisis.

The argument here is not that liberalization is bad. Rather, it is that a change in economic strategy has to be implemented systematically and carefully so that there is a congruence between the economic framework set by the state and the approach used by firms. Given the developmental interventionist approach that emerged in the 'miracle' economies during the Cold War years, a rapid, ill-coordinated change to a more neoliberal economic approach, advocated by the US government and the international organizations it controlled, was likely to end in disaster. The examples of Taiwan and Singapore, which opened up their economies to the wider international market forces in a more systematic and nuanced manner and which were able to withstand the pressures exerted by the Asian crisis, provide a contrast to the travails of Thailand, Malaysia and South Korea. The example of Indonesia is also instructive. Like its Southeast Asian neighbours, Indonesia went through a period of economic liberalization during the 1990s. However, the process was plagued by blatant and extensive corruption as well as inconsistent and erratic policy implementation. Moreover, Indonesia lacked the well-developed administrative infrastructure of the seven 'miracle' economies and its industrial and financial sectors were similarly relatively immature. Once the crisis hit, not only was the Indonesian government incapable of dealing with the immediate issues – as were the other crisis-hit governments – but it found that it was extremely difficult to develop, and even more importantly implement, a strategy by which it could get out from under the economic and social catastrophe that had enveloped the country. Indeed, unlike the 'miracle' economies that were hit by the crisis, Indonesia kept on haemorrhaging substantial amounts of capital through to 2001 (Bartels and Freeman 2004: 4, 6).

Regionalism

Regionalism in East and Southeast Asia – an area stretching from Japan to Singapore, and increasingly referred to simply as East Asia – owes much to the sequence of geopolitical events that have engulfed the region over the last seventy years or so. Just as the Asian economic crisis cannot be fully understood without reference to the political and economic institutions that emerged during the Cold War and the impact of the end of the Cold War, so the development of regionalism in East and Southeast Asia cannot be fully comprehended without an appreciation of how the Cold War and the various domestic wars helped to bring the region together. First, many of the countries of East and Southeast Asia have gone through similar experiences in the recent past. The Second World War; the regional wars and the overarching Cold War, which brought a strong US presence to the region; and the wave of Japanese investment that swept through East and Southeast Asia during the 1980s and 1990s all had an impact on the region's economies. Most importantly, despite the many differences in the way in which the main economies developed, there was a general similarity to the sequence of policies adopted by the governments of the 'miracle' economies. The devastation of war was followed by the recovery phase during which the infrastructure was developed, and, in a number of cases, the agricultural sector refurbished. Then, a period of import-substitution industrialization was followed by a turn to export-manufacturing industrialization. Thereafter, economic liberalization was implemented which proved to be the prelude to a major economic crisis and eventual economic recovery. In other words, the governments of the region have gone through a comparable set of historical experiences and phases of economic development. This common background means that they share many of the same challenges in managing the future expansion of their economies.

Second, despite some important differences, as the analysis in this study attests, a number of the key domestic political and economic institutions and policies which developed out of the geopolitically driven events that engulfed the region, are broadly similar. Each of the Asian 'miracle' economies has – at least by the standards of the developing world – a relatively strong centralized government that emerged out of the need to mobilize resources to conduct, or prepare for, war. During the Cold War years these governments adopted a mercantilist approach to rapid economic development. State intervention in the economy and society was geared towards building state power to face down the threat of communism. Strong state–business links were forged. Civil society remained relatively weak, with labour organizations essentially neutered. And social programmes were kept to a bare minimum. Ironically, two of the more recent contributors to the East Asian regional project, China and Vietnam, have started to evince a comparable developmental trajectory to that of the seven successful Asian economies. Although on the opposite side to the 'miracle' economies during the Cold War, both China and Vietnam also developed strong interventionist states to mobilize resources to prepare for, and fight, wars. As a consequence some of their institutions and policies are similar to those of a number of their neighbours. Certainly, their switch from an import-substitution industrialization strategy to an export-oriented approach follows the strategy adopted by Asia's 'miracle' economies. Indeed, 'State practice at the local and central levels in China resembles that of developmental states in Northeast Asia. In particular, China is becoming increasingly similar to Taiwan in its early developmental stage' (Zhu 2003: 158).

Third, recent East and Southeast Asian historical experiences, common institutional influences and some similar cultural characteristics have combined to produce a form of capitalism that is quite distinct from either Western European or North American capitalism (Stubbs 1998). This form of capitalism is rooted in business networks and is characterized by strong state–business links. It emphasizes production rather than consumption, and results – in terms of rapid economic growth – rather than ideology and tends to place a premium on market share as opposed to short-term profits. This form of capitalism is also based more on social obligation and social trust than on the rule of law (Hamilton 1991; Harianto 1993; Orrù 1991; Stubbs 1998). Importantly, East Asia's emerging form of capitalism was given a major boost by the flood of FDI that spread through the region in the post-Plaza Accord period. Japanese FDI led the way, especially in Southeast Asia and China, but ethnic Chinese investors were also very active in the region. For example, Taiwanese businesses invested heavily in Malaysia, Singapore firms played a major role in the development of Vietnam, and Hong Kong and Taiwanese business people invested in China as the government opened up the Chinese economy. These cross-cutting investment patterns helped to knit the region's economy together by underscoring the common elements of the various forms of Asian network capitalism and by promoting a rapid increase in intra-East Asian trade.

In many ways the Cold War masked the emerging sense of regionalism in East and Southeast Asia. The American practice of 'hub and spoke' alliances, whereby the US government established a series of bilateral agreements with its major allies in the region, tended to inhibit intra-regional relations. However, once the Cold War ended and multilateralism began to take hold in East and Southeast Asia, the idea of an East Asian approach to economic development and regional issues came to the fore. Indeed, the Asia Pacific Economic Cooperation (APEC) forum, which was inaugurated in 1989, and which brought together member economies from both sides of the Pacific Ocean, ended up being divided between the Anglo-American members, such as the US, Australia, Canada and New Zealand, and a number of Asian members, such as Japan, China and Malaysia. The disagreement revolved around the pace, direction and nature of the economic liberalization programme to be followed by APEC members (Gallant and Stubbs 1997; Higgott and Stubbs 1995). By the late 1990s it was obvious that APEC brought two regions of the world together – North America (including Australia and New Zealand) on the one hand and East Asia on the other – and that it was best to view it 'as a *trans*-regional rather than a regional body' (Ravenhill 2000: 329, emphasis in the original). Overall, then, by the 1990s there appeared to be emerging what Yoichi Funabashi (1993) termed 'an Asian consciousness and identity' or what others began to refer to as 'neo-Asianism', 'an Asian renaissance', and a 'sense of East Asian identity' (Higgott and Stubbs 1995: 530–1; see also Anwar 1997; Tay 2001).

Yet in the early 1990s there was little interest among East and Southeast Asian governments in developing a state-driven institutional framework that might bring the region together to find regional solutions to regional economic problems and give regional governments a more coherent voice in the global political economy. The regionalization that was taking place in East and Southeast Asia was based on the market-driven cooperation that was taking place among Chinese and Japanese business networks investing in different parts of the region and developing regional trading links

(Borrus, Ernst and Haggard 2000). The lack of enthusiasm for state-led regionalism was demonstrated when in late 1990, Malaysian Prime Minister Mahathir proposed the establishment of an East Asian Economic Grouping or Caucus (EAEG/EAEC). His proposal was given a cool reception by his neighbours, in good part because of the opposition of the US government, which feared being excluded from any new regional arrangement. The EAEC was eventually adopted as a caucus within the APEC framework and essentially put on the backburner.

All this changed with the Asian economic crisis of 1997–8 (Bowles 2002; Higgott 1998). Many East Asian governments, were resentful of both the IMF's botched initial attempts to manage the Asian crisis and the American government's veto of a proposed Asian Monetary Fund that could have provided a regional vehicle for dealing with the crisis. Asian governments then looked around for alternative ways of averting or better managing a possible future crisis. The best vehicle for regional economic cooperation appeared to be the embryonic ASEAN Plus Three (APT) framework. This framework emerged out of need for the Asian members of the first Asia–Europe Meeting (ASEM), held in Bangkok in March 1996, to caucus in order to agree on a common Asian position. ASEAN members, as the initiators of the ASEM, asked China, Japan and South Korea to join them as the Asian representatives. The decision at the Bangkok meeting to hold a second ASEM summit in London in 1998 required a more formal commitment for senior official, economic ministers and foreign ministers to get together on a regular basis to plan for the London summit and deal with ongoing ASEM issues. At the ASEAN summit in Kuala Lumpur in 1997 the first informal meeting of the APT heads of government was held. Annual meetings of heads of government, as well as meetings of various officials and ministers, have taken place ever since (Stubbs 2002).

The APT framework provides a forum within which a number of projects have been undertaken. Building on the work of the East Asian Vision Group, a collection of eminent individuals from the member countries who set out a road map for a more integrated regional economy, progress has been made on a number of fronts. One of the main projects has been the Chiang Mai Initiative (CMI). The CMI set the stage for a series of bilateral currency-swap arrangements that would provide a safety net for any regional currency under attack. Progress on assembling the web of bilateral agreements has been slow but steady. The end goal is to convert the bilateral agreements so that any APT member can tap into the massive currency reserves held by central banks around East Asia. A parallel, although much more recent, development has been the Asian Bond Market Initiative. It would allow Asian savings to be directly channelled into Asian economies by way of public and private sector bonds rather than be cycled through the US (Fukushima 2004; Mays and Preiss 2003). At the same time, the APT has provided the framework for the development of the ASEAN–China Free Trade Agreement, the ASEAN–Japan comprehensive economic partnership and a series of bilateral free trade agreements among APT members. At least one APT leader has suggested that the aim should be to create an East Asian Free Trade Area (Goh 2003).

There is good reason to believe that the APT will emerge as the key organization in East Asia. But this is certainly not inevitable. APEC is still functioning. Its aim of free trade for all its developed members by 2010 and for developing members by 2020 is a goal around which to rally support. Moreover, a number of the new bilateral free trade agreements are between APT members and governments external to East Asia (Dent 2004). This development could undermine the cohesion of East Asia as a region. However, the long-term trends favouring regional integration, which go back to the Cold War years and which indicate the need for an organization to give the East Asian region an institutional focus, will prove too powerful to ignore. These trends, reinforced by growing intra-regional FDI, production networks and trade flows, plus region-based competition from the European Union and the North American Free Trade Agreement, strongly suggest that the APT will evolve into a globally significant regional economic grouping.

Conclusion

The winding down of the Cold War had important implications for Asia's 'miracle' economies. Most significantly, as the threat of war receded, the external and internal pressures for change mounted. With the reduction in the communist threat, the American government clearly felt that it was no longer obligated to support its Asian allies unreservedly. Gradually pressure was applied, both directly and through US-dominated international organizations such as the IMF, the World Bank and the OECD, for a liberalization of the economy and a democratization of the political process. Similarly, internal pressures for change increased as the need to rally around the hegemonic project of defence against the communist enemy subsided. The sustained and rapid growth in the economy also produced its own tensions and demands for reforms. At the same time technocrats within a number of the bureaucracies of the seven successful societies were arguing strongly for policies that would create a more open, less regulated, economy.

Economic, and in some cases political, liberalization occurred in each of the seven successful Asian economies. However, economic liberalization was not always undertaken in a coherent, systematic way. In Thailand and South Korea in particular, where a disjointed process of democratization parallelled economic liberalization, the economies were opened up in an *ad hoc*, piecemeal manner by governments that lacked an overarching strategy. In other instances, most notably in Taiwan and Singapore, economic liberalization was more coherent and consistent. The process took into account the need to balance increased openness with corresponding prudential regulation. It became clear that economic liberalization, especially liberalization of the financial sector, was a recipe for disaster without a commensurate ability to monitor and regulate the resulting economic activities.

Although it was not the only cause, the ill-thought-out programmes of economic liberalization in some of the economies of East and Southeast Asia paved the way for the economic crisis of 1997–8. It was perhaps not surprising that the crisis should have begun in Thailand and spread to Malaysia and Indonesia, both of which had developed a set of economic liberalization policies very similar to those adopted by the Thai government. It then spilt over into South Korea, which had its own unique problems. The degree to which the economies most affected by the crisis unravelled so quickly was a surprise to everyone. However, the herd instinct of investors, the misguided initial policies of the IMF, the inability of governments to respond quickly enough to the unfolding crisis, and widespread corruption, all contributed to the economic, social and political turmoil that ensued. The Asian economic crisis demanded a reassessment of how the old state-led developmental approach to economic growth was adapted to the changing global economy. Moreover, it clearly showed that simply opening up an economy to the forces of globalization without maintaining important safeguards was not the approach to take.

And while liberalization was an attempt to move Asian economies down the road towards a US style of capitalism, the opening up of the successful 'miracle' economies and the subsequent Asian economic crisis did not hasten a major convergence of Asian capitalism around a 'Western form of free market capitalism' as so many US policy makers and commentators predicted (eg. Greenspan 1998, quoted in Hamilton 1999: 45–6; Kristof 1998: A1, D3). Certainly, there have been some reforms which have brought the Asian economies closer to a form of Western neoliberal capitalism. Overall, however, the Asian economies have retained many of the essential characteristics that were developed during the Cold War, high-growth period. As Mark Beeson (2002:19) points out in his analysis of institutional change in East Asia, 'the specific institutional arrangements that underpinned the region's distinctive social systems of production became a deeply embedded and generally legitimate part of the social fabric of individual nations'. His point that 'historical circumstances impart a degree of path dependency to institutional development' echoes the argument that is made in this analysis (Beeson 2002: 17). And, significantly, in the wake of the Asian crisis, it has been generally agreed that rather than reducing state regulation, economies need to be more and better regulated in order to lessen the risks associated with any increased access to the global economy. Indeed, in reregulating their economies, governments such as those in Thailand and South Korea have fallen back on the institutional forms that brought them economic success during the Cold War years.

A similar argument can be made about how the Cold War-shaped political and economic institutions in the seven successful economies have helped to encourage East Asian regionalism. While there are obviously many differences among the 'miracle' economies, the common historical experiences and the similar institutional and policy responses to these experiences have tended to give the governments of the region a shared understanding of the challenges they face. Path dependency has ensured that even though individual governments have made policy choices that take each of their economies on a slightly different trajectory, there is still enough of a common approach to economic development that members of the APT can see the advantages of working together. The regionalism of the state-directed, export-oriented economies of East Asia clearly has its roots in the high-growth period of the Cold War.

8
Conclusion

This analysis argues that the geopolitical history of East and Southeast Asia had a major impact on the economic success of the seven 'miracle' economies of Japan, South Korea, Taiwan, Hong Kong, Singapore, Malaysia and Thailand. The series of 'hot' wars that preoccupied the region from the Second World War onwards, in conjunction with the all-encompassing Cold War, significantly shaped the political and economic institutions that emerged in the seven highly successful Asian economies. No analysis of the political economy of East and Southeast Asia over the last half century is complete without considering the Cold War, the sequence of 'hot' wars that occupied the region, and the role of the US as it sought to contain the spread of Asian communism. This concentration on the historical, geopolitical context brings into sharp focus our understanding of the reasons for the success of the seven 'miracle' economies. It forces us to rethink the way we examine East and Southeast Asia's remarkable economic success and the 1997–8 economic crisis.

Although the seven successful Asian economies all produced sustained periods of high rates of growth, each had very distinctive backgrounds and characteristics which made it very different from the others. South Korea and Taiwan were part of Japan's colonial empire until its defeat at the end of the Second World War. Malaya/Malaysia, Singapore and Hong Kong were part of the British Empire until Malaya was granted independence in 1957, Singapore was folded into Malaysia in 1963 and Hong Kong was handed back to the Chinese in 1997. Thailand was formally independent, although it came under considerable foreign influence at various times in its

218

history. Nor can it be said that US influence among the seven economies was similar. Japan, South Korea, Taiwan and Thailand were
major allies of the US; Hong Kong, Singapore and Malaysia had
relatively limited relations with the Cold War superpower. And
there is a vast range in terms of the size of each of the economy's
populations. Japan is more than twice the size of Thailand, three
times the size of South Korea and forty times the size of Singapore.
Neither Hong Kong nor Singapore have an agricultural sector, while
Thailand and Malaysia have substantial agricultural lands. Moreover, within each economy the nature of the enterprises was different.
For example, small- and medium-sized firms dominated in Hong
Kong and Taiwan, whereas large conglomerates controlled the
economies of South Korea and Japan (Clark and Chan 1992a).

Yet, despite their many differences, all seven economies were
immensely successful in very comparable ways. The common
denominator in steering the seven economies down similar pathways
to success was the series of wars that consumed East and Southeast
Asia and the general geopolitical context which provided both the
resources and the incentives for achieving rapid economic growth.
Over many centuries war has demonstrated its capacity to shape the
way events unfold. The history of the political economy of East and
Southeast Asia over the last sixty years of the twentieth century
shows that this region is no exception. Indeed the region experienced
all three effects of war: the destructive and disintegrative effects; the
formative and developmental effects; and the reformative and redistributive effects. However, crucial to the impact of the various wars
on the political economy of the region was the sequence of effects.
The destructive and disintegrative effects of the Second World War
were followed by the formative and developmental effects of the
Korean War and early years of the Cold War, and then by the
reformative and redistributive effects of the later Cold War years
and the Vietnam War. The series of wars that beset East and Southeast
Asia from the Second World War onwards, then, provided a unique
context which shaped the economic development of the region's
successful economies in critical ways.

Hence, driven by the sequence of geopolitical events that overtook the region, each of the 'miracle' economies went through
roughly the same phases of economic development. The historical
institutionalist approach employed in the analysis highlights these
phases. The approach emphasizes how the context of the Cold War

and the various 'hot' wars shaped the way in which the political and economic institutions developed and prompted states to adopt roughly similar routes to economic development. In turn economic success produced positive feedback which cemented the institutions in place and reinforced the commitment of governments to a broad policy of state-facilitated export-manufacturing industrialization. The phases through which the economies were moved by their governments in response to similar geopolitical circumstances tended to be very similar. Moreover, the combination of state intervention; large inward capital flows generated by the various wars; and the incentive to rally around a hegemonic project, which was prompted by the threat of communism, were all significant factors in the success of the rapid economic growth strategies.

Phases of Development

The five 'ideal' phases through which the 'miracle' economies went on their way to economic success can be briefly set out. The first phase was initiated by the outbreak of conflict in the Pacific theatre in December 1941. During the Second World War and its aftermath, intense wartime fighting led to extensive dislocation and, in places, even the total destruction of the social institutions that had honeycombed and given structure to the society. Civilian loss of life, widespread casualties and forced migration as people fled combat zones undermined the stable social relations that had characterized the seven Asian societies leading to the outbreak of war. Also severely weakened were the political and administrative institutions. With capital cities under attack or occupied, the traditional patterns of administration were often disrupted and the machinery of government left in disrepair. Similarly, the economy was severely strained by the disruption of the labour force, the destruction of the economic infrastructure, and the limitations placed on production. Problems also arose with the supply of inputs for agriculture and with the loss of stable markets. Overall, this first phase in producing the seven future 'miracle' economies was characterized by the destructive and disintegrative effects of war.

The second phase was initiated, in the late 1940s, by the onset of a series of communist-inspired guerrilla wars around the region. These guerrilla wars and the Korean War, which began in 1950, marked the spread of the Cold War to Asia. The perception in the US and around the region was that there was a very high likelihood of either an external attack from one of Asia's communist countries or the launching of an internal war by armed communist guerrilla groups. The result, or 'legacy', of this perceived crisis, or 'critical juncture' (Collier and Collier 1991), was the buildup of the state's administrative and coercive capacity in order to mobilize resources and confront the communist threat. Crucial to the construction of this capacity was the combination of the motivation to build up the state and develop the economy created by the imminent threat and the availability of the necessary funds. Both the coercive and civil aspects of the state's formal institutional capacity were rapidly expanded in the drive to prepare for any open conflict with Asian communism. Moreover, increased state capacity took place in the context of a weak, fragmented society which was a legacy of the first phase of the 'miracle' economies' development. Fragmented and weak societies allowed for considerable state autonomy during this second phase. In addition, a further response was to reinvigorate the economy. A sound economic base was recognized to be not only a critical factor in assembling a strong military, but was also, in itself, a way of ensuring that communism's appeal went unheeded. In rebuilding the economy, emphasis was placed on revitalizing the agricultural sector and on developing an import-substitution strategy. Generally, then, the second phase of the model was driven by the formative and reformative aspects of war.

The third phase was initiated when questions were raised about the sustainability of the import-substitution strategy adopted by governments in phase two. A stagnating economy and looming balance of payments problems produced a minor critical juncture so that immediate action was required. To ensure that the economy and the society remained strong, and hence, able to repel the threat from communism, a switch to a greater emphasis on an export-oriented industrialization strategy was necessary. Institutions and policies were developed that supported the export of manufactured goods into the global market. And capital was made available by way of US military procurement, military or economic aid, or through FDI. The adoption of this strategy was not a signal to abandon the institutions providing the infrastructure for the import-substitution strategy. Rather, it meant encouraging an export-oriented strategy for specific industrial sectors where a market could be found in the international economy. The general result was that economic policies 'came to have a distinctly mercantilist cast' (Haggard 1990: 99). Moreover, as the economy developed and economic institutions took root, the state autonomy of phase two was transformed into a more cooperative state–business relationship. This phase, too, was driven by the formative and reformative aspects of war.

The fourth phase was characterized by a deepening of the industrialization process and an extension of the export-oriented strategy initiated in the third phase. Secondary import-substitution industries were developed so as to replace imported iron, steel, chemicals, artificial fibres and similar goods. The overall economy acquired the ability to develop more capital-intensive and high-technology-intensive industrial sectors and to produce a new generation of exports such as electronic goods and transportation equipment. Moving up the technological ladder in order to supply growing international markets was an important aspect of this phase. Of course, crucial to both the third and fourth phases of development for the 'miracle' economies was the fact that the reformative effects of the Cold War meant that successive American administrations were prepared to overlook the protectionist import-substitution policies of the East and Southeast Asian economies and keep the United States market fully open to exports from the region. Equally significant was access to increased amounts of capital. Again this came from increased FDI, and in some cases economic aid, either from the US or Japan.

The fifth and last phase covers the period during which the relatively mature institutions and entrenched policies of previous phases faced a series of crises which produced pressures for change. Most crucially, the gradual reduction in the communist threat and the eventual end of the Cold War prompted the US government to pressure the governments of East and Southeast Asia to open up their economies and their political systems. With the waning of the communist threat, US officials no longer felt bound to give their unconditional support to authoritarian regimes following mercantilist economic policies. American pressure for greater liberalization was supported by influential groups of local technocrats, many of whom had been trained in the US. At the same time a significant number of the institutions and policies that had supported the mercantilist approach to economic development remained in place. Economic liberalization, in its various guises, was accompanied by rising flows of capital. Initially, this capital was in the form of FDI, especially after the Plaza Accord increased the value of the yen against the dollar and Japanese companies looked to other parts of East and Southeast Asia for low-cost platforms from which to export their manufactured products to North America and Europe. However, during the 1990s, increasing amounts of capital were transferred into the region in the form of short-term loans as investors around the world sought to exploit the region's high growth rates. The 1997–8 crises severely interrupted economic growth but the 'miracle' economies were able to bounce back. Significantly, the institutions established over an extended period of time and the policies that the governmental institutions espoused were reshaped by these crises, but were not as radically transformed as some analysts, especially those in the United States, had expected. This period underscores the staying power of institutions and the degree to which relatively mature institutions and policies are slow to change despite strongly articulated reasons and powerful pressures to do so.

None of the seven successful East and Southeast Asian economies followed exactly this idealized sequence of economic development. Indeed, each departs from the model set of phases in significant ways. There are a number of reasons why. First, the distinctive backgrounds and characteristics of each economy ensures that the starting point and the trajectory to success were slightly different. Second, each economy's location within the region affected the way in which the two major wars, the Korean War and the Vietnam War, and America's military involvement in the Cold War influenced its economic growth. Third, the timing of the Korean and Vietnam Wars also had an impact on when sustained rapid economic growth took off in particular economies. For example, those most affected by America's involvement in the Korean War tended to start their ascent to economic success earlier than those for whom the Vietnam War was key to their prosperity. Hence, although the seven economies did extremely well, the extent of their success, the speed with which that success was achieved, and the industrial platform on which the success was built all varied, despite each economy being based on export industrialization and going through roughly the same phases of economic development.

Strong States, Capital and Markets

In this analysis of the sequence of wars that gripped East and Southeast Asia and led to the rapid and sustained economic growth of the seven 'miracle' Asian economies, three factors stand out. First, vital to the success of each economy was the emergence of a strong state able to maintain internal social stability, face down external threats, and plan and implement a relatively coherent and effective economic strategy for rapid economic growth. As Dani Rodrik (1998: 99) has pointed out, 'No one who studies economic development will be surprised to learn that the quality of government institutions matters for growth.'

Importantly, the set of conditions for the development of strong states, laid out in the introductory chapter, were met for each of the seven 'miracle' economies. First, the Second World War and its aftermath produced widespread social dislocation which severely weakened, and in some cases even broke apart completely, the existing system of social control. Second, the onset of the Cold War created a situation in which the US, which emerged from the Second World War as one of two superpowers, defined its interests in confronting communism to include support for a concentration of social control – in other words, authoritarian governments – in its main allies in Asia. Third, the outbreak of several regional communist-inspired guerrilla wars and the Korean War drove home for everyone in the region the imminent and serious internal and external military threat posed by Asian communism. Fourth, either through aid from the US or through the commodity boom generated by the Korean War, each of the 'miracle' economies was provided with funds, and in some cases skilled manpower and organizational and technical knowledge, to develop effective institutions. Fifth, the need to mobilize resources and build a security apparatus able to ward off the communist threat, combined with the weakness of social forces, prompted the creation of state institutions with the autonomy, skills and capacity to execute the leadership's overall strategy. And, sixth, in each of the 'miracle' economies a relatively skilled leadership group emerged that was able to take advantage of the prevailing conditions to build strong state institutions.

The strong states that were generated by this sequence of events in East and Southeast Asia generally had two sides to them. First, there was the coercive side of the state apparatus. This element of the state was built up in response to the perceived internal and external threats and included various mixes of military, police and intelligence capabilities. The coercive institutions also kept domestic social order, sometimes by using intimidation and violence. Second, was the civil or bureaucratic side of the state. While initially the main purpose of the bureaucracy was to mobilize resources to prepare for, or engage in, war, it became a crucial player in the development of each of the 'miracle' economies. Leaders were able to use the bureaucracy in order to undertake what has been termed in this study 'developmental interventionism'. The idea was to promote rapid economic growth initially through import-substitution industrialization and later through export-oriented industrialization.

The governments of the seven successful Asian economies intervened in four broad economic areas. First, all governments invested heavily in the physical infrastructure of their economies, including, for example, roads, railways, port facilities, electrical generating capacity, water supplies and irrigation. Many of these infrastructure projects were originally built to serve military needs and then converted to support economic development. Second, all governments invested in the human infrastructure required to advance their economies. For example, they emphasized developing the general education systems, skills training, the provision of cheap labour either with the help of land reform or subsidized housing, and the management of immigration. At the same time, often because of concerns about the links between communism and trade unions, governments severely restricted the activities of organized labour. Third, all governments intervened to regulate, and in many cases directly manage, the distribution of capital within their economies. The bank-based financial systems that characterized the 'miracle' economies were closely controlled by governments; interest rates were regulated and credit selectively allocated to promote government economic strategies. Finally, each government developed an industrial strategy through varying degrees of government intervention. For Hong Kong, the level of government intervention was relatively low with land use and trade promotion the most prominent aspects of the colonial administration's policy. In contrast, the governments of Japan, South Korea and Taiwan intervened extensively to promote chosen industries – such as steel, shipbuilding or car manufacturing- and even particular companies. In Singapore, Malaysia and Thailand government intervention was crucial to the success of industries such as electronics assembly and computer components (Jomo 2001). Overall, therefore, government intervention to manage and direct economic development was crucial to the economic success of the seven 'miracle' economies.

Was there a point at which the developmental state was no longer able to intervene effectively in the economy to promote rapid economic growth? This, of course, is an important question and some analysts have argued that this point was reached during the 1980s and 1990s when it appeared that governments were forced to limit the role of the state and rely more and more on opening up their economies to market forces (Pang 2000). Linda Weiss (2003) disagrees. She argues that the developmental states have maintained an adaptive capacity that has allowed them to continue to play an import role in economic development. Certainly, there is mounting evidence to show that in the post-crisis period increased state intervention to regulate liberalized economies did occur. Aspects of the developmental state were reinvigorated in order to bring some stability and predictability back to the battered economies.

The emergence of strong, relatively autonomous states in each of the 'miracle' economies also allowed for a comparatively smooth transition from an import-substitution industrialization strategy to an emphasis on export oriented industrialization. The political coalitions that usually emerged around import-substitution industrialization were, in the 'miracle' economies, unable to exert enough influence to prevent the shift to a primarily export-oriented strategy. Import-substitution was not, however, abandoned altogether. Indeed, those domestic industries supplying the local market continued to be protected and often subsidized in one way or another. Nonetheless, in each case a crisis forced the government to put greater emphasis on export manufacturing. The crisis arose either from a looming balance of payments problem, with foreign currency income of various kinds not covering foreign currency expenditures, or from some other predicament that weakened the economy or the society and threatened the 'miracle' economy's overall security.

Each of the seven economies moved to a primarily export-oriented approach at different times. Some took longer to make the transfer to the new strategy than others. Hong Kong, as an entrepôt with no import or export taxes, geared its manufacturing towards exports from the arrival of the textile machinery and skilled refugees from civil war-ravaged Shanghai in the late 1940s. Japan began to adopt an export-oriented stance with the introduction of the Dodge Line in 1949 and confirmed its commitment to encouraging exports during the Korean War. Both economies were trying to lift themselves out of post-Second World War recessions. Taiwan, South

Korea and Singapore all shifted to an emphasis on export promotion in the early to mid-1960s just as the Vietnam War got under way. The governments of all three economies saw they were increasingly vulnerable in the face of impending balance of payments problems. Malaysia moved relatively slowly during the 1970s to encourage export manufacturing with the 1985–6 recession forcing a completion of the process. Similarly, the 1985–6 slowdown in the regional economy prompted Thailand to place greater emphasis on export manufacturing. In each case the key to the shift from import-substitution to an export-oriented approach to economic development was the relative autonomy and capacity of the state to oversee the policy changes that were needed to implement the new export-oriented strategy.

The emergence of the war-driven, strong institutional states was also critical to the way state–business relations developed. Initially, as the state institutions were quickly bolstered to deal with the imminent threat from communism, the state was very much in command. Slowly this relationship evolved into what Evans (1992; 1995) terms 'embedded autonomy'. As the economy grew, largely at the direction of the state, state institutions and agencies developed links into the business community that allowed them to steer the economy down the road to rapid growth. The robust state–business linkages were reinforced by the demands of preparing for a possible war, a situation which invariably brings governments and businesses closer together, and also by the fact that in East and Southeast Asia the rigid public–private distinction in economic affairs is not generally recognized. However, over time rapid growth produced a larger, more complex economy and the state's capacity to drive the economy was gradually reduced. Yet, it did not recede altogether. Indeed, in all the seven 'miracle' economies governments still play a crucial guiding role. Institutional inertia, habit and a strong record of past successes have combined to ensure that state intervention has not been totally abandoned (Beeson 2002).

Of course, as with all other aspects of their development, the seven successful Asian economies each experienced a different evolution of state–business relations. The links between state institutions and the business community in Japan, South Korea and Taiwan, where domestic firms were prominent, were unlike those that developed in places like Singapore and Hong Kong, where foreign corporations played a major role in the economy. The important point is, however, that the early emergence of the strong state ensured that governments had the upper hand in guiding economic progress during the formative years of each of the 'miracle' economies. And this highly successful relationship has produced a legacy of active state involvement in economic development that remains to this day.

The second factor that stands out as vital to the rapid and sustained growth of the 'miracle' economies was the successive, war-induced waves of capital that flooded East and Southeast Asia in the decades following the Second World War. The first influx of capital was the product of the exodus of capital and other assets from Shanghai as a result of the Chinese civil war and benefited mainly Hong Kong and Taiwan. The massive wave of capital into the region that came with the outbreak of the Korean War quickly followed. Direct American spending on fighting the Korean War proved an invaluable catalyst to the Japanese and Taiwanese economies and served to build up the military in both Taiwan and South Korea. Indirectly, US spending to increase stockpiles of vital war materials, most notably natural rubber and tin, had a major impact on the economies and institution building of Malaya, Singapore and, to a limited extent, Thailand. During the height of the Cold War in Asia, from the end of the Korean War to the mid-1960s, a steady flow of American military and economic aid provided another wave of capital for Japan, South Korea, Taiwan and Thailand. American spending on the Vietnam War produced the next wave of capital to flood into East and Southeast Asia and gave a major economic boost to all seven 'miracle' economies.

In the early 1970s the nature of the capital that entered East and Southeast Asia began to change. Alerted to the potential of the region as a low-cost manufacturing centre by businessmen visiting parts of East and Southeast Asia in connection with the Vietnam War, the flow of US, and increasingly Japanese, FDI into Hong Kong, Taiwan, South Korea and the three Southeast Asian economies gradually increased. Japanese aid to Malaysia and Thailand also rose significantly as the government came to appreciate the strategic significance of Southeast Asia as a source of raw materials and as a region straddling its maritime trading routes. However, it was the flood of FDI that was triggered by the appreciation of the yen from 1985 onwards, and the resulting search by Japanese companies for low-cost export-manufacturing platforms, that proved to be especially consequential for the three Southeast Asian economies. This wave of capital into the region was augmented by Japanese firms' competitors from Asia, Western Europe and North America also investing in the Southeast Asian economies. Overall, then, East and Southeast Asia experienced a unique series of capital inflows which proved to be crucial in promoting rapid and sustained economic growth in the seven 'miracle' economies.

Yet capital inflows by themselves did not guarantee economic prosperity. The key was the ability of the state to harness the inflow of capital and put it to productive use. Having relatively strong and autonomous states with a clearly defined goal of defending their governments and their societies against communism was key to employing the capital windfalls to good effect. Nationalism, invariably a product of war, helped to channel the resources towards the hegemonic project of defence through economic strength. Moreover, while corruption was clearly a problem it did not become so debilitating as to derail the government's overall strategy. The communist threat imposed a certain discipline on everyone, because failure to successfully confront the danger was widely believed to invite catastrophe. The productive activities into which capital was channelled by the governments of the various 'miracle' economies included increasing agricultural production, developing the economy's physical and human infrastructure, promoting industrial activity and then upgrading industrial production.

Capital and other available resources were directed notably into productive activities but just as significantly into projects that generated 'growth with equity' (World Bank 1993). The relatively good distribution of wealth was achieved slightly differently in each economy. For example, in Taiwan and South Korea land reform helped to raise living standards and redistribute rural assets to those who had previously been tenants or who held very small parcels of land. In Singapore and Hong Kong the provision of heavily subsidized housing performed a similar function to land reform in terms of ensuring urban workers a basic standard of living. In a number of societies the manner by which capital was injected into growing economies proved decisive in bringing about equitable growth. The boom in rubber and tin prices associated with the Korean War put money directly into the hands of rubber smallholders, tappers, estate workers and tin mine labourers who then formed the vast majority of workers in Malaya. The boom also benefited Singaporean and, to a lesser extent, Thai workers. This situation was in marked contrast to economic booms in capital-intensive industries, such as petroleum or copper mining, where the impact does not necessarily reach into all parts of the economy and society. Later the labour-intensive industrialization, which took place in all of the 'miracle' economies, again put money into the hands of workers, a significant portion of whom had, up until that point, been engaged in subsistence agriculture. And as the supply of labour grew tighter, and the demand for higher-skilled labour increased, so wages rose, helping to maintain 'growth with equity'.

The third factor essential to the rapid and sustained growth of the seven 'miracle' economies was the availability of markets. Goods produced for export need markets. The decision by successive American governments to allow manufactured goods from the seven 'miracle' economies to be freely imported was critical to their successful development. In the years after the Second World War, the industrialized countries structured their tariffs to encourage the importation of raw materials from the developing world for processing and turning into manufactured products. These finished products were then exported back to the developing world. America was prepared to depart from this practice for political reasons. The Cold War gave successive US administrations strong incentives to ensure that its allies in Asia developed strong economies. Japan, South Korea, Taiwan, Hong Kong and Singapore were all short of raw materials and had to rely on the export of manufactured products. Hence, the US admitted Asian manufactured goods into its economy so as to guarantee the economic, and therefore military, security of these vital bulwarks against the spread of Asian communism.

The US allowed Asian manufactured goods into its market from the very beginning of the Cold War. During the Korean War the US military provided a major market for Japanese products. The US also opened its domestic market to Hong Kong and Japanese goods during the 1950s. Later, as the US economy expanded with the spending on the Vietnam War, the US became a key market for Taiwan, South Korea and Singapore as they turned from an import-substitution to an export-oriented economic development strategy. America continued to keep its markets open even during the turbulent times of the 1970s and 1980s. As Malaysia and Thailand developed their export-manufacturing capacity, they too were able to take advantage of the relatively open US market. Equally important was the emergence of the Southeast Asian market created by US Vietnam War-related spending in the region. Again it was Japan, South Korea,

Taiwan, and to a lesser extent Singapore, that benefited most. And as the economies of East and Southeast Asia grew, so regional markets opened up. Overall, then, the sequence of geopolitical events ensured that the seven successful East and Southeast Asian economies had markets for their developing export-manufacturing industries. Indeed, although they have faded a little, the trade patterns, especially the links to the US, established during the Cold War years are still of considerable importance to Asia's 'miracle' economies many years later.

Each of the three factors – strong state, waves of capital and access to markets – that were key to the success of Asia's 'miracle' economies was the product of the sequence of wars in the region from the Second World War onwards. The way in which the three factors combined was also a consequence of these wars. This point is underscored by comparing the seven successful economies with others in the region, most notably Indonesia and the Philippines, that were not so successful. None of the other institutional states in the region had either the autonomy or the capacity that were displayed by the institutional states of the seven 'miracle' economies. Rodrik (1998: 94) notes that 'In the Philippines and Indonesia, it is poor institutions that were primarily responsible for lacklustre performance' in terms of economic growth. Hamilton-Hart (2002: 183) reinforces this point by demonstrating that the 'governing capacity' of Indonesia and the Philippines was way below that of the successful Asian economies.

With relatively weak institutional states, the governments of both Indonesia and the Philippines failed to make good use of the available capital. For example, between 1962 and 1983 the US government gave US$3 billion to the Philippines in the form of military and economic assistance (Boyce 1993 1; see also Kang 2002: 42–3). However, the vast sums of US aid were generally dissipated by a weak state that allowed its revenues to be syphoned off by societal powerbrokers. As a consequence, the government failed to institute the kind of land reform, agricultural improvements, physical and human infrastructure projects, and industrial development that were emphasized by the strong, interventionist governments of the 'miracle' economies. Similarly, in Indonesia the relatively weak state became dependent on the petroleum industry as oil prices boomed during the 1970s (Karl 1997: 190–213). Corruption increased as revenue rose and, while some investments were made in agricultural as well as physical and human infrastructure projects, generally the government proved incapable of channelling the windfall oil revenues into areas of the economy in a sustained enough fashion to provide long-term benefits.

For no other country in the world was the sequence of geopolitical events so advantageous during the second half of the twentieth century as they were for the seven successful Asian economies analysed in this study. As American real estate agents are wont to say, the key was 'location, location, location'. In neither Africa nor Latin America was the threat from communism sufficiently grave and imminent to promote the strong states or to encourage the US to provide aid on the scale it did to the frontline states in East and Southeast Asia. The one country that was possibly in a similar position to the seven Asian economies was Israel. Israel built up a strong state in response to an external threat and received massive amounts of capital in the form of US aid and remittances from Jewish communities around the world. However, because it was not until 1991 that the US fought a war in the region, the comparison obviously has its limitations. The experience of the seven 'miracle' economies is, therefore, unique and unlikely to be repeated in the future.

Cold War Developmentalism versus Post-Cold War Liberalism

The developmental economic strategy that grew out of the geopolitical context of East and Southeast Asia set the 'miracle' economies on a trajectory of rapid and sustained growth. It was a strategy that echoed aspects of mercantilism and the work of theorists such as Alexander Hamilton and Friedrich List. The parallels between Asian developmentalism during the years from 1941 to the late 1970s and the European mercantilism of the seventeenth and eighteenth centuries are perhaps not surprising given that war and the threat of war were pervasive in both periods. In each case the government's aim was to strengthen the economy and reinforce the capacity of the state so that the society would have the resources to defend itself against an external threat (Buck 1942; Ekelund and Tollison 1997). Economic growth was not seen as an end in itself but rather as a means to building the state and increasing the security of the community.

Adapting some of the ideas of mercantilism to nineteenth-century America and Germany respectively, Hamilton and List argued for some forms of protectionism in order to promote industrialization in relatively weak economies. In particular, both Hamilton and List 'argued that national security generally required the development of a manufacturing base' (Harlen 1999: 740). Capital was needed to be channelled into industrial development and tariff protection was vital so that infant industries could be nurtured. The ideas espoused by Hamilton, List and others found their way to Japan mostly via Germany and the German Historical School (Fallows 1994: 179–240; Morris-Suzuki 1989; Pempel 1999: 139; Woo-Cumings 1999: 4–5). From Japan they spread to other parts of East and Southeast Asia. While the developmental economic policies of the governments of the 'miracle' economies were clearly a response to the regional and international geopolitical events, their reputable intellectual basis also helped them become firmly embedded in the political and economic life of East and Southeast Asia.

But the main reason that developmental economic policies became so deeply entrenched in the political economy of the successful Asian economies was that they generated widespread prosperity. As the governments of the seven 'miracle' economies responded to the communist threat, the economic policies they introduced became institutionalized. The result was a self-reinforcing positive feedback process. The developmental interventionist policies of the various governments succeeded in providing domestic social stability, security against external threats, and high levels of economic growth. Indeed, the three positive outputs fed on each other to create a virtuous circle of economic development. Social stability and security helped to provide the basis for economic growth. In turn, economic growth encouraged greater social stability and generated the resources to strengthen defences against the external threat. Moreover, as the developmental policies proved successful, cultural influences, like local norms and business practices, meshed with and helped to shape the emerging institutions (Orrù, Biggart and Hamilton 1991). Equally, other institutions and political and economic actors adapted to the successful developmental policies and in doing so reinforced their central role in the development of the 'miracle' economies. In all seven successful Asian economies, increased prosperity underscored the legitimacy of the developmental policies. And with their success and the widespread support they received came increased pressure to continue down the path to further rapid economic growth prescribed by these same policies and the institutions implementing them.

However, during the 1980s the intensity of the Cold War in Asia abated; the security lid was gradually lifted off the pressure cooker that was the region's 'miracle' economies. As a result, demands for change started to emerge. The American government began to campaign for greater economic and political liberalization. At the same time, rapidly expanding economies and a rising interest in greater political participation intensified demands for the seven successful Asian societies to liberalize their economies and open up their political institutions.

The push to liberalize was not uniform across all seven economies. In part this was because the perception of the change in the threat to each economy was different. The weaknesses in the North Korean economy and the regime that governed it were becoming evident. This turn of events eased the fears of North Korea's immediate neighbours, Japan and South Korea. China's improved relations with the West also helped to assuage Japanese concerns, but the growing strength of the Chinese economy and military perpetuated Taiwan's suspicions of the mainland's intentions. In Southeast Asia Vietnam's occupation of Cambodia slowly stabilized and presented less of a threat to Thailand. In Malaysia the internal communist threat faded appreciably; however, the government remained troubled about underlying communal tensions between Malays and non-Malays. For Singapore's leaders the size of their country continued to make them feel vulnerable despite the receding communist threat. And Hong Kong became caught up in the negotiations between Britain and China over the transfer of sovereignty in 1997. As a result of the breakdown in the overarching Cold War structure, then, each of the seven successful Asian governments opened up its economy in different ways and to differing degrees.

The differences in economic liberalization were compounded by differences in political liberalization. Japan, Malaysia and Singapore already held regular elections and the leaders thought of their countries as reasonably democratic. There were limited political reforms in these countries. However, South Korea, Taiwan and Thailand had authoritarian governments and so the pressure on their political leaders to institute change by democratizing their political systems was much greater. In South Korea and Thailand in particular, the process of democratization tended to be disjointed and led to increased levels of corruption as well as the erratic implementation of economic policies.

Hence, the degree to which the liberalization of the various 'miracle' economies took place and the extent to which the process was properly regulated varied markedly. The more piecemeal the process and the less it was adequately regulated, the more vulnerable it was to swings in the international economy. This vulnerability was borne out by the events of the Asian economic crisis of 1997–8. The liberalized economic and political institutions in Thailand, Malaysia, Indonesia and South Korea proved incapable of dealing with the changing nature of international financial flows and the tendency of short-term capital to flood in and out of economies. Tellingly, the 'miracle' economies of Thailand, Malaysia and South Korea were much better able to pull themselves out of the crisis-induced recession than Indonesia. Part of this process entailed reregulation and a return to some aspects of the old developmental economic policies.

Recent events, then, have clearly demonstrated that there are two main economic strategies that have support within the successful Asian economies (Stubbs 2000). On the one hand there is the Cold War developmental approach. It emphasizes state intervention in order to protect key import-substitution industries and give a comparative advantage to export-manufacturing sectors. This strategy still has considerable resonance among sections of the bureaucracy; many, including legislators, associated with domestic industries that benefited from import-substitution tariff protection or export subsidies; and politicians and others concerned about social equity issues that might affect the stability of the society. The developmental approach has been embedded in an institutional continuity and reinforced by powerful actors who benefit from the resulting policies and who gain a measure of legitimacy from their success. It is also buttressed by the wider community's appreciation that it has provided social stability and an increasing level of prosperity. Importantly, then, developmental institutions, and the policies that they are responsible for, are still very much part of the political economy of the 'miracle' economies.

On the other hand, liberalism has also taken route in the 'miracle' economies. The idea that the market, not the state, constitutes the most effective and productive way of organizing economic relations and that, therefore, policies should be followed that open up the economy to market forces through deregulation and privatization, has been adopted by the governments of the successful economies. In addition, liberalism focuses on the need to encourage the free flow of trade and capital so as to exploit the perceived mutual gains from participating in the global economy. Liberalism has been promoted most strongly in the Asian 'miracle' economies by, amongst others, Western-trained technocrats, many of whom inhabit key economic planning agencies; economists in universities and policy think-tanks; and those associated with export-dependent and multinational corporations – especially European and American-based companies – who fear that local, domestic protectionism may jeopardize their attempts to gain access to foreign markets. This liberal reformist approach was especially influential during the 1980s and 1990s up to the Asian crisis of 1997–8.

In the wake of the Asian crisis those advocating these two approaches have tended to find compromises and ways of working together in an attempt to manage the forces of globalization as advantageously as possible. Etel Solingen (2004) refers to this as a 'hybrid' coalition of political interests. It has been the basis on which reforms have been undertaken to deal with the fallout from the crisis and to swing support behind the ASEAN Plus Three regional project (Beeson 2005; Hughes 2005; Stubbs 2002). The developmental approach that emerged during the Cold War years still has a significant influence on the political economy of the seven Asian 'miracle' economies. Its durability indicates that institutional continuity, or path dependency and positive reinforcing feedback, must be considered when analysing contemporary political and economic events in East and Southeast Asia.

The explanation that runs through this analysis clearly builds on previous sets of explanations for the success of Asia's 'miracle' economies. The American-hegemony approach underscores the crucial role played by the US in defining the overall strategic, Cold War context and in injecting massive amounts of capital and other resources into East and Southeast Asia in order to contain Asian communism. The statists stress the importance of the strong centralized state that intervenes to direct the economy. The Japan-centred explanations focus our attention on the role that Japanese colonialism played in creating some of the institutions and practices that later re-emerged in Taiwan and South Korea in the post-Second World War years. It also highlights the extent to which Japanese FDI and aid boosted the Southeast Asian 'miracle' economies during the 1980s and 1990s. The neoclassical economic explanations emphasize the export-orientation of the successful economies and the way in which increasingly advanced technologies were incorporated into the process of industrialization that led to rapid economic growth. Finally, the cultural explanation points to the importance of the economic and political institutions and policies that propelled the 'miracle' economies down the path to rapid and sustained economic growth being compatible with local cultural norms and practices.

However, the analysis in this study goes beyond previous explanations. An examination of the sequence of major geopolitical events in East and Southeast Asia from the beginning of the Second World War to the present day has been combined with an historical institutionalist approach to produce a more compelling account of the political economy of the region. By focusing on the political and economic institutions that were developed as a result of the Cold War and the various 'hot' wars that flared up in East and Southeast Asia, the analysis has been able to integrate both the international and domestic factors that promoted growth in the region and that have been at the centre of other explanations. Indeed, explanations which involve only one level of analysis are generally incomplete. Moreover, rather than concentrating, as others have done, on one or two of the successful Asian economies, this analysis has laid out an instructive, comparative account of the main achievements and failures of *all* seven of Asia's 'miracle' economies.

Lessons for the Global Political Economy

What lessons, then, does the development of Asia' seven 'miracle' economies hold for the wider study of the international political economy – increasingly referred to as the global political economy – and for the implementation of economic development policies in other parts of the world? First, the analysis in this study underscores the value of taking a longitudinal view of the global political economy and economic development. It may be useful in some circumstances to undertake an analysis of the political economy of a state or region at a particular point in time; however, most analyses will benefit immensely from an historical perspective that shows the long-term trends that lie behind the day-to-day changes affecting the political economy of a society or group of states. In any study of events in the rapidly changing global political economy 'history matters'.

Second, while the study of international political economy has been good at exploring the reciprocal two-way relationship between political authority on the one hand and economic institutions and practices on the other, it has not always succeeded in incorporating security issues into analyses of the emerging global political economy. This analysis of the economic rise of East and Southeast Asia demonstrates how crucial the security dimension can be to the way in which economies develop or decline. This link between economic development and national security is widely recognized in East and Southeast Asia. For example, economic security is a central component of what the Japanese refer to as 'comprehensive security'. Similarly, the ASEAN notion of 'regional resilience', originally developed as 'national resilience' by the Indonesians, also has economic security as a key component. In other words, there is a consensus within the region that there are significant complementary connections between a strong economy and a society's general security. Analysts of the international global economy should be more alert to the need to take into account the security dimension in their empirical analyses no matter what part of the world they are examining.

Third, this study underlines the high degree of interdependence between events in the international political economy and what happens in the domestic political economy. The regional 'hot' wars and the global Cold War shaped the political and economic institutions of Asia's 'miracle' economies in significant ways. In turn the rapid and sustained economic growth of Asia's successful economies was influential in promoting regional stability and eventually the emergence of East Asian regionalism as well as creating positive attitudes towards East and Southeast Asia among the major global players such as the governments of the US and key European countries. Significantly, the impact of the global political economy on Asia's 'miracle' economies had both positive and negative effects. The exercise of American hegemony and later Japan's search for low-cost export-manufacturing sites brought capital into the region which provided the catalyst for sustained rapid growth. Indeed, in many ways the successful economies of East and Southeast Asia can be said to have been among the early beneficiaries of the contemporary form of globalization as highly mobile capital searched for ever higher profits. Yet globalization also brought about the Asian economic crisis as short-term investment first flooded into the region and then fled *en masse* when news of the rapidly depreciating value of the Thai baht quickly spread across the globe. But equally, domestic events within the states of East and Southeast Asia have contributed to important developments at the regional level. Indeed, regionalism has emerged in good part because domestic political coalitions within East and Southeast Asia have seen the value of working together to manage the forces of globalization and cooperating to deal with common economic challenges. It is important, then, that analysts fully recognize the interdependence of domestic and international factors as they analyse the emerging global political economy.

Fourth, this study underscores the importance of institutions in 'translating political inputs into political outcomes' (Hay 2002: 14). The emerging political and economic institutions that were a product of the Cold War and the various 'hot' wars in East and Southeast Asia were central to the development of the interventionist state and to the rapid economic growth that was characteristic of the seven 'miracle' economies. The analysis in this book has emphasized the way in which the external regional and international geopolitical environment was translated into domestic policies that resulted in strong, sustained economic growth rates. The criticism of institutional analyses is that they are better at explaining stability and continuity than transformations, upheavals and change. However, studies of the political economy of East and Southeast Asia over the last decade or so have been replete with analyses of how the forces of globalization, liberalization and democratization have brought about changes to the region. Yet in many ways the region has been relatively slow to change. Or, where changes and reforms have been implemented they have proved short-lived, with policies and practices often reverting to former ways. The stress in this analysis on the institutional factor helps us to understand why change can be so slow to emerge. Institutions that support particular routines, practices and conventions that have been embedded for many years within a society are usually difficult to reform or replace. Analysts interested in the transformative powers of the forces of globalization might do well to note the powers of resistance exhibited by mature, socially and politically embedded institutions. The argument here is not that the ability of institutions to remain in place and continue to influence events is good or bad for a society, but rather that the ability of institutions to promote stability, continuity and coherence in various domestic political economies as well as in the global political economy should not be underestimated.

Finally, this analysis highlights the importance for East and Southeast Asia's success of the mobilization of substantial amounts of capital and the development of effective state capacity in order to promote economic development. During the second half of the twentieth century neither other parts of Asia nor Africa, Latin America or the Middle East experienced the combination of capital inflow and strong states that propelled the 'miracle' economies to such high levels of economic growth. As a result the economic development of the states in these regions was generally less successful than in East and Southeast Asia. This analysis suggests that war is the decisive factor which drew capital into East and Southeast Asia and provided the motive for the creation of strong states. However, the sequence of wars that engulfed the region was a unique occurrence. Therefore, it is difficult to draw too many lessons from the success of the 'miracle' economies. Yet it is clear that the world must find some way of ensuring that the countries of the developing world are provided with the necessary capital to initiate economic development and at the same time build sufficient state capacity to maintain social stability and advance rapid economic growth. This is a conundrum that those interested in the emerging global political economy must address.

The aim of the book, then, has been to make the argument that we need to rethink the way we analyse Asia's economic success and the traumatic events of the crisis of 1997–8. Certainly, the analysis emphatically underscores the point that any future study of the region's sustained, rapid economic growth and the overall success of the seven 'miracle' economies, as well as the economic crisis of 1997–8, cannot be complete without taking into consideration the way the Cold War and the series of 'hot' wars shaped their domestic political and economic institutions and made such a critical contribution to East and Southeast Asia's remarkable economic development.

Bibliography

Abbot, J.P. (2003) *Developmentalism and Dependency in Southeast Asia: The Case of the Automotive Industry* (London: RoutledgeCurzon).

Acheson, D. (1969) *Present at the Creation: My Years in the State Department* (New York: Norton).

Adams, T.F.M. and I. Hoshii (1972) *The Financial History of the New Japan* (Tokyo: Kodansha).

Ahn C-s and Jaung H. (1999) South Korea in I. Marsh, J. Blondel and T. Inoguchi (eds), *Democracy, Governance and Economic Performance: East and Southeast Asia* (Tokyo: United Nations University Press), 137–66.

Allen, G.C. (1962) *A Short Economic History of Modern Japan 1867–1937: With a Supplementary Chapter on Economic Recovery and Expansion 1945–1960* (London: George Allen & Unwin).

Allen, G.C. (1965) *Japan's Economic Expansion* (London: Oxford University Press).

Allinson, G.D. (1993) 'The Structure and Transformation of Conservative Rule' in A. Gordon (ed.), *Postwar Japan as History* (Berkeley: University of California Press), 123–44.

Allinson, G.D. (1997) *Japan's Postwar History* (Ithaca: Cornell University Press).

Amsden, A.H. (1989) *Asia's Next Giant: South Korea and Late Industrialization* (New York: Oxford University Press).

Amsden, A.H. (1994) 'Why Isn't the Whole World Experimenting with the East Asian Model to Develop? Review of *The East Asian Miracle*', *World Development* 22 (No. 4), 627–33.

Anwar I. (1997) *The Asian Renaissance* (Singapore: Times Books International).

Aoki, M. (1987) 'The Japanese Firm in Transition' in K. Yamamura and Y. Yasuba (eds), *The Political Economy of Japan, Volume 1: The Domestic Transformation* (Stanford: Stanford University Press), 263–88.

Appelbaum, R.P. and J. Henderson (1992) 'Situating the State in the East Asian Development Process', in R.P. Appelbaum and J. Henderson (eds), *State and Development in the Asian Pacific Rim* (Newbury Park: Sage Publications), 1–26.

Arrighi, G. (1996) 'The Rise of East Asia: World-Systemic and Regional Aspects', *International Journal of Sociology and Social Policy* 16 (7/8), 6–44.

ASEAN (2002) *Investment Statistics* (Jakarta: ASEAN Secretariat).

ASEAN Centre (various issues) *ASEAN–Japan Statistical Pocketbook* (Tokyo: ASEAN Promotion Centre on Trade, Investment and Tourism).

Asia Development Bank (1992) *Asia Development Outlook 1992* (Manila: Asia Development Bank).

Athukorala, P.-c. (1999) 'Swimming Against the Tide: Crisis Management in Malaysia', in H.W. Arndt and H. Hill (eds), *Southeast Asia's Economic Crisis: Origins, Lessons, and the Way Forward* (Singapore: Institute of Southeast Asian Studies).

Balakrishnan, N. (1989) 'The Next NIC', *Far Eastern Economic Review*, 7 September, 96–8.

Balassa, B. (1980) 'The Newly Industrializing Countries After the Oil Crisis', *World Bank Staff Working Papers*, No.437.

Balassa, B. (ed.) (1981) *The Newly Industrializing Countries in the World Economy* (New York: Pergamon Press).

Balassa, B. and Associates (eds) (1982) *Development Strategies in Semi-Industrial Economies* (Baltimore: Johns Hopkins University Press).

Barlow, C. (1978) *The Natural Rubber Industry: Its Development, Technology, and Economy in Malaysia* (Kuala Lumpur: Oxford University Press).

Bartels, F.L. and N.J. Freeman (2004) 'Introduction to Foreign Direct Investment in Southeast Asia', in N.J. Freeman and F.L. Bartels (eds), *The Future of Foreign Direct Investment in Southeast Asia* (London: RoutledgeCurzon), 1–14.

Bean, R. (1973) 'War and the Birth of the Nation', *Journal of Economic History* 33: 203–21.

Beeson, M. (2001) 'Globalisation, Governance, and the Political-Economy of Public Policy Reform in East Asia', *Governance* 14 (4), 481–502.

Beeson, M. (2002) 'Theorising Institutional Change in East Asia', in M. Beeson (ed.), *Reconfiguring East Asia: Regional Institutions and Organisations After the Crisis* (London: RoutledgeCurzon), 7–30.

Beeson, M. (2004) 'The Rise and Fall (?) of the Developmental State: The Vicissitudes and Implications of East Asian Interventionism?', in L. Low (ed.), *Developmental States: Relevant, Redundant or Reconfigured?* (New York: Nova Science Publishers).

Beeson, M. (2005) 'Politics and Markets in East Asia: Is the Developmental State Compatible with Globalisation?', in R.Stubbs and G.R.D. Underhill (eds), *Political Economy and the Changing Global Order*, 3rd edn (Toronto: Oxford University Press).

Bell, S. (2003) 'Great Ideas of Central Banking: Values, Ideas and the Transformation of Central Banking and Monetary Policy in Australia', in I. Holland and J. Fleming (eds), *Government Reformed: Values and New Political Institutions* (Aldershot: Ashgate), 23–42.

Benoit E. (1971) 'The Impacts of the End of the Vietnam Hostilities and the Reduction of British Military Presence in Malaysia and Singapore', in Asia Development Bank, *Southeast Asia's Economy in the 1970s* (London: Longman), 582–671.

Berger, M.T. (2004) *The Battle for Asia: From Decolonisation to Globalization* (Abingdon: RoutledgeCurzon).

Bernard, M. (1989) *Northwest Asia: The Political Economy of a Postwar Regional System*, Asia Papers No.2 (Toronto: University of Toronto–York University, Joint Centre for Asia Pacific Studies).

Bernard, M. (1994) 'Post-Fordism, Transnational Production, and the Changing Global Political Economy', in R. Stubbs and G.R.D. Underhill (eds), *Political Economy and the Changing Global Order* (Toronto: McClelland and Stewart), 216–29.

Bernard, M. (2000) 'Post-Fordism and Global Restructuring', in R. Stubbs and G.R.D. Underhill (eds), *Political Economy and the Changing Global Order* (Toronto: Oxford University Press), 152–62.

Bernard, M. and J. Ravenhill (1995) 'Beyond Product Cycles and Flying Geese: Regionalization, Hierarchy, and the Industrialization of East Asia', *World Politics* 47 (January), 171–209.

Bevacqua, R. (1998) 'Whither the Japanese Model? The Asian Economic Crisis and the Continuation of Cold War Politics in the Pacific Rim', *Review of International Political Economy* 5 (Autumn), 410–23.

Bhagwati, J.N. (1978) *The Anatomy and Consequences of Exchange Control Regimes* (Cambridge, Mass.: Ballinger for the National Bureau of Economic Research).

Bhagwati, J. (1998) 'The Capital Myth: The Difference Between Trade in Widgets and Dollars', *Foreign Affairs* 77 (May–June), 7–13.

Biggart, N.W. and G.G. Hamilton (1997) 'Explaining Asian Business Success: Theory No.4', in M. Orrù, N.W. Biggart and G.G. Hamilton, *The Economic Orgainzation of East Asian Capitalism* (Thousand Oaks: Sage), 97–110.

Block, F. (1977) 'The Ruling Class Does Not Rule: Notes on the Marxist Theory of the State', *Socialist Revolution* 7: 6–28.

Bond, B. (1983) *War and Society in Europe, 1870–1970* (Leicester: Leicester University Press).

Booth, A. (2002) 'Rethinking the Role of Agriculture in the "East Asian" Model: Why is Southeast Asia Different from Northeast Asia?', *ASEAN Economic Bulletin* 19(1), 40–51.

Borden, W.S. (1984) *The Pacific Alliance: United States Foreign Economic Policy and Japanese Trade Recovery, 1947–1955* (Madison: University of Wisconsin Press).

Borrus, M., D. Ernst and S. Haggard (2000) 'Introduction: Cross-Border Production Networks and the Industrial Integration of the Asia-Pacific Region', in M. Borrus, D. Ernst, and S. Haggard (eds), *International Production Networks in Asia: Rivalry or Riches?* (London: Routledge).

Borthwick, M. (1992) *Pacific Century: The Emergence of Modern Pacific Asia* (Boulder: Westview Press).

Bowen, J.P. (1984) *The Gift of the Gods: The Impact of the Korean War on Japan* (Old Dominion Graphics Consultants).

Bowie, A. and D. Unger (1997) *The Politics of Open Economies: Indonesia, Malaysia, the Philippines and Thailand* (Cambridge: Cambridge University Press).

Bowles, P. (2002) 'Asia's Post-Crisis Regionalism: Bringing the State Back In, Keeping the (United) States Out', *Review of International Political Economy* 9 (May), 230–56.

Boyce, J.K. (1993) *The Philippines: The Political Economy of Growth and Improvement in the Marcos Era* (Honolulu: University of Hawaii Press).

Breslin, S.G. (1996) 'China: Developmental State or Dysfunctional Development', *Third World Quarterly* 17 (No.4), 689–706.

Breslin, S. (2000) 'China: Geopolitics and the Political Economy of Hesitant Integration', in R. Stubbs and G.R.D. Underhill (eds), *Political Economy and the Changing Global Order*, 2nd edn (Toronto: Oxford University Press), 392–405.

Breslin, S. (2005) 'China and the Political Economy of Global Engagement', in R. Stubbs and G.R.D. Underhill (eds), *Political Economy and the Changing Global Order*, 3rd edn (Toronto: Oxford University Press).

Brown, C. (1997) *Understanding International Relations* (New York: St Martin's Press).

Buck, P.W. (1942) *The Politics of Mercantilism* (New York: Henry Holt and Co.).

Burgess, E. (1972) 'Hong Kong Electronic Exports Zing', *The Christian Science Monitor*, 4 January.

Burns, J.P. (1991) 'Diminishing *Laissez-Faire*', in S.M. Goldstein (ed.), *Mini Dragons: Fragile Miracles in the Pacific* (Boulder: Westview Press), 104–43.

Burton, J. (2004) 'Malaysia Currency Peg Gets IMF Nod', *Financial Times*, 26 March, 6.

Buzan, B., O.Weaver and J.de Wilde, (1998) *Security: A New Framework for Analysis* (Boulder: Lynne Rienner).

Calder, K.E. (1993) *Strategic Capitalism: Private Business and Public Purpose in Japanese Industrial Finance* (Princeton, NJ: Princeton University Press).

Caldwell, J.A. (1974) *American Economic Aid to Thailand* (Lexington, Mass.: Lexington Books).

Campbell, J.L. (1998) 'Institutional Analysis and the Role of Ideas in Political Economy', *Theory and Society* 27: 377–409.

Castells, M. (1992) 'Four Asian Tigers with a Dragon Head: A Comparative Analysis of the State, Economy and Society in the Asian Pacific Rim', in R.P. Appelbaum and J. Henderson (eds), *States and Development in the Asian Pacific Rim* (Newbury Park: Sage), 33–70.

Castells, M. (1996) *The Information Age: Economy, Society and Culture; Volume I: The Rise of the Network Society* (Oxford: Blackwell).

Cerny, P.G. (2004) 'Political Economy and the Japanese Model in Flux: Phoenix or Quagmire?', *New Political Economy* 9(1) (March), 101–11.

Cha, S.H. (2003) 'Myth and Reality in the Discourse of Confucian Capitalism in Korea', *Asian Survey* 43 (No.3, May–June), 485–506.

Chai-Anan, S., S. Kusuma and B. Suchit (1990) *From Armed Supression to Political Offensive* (Bangkok: Institute of Security and International Studies, Chulalongkorn University).

Chan H.C. (1971) *Singapore: The Politics of Survival, 1965–67* (Kuala Lumpur: Oxford University Press).

Chan H.C. (1975) 'Politics in an Administrative State: Where Has the Politics Gone?' in Seah C.M. (ed.), *Trends in Singapore* (Singapore: Singapore University Press), 31–68.

Chan H.C. (1987) 'Political Parties' in J.S.T. Quah, Chan H.C. and Seah C.M. (eds) *Government and Politics of Singapore* (Singapore: Oxford University Press), 146–72.

Chan, W.K.K. (1982) 'The Organizational Structure of the Traditional Chinese Firm and Its Modern Reform', *Business History Review* 56: 218–35.

Chang H.-J. (1994) *The Political Economy of Industrial Policy* (New York: Cambridge University Press).

Chang H.-J. (1998) 'South Korea: The Misunderstood Crisis' in K.S. Jomo (ed.), *Tigers in Trouble: Financial Governance, Liberalisation and Crises in East Asia* (London: Zed Press), 222–31.

Chapman, W. (1991) *Inventing Japan: An Unconventional Account of the Postwar Years* (New York: Prentice-Hall).

Charoenloet, V. (1991) 'Thailand in the Process of Becoming a NIC: Myth or Reality?', *Journal of Contemporary Asia* 21 (1), 31–41.

Cheah B.K. (1983) *Red Star Over Malaya: Resistance and Social Conflict During and After The Japanese Occupation, 1941–1946* (Singapore: Singapore University Press).

Chee P.L. and Lee P.P. (1979) *The Role of Japanese Direct Investment in Malaysia*, Occasional Paper No.60 (Singapore: Institute of Southeast Asian Studies).

Chen, E.K.Y. and R.C.W. Ng (1999) 'The Financial Sector and Economic Development in Hong Kong: Implications for Developing Countries', in S. Masuyama, D. Vandenbrink and S.Y. Chia (eds), *East Asia's Financial Systems: Evolution and Crisis* (Tokyo: Nomura Research Institute), 200–30.

Chen, E. and R. Ng (2001) 'Economic Restructuring of Hong Kong on the Basis of Innovation and Technology', in S. Masuyama, D. Vandenbrink and S.Y. Chia (eds), *Industrial Restructuring in East Asia: Towards the 21st Century* (Tokyo: Namura Research Institute).

Chen, J. (2001) *Mao's China and the Cold War* (Chapel Hill: University of North Carolina Press).

Cheng, T.-J. (1990) 'Political Regimes and Development Strategies: South Korea and Taiwan', in G. Gereffi and D.L. Wyman (eds), *Manufacturing Miracles: Paths to Industrialization in Latin America and East Asia* (Princeton, NJ: Princeton University Press), 139–78.

Cheng, T.-j. and C.-l. Lin (1999) 'Taiwan: A Long Decade of Democratic Transition', in J.W. Morley (ed.), *Driven by Growth: Political Change in the Asia–Pacific Region* (Armonk: M.E. Sharpe), 224–54.

Chia S.Y. (2001) 'Singapore: Towards a Knowledge-Based Economy', in S. Masuyama, D. Vandenbrink and Chia S.Y. (eds), *Industrial Restructuring in East Asia: Towards the 21st Century* (Tokyo: Namura Research Institute), 169–208.

Chin P. (2003) *My Side of History* (Singapore: Media Masters).

Choi, A.H.-K. (1994) 'Beyond Market and State: A Study of Hong Kong's Industrial Transformation', *Studies in Political Economy* 45 (Fall), 38–64.

Choi, A.H. (1999) 'State–Business Relations and Industrial Restructuring', in T.-W. Ngo (ed.), *Hong Kong History: State and Society Under Colonial Rule* (London: Routledge), 141–61.

Chomchai, P. (1975) 'Thailand', in S. Ichimura (ed.), *The Economic Development of East and Southeast Asia* (Honolulu: University of Hawaii Press), 129–78.

Chow, S.C. and G.F. Papanek, (1981) 'Laissez-Faire, Growth and Equity – Hong Kong', *Economic Journal* 91: 466–85.

Chowdhury, A. and I.Islam (1993) *The Newly Industrialising Economies of East Asia* (London: Routledge).

Christopher, R.C. (1983) *The Japanese Mind: The Goliath Explained* (New York: Linden Press/Simon & Schuster).

Clayton, J.L. (ed.), (1970) *The Economic Impact of the Cold War: Sources and Readings* (New York: Harcourt, Brace and World Inc.).

Clark, C. and S. Chan (eds) (1992) *The Evolving Pacific Basin in the Global Political Economy: Domestic & International Linkages* (Boulder: Lynne Rienner).

Cole, D.C. (1980) 'Foreign Assistance and Korean Development', in D.C.Cole, Y.Lim and P.W. Kuznets (eds), *The Korean Economy – Issues of Development*, Korea Research Monograph No.1 (Berkeley: Institute of East Asian Studies, University of California), 1–29.

Cole, D.C. and P.N. Lyman (1971) *Korean Development: The Interplay of Politics and Economics* (Cambridge, Mass.: Harvard University Press).

Collier, R.B. and D. Collier (1991) *Shaping the Political Arena : Critical Junctures, the Labor Mouvement and Regime Dynamics in Latin America* (Princeton, NJ: Princeton University Press).

Cox, R.W. (1987) *Production, Power and World Order: Social Forces in the Making of History* (New York: Columbia University Press).

Cox, R.W. (1997) 'A Perspective on Globalization', in J.H. Mittleman (ed.), *Globalization: Critical Reflections* (Boulder: Lynne Rienner), 21–30.

Crouzet, F. (1964) 'Wars, Blockade and Economic Change in Europe, 1792–1815', *Journal of Economic History* 24: 567–88.

Cumings, B. (1981) *The Origins of the War in Korea: Volume I, Liberation and the Emergence of Separate Regimes, 1945–1947* (Princeton, NJ: Princeton University Press).

Cumings, B. (1984a) 'The Origins and Development of the Northeast Asian Political Economy: Industrial Sectors, Product Cycles and Political Consequences', *International Organization* 38, No.1 (Winter), 1–40.

Cumings, B. (1984b) 'The Legacy of Japanese Colonialism in Korea', in H.R. Myers and M.R. Peattie (eds), *The Japanese Colonial Empire: 1885–1945* (Princeton, NJ: Princeton University Press), 478–96.

Cumings, B. (1990) *The Origins of the Korean War: Volume II, The Roaring of the Cataract, 1947–1950* (Princeton, NJ: Princeton University Press).

Cumings, B. (1999a) 'Still the American Century', *Review of International Studies* 25 (Special Issue December), 271–99.

Cumings, B. (1999b) 'The Asian Crisis, Democracy, and the End of "Late" Development', in T.J. Pempel (ed.), *The Politics of the Asian Economic Crisis* (Ithaca: Cornell University Press), 17–44.

Curtis, G.L. and S.-J. Han (eds) (1983) *The U.S.–South Korean Alliance: Evolving Patterns in Security Relations* (Lexington, MA Lexington Books).

Dahl, R. (1961) *Who Governs?* (New Haven, CT: Yale University Press).

Davies, D. (1972) 'Malaysia: The Three Year Recovery', *Far Eastern Economic Review*, 6 (May), 12–14.

De Guzman, R.P., A.B. Brillantes Jr., and A.G. Pacho (1988) 'The Bureaucracy', in R.P. De Guzman and M.A. Reforma (eds), *Government and Politics of the Philippines* (Singapore: Oxford University Press), 180–206.

Deane, P. (1975) 'War and Industrialisation', in J.M.Winter (ed.), *War and Economic Development*, pp.91–102.

Deans, P. (2000) 'The Capitalist Developmental State in East Asia', in R.P. Palan and J.P. Abbott (eds), *State Strategies in the Global Political Economy* (London: Pinter), 78–102.

Deans, P. (2004) 'The People's Republic of China: The Post-Socialist Developmental State', in L. Low (ed.), *Developmental States: Relevant, Redundant or Reconfigured?* (New York: Nova Science Publishers).

Dent, C. (2004) 'The New Economic Bilateralism and Southeast Asian: Region-Convergent or Region-Divergent', IPEG Papers in Global Political Economy, No.7 (April), www.bisa.ac.uk/groups/ipeg/ipegpapers.htm. (21.3.05).

Deyo, F.C. (1987) 'Coalitions, Institutions, and Linkage Sequencing – Towards a Strategic Capacity Model of East Asian Development', in F.C. Deyo (ed.), *The Political Economy of the New Asian Industrialism* (Ithaca: Cornell University Press), 227–47.

Deyo, F.C. (1989) *Beneath the Miracle: Labor Subordination in the New Asian Industrialism* (Berkeley: University of California Press).

Doner, R.F. (1991) 'Approaches to the Politics of Economic Growth in Southeast Asia', *The Journal of Asian Studies* 50 November, 818–49.

Doner, R.F. and G. Hawes (1995) 'The Political Economy of Growth in Southeast Asia and Northeast Asia', in M. Dorraj (ed.), *The Changing Political Economy of the Third World* (Boulder: Lynne Rienner), 145–86.

Donnelly, M.W. (2004) 'The Politics of Uncertainty in Japan', *Behind the Headlines* 61 (3), 1–20.

Dore, R. (1997) 'The Distinctiveness of Japan', in C. Crouch and W. Streeck (eds), *The Political Economy of Modern Capitalism* (Thousand Oaks: Sage), 19–32.

Dower, J.W. (1979) *Empire and Aftermath: Yoshida Shigeru and the Japanese Experience, 1878–1954* (Cambridge, MA: Harvard University Council on East Asian Studies).

Dower, J.W. (1999) *Embracing Defeat: Japan in the Wake of World War II* (New York: W.W. Norton).

Drabble, J.H. (2000) *An Economic History of Malaysia, c.1800–1990: The Transition to Modern Economic Growth* (Basingstoke: Macmillan).

Easterly, W. and R. Levine (1996) 'Africa's Growth Tragedy: Policies and Ethnic Divisions', Mimeo, The World Bank, Washington DC (May).

Economist Editorial (1989) 'The Fifth Tiger', *The Economist*, 28 October, 17.

Economist, The (1998) 'A Survey of East Asian Economies: Six Deadly Sins', 7 March, 12–14.

Editorial Staff (1971) 'Singapore Investments: Investment in Singapore', *Asian Research Bulletin* 1–30 November.

Eisenstadt, S.N. (1996) 'Some Observations on the Transformation of Confucianism (and Buddhism) in Japan', in W.-M. Tu (ed.), *Confucian Traditions in East Asian Modernity: Moral Education and Economic Culture in Japan and the Four Mini-Dragons* (Cambridge, MA: Harvard University Press), 175–201.

EIU (1968) *The Economic Effects of the Vietnamese War in East and South East Asia*, QER Special No.3 (London: The Economist Intelligence Unit, November).

Ekelund, R.B. and R.D. Tollison (1997) *Politicized Economies: Monarchy, Monopoly and Mercantilism* (College Station: Texas A & M University Press).

Elliott, T.H. (1973) 'Multinational Corporations: Background Papers, Multinational Corporations in Developing Countries', *Asian Research Bulletin*, 1–31 July.

Elshtain, J.B. (1987) *Women and War* (New York: Basic Books).

Esman, M. (1972) *Administration and Development in Malaysia: Institution Building and Reform in a Plural Society* (Ithaca: Cornell University Press).

Euh, Y.-D. and J.C. Baker (1990) *The Korean Banking System and Foreign Influence* (London: Routledge).

Evans, P. (1992) 'The State as Problem and Solution: Predation, Embedded Autonomy, and Structural Change', in S. Haggard and R.R. Kaufman (eds), *The Politics of Economic Adjustment* (Princeton, NJ: Princeton University Press), 139–81.

Evans, P.B. (1995) *Embedded Autonomy: States and Industrial Transformation* (Princeton, N.J.: Princeton University Press).

Fallows, J. (1994) *Looking for the Sun: The Rise of the New East Asian Economic and Political System* (New York: Pantheon Books).

Fan, S.-C. (1975) 'Hong Kong', in S. Ichimura (ed.), *The Economic Development of East and Southeast Asia* (Honolulu: University Press of Hawaii), 229–67.

FEER (1975) 'Washington Feels the Asian Pulse', *Far Eastern Economic Review* (13 June).

FEER (1987) *Asia 1987 Yearbook* (Hong Kong: Far Eastern Economic Review).

Fleming, D.F. (1961) *The Cold War and Its Origins, 1917–1960*, 2 Vols (Garden City, NY: Doubleday).

Francks, P. (1992) *Japanese Economic Development: Theory and Practice* (London: Routledge).

French, H.W. (2003) '100,000 People Perished, But Who Remembers?', *New York Times*, 14 March.

Friedman, M. (1981) *Free to Choose* (London: Pelican).

Fukuda, K.J. (1988) *Japanese-Style Management Transferred: The Experience of East Asia* (London: Routledge).

Fukushima, K. (2004) 'Challenges for Currency Cooperation in East Asia', *Asia-Pacific Review* 11 (May), 20–45.

Funabashi, Y. (1993) 'The Asianization of Asia', *Foreign Affairs* 72 (November/December), 75–85.

Gallant, N. and R. Stubbs (1997) 'APEC's Dilemmas: Institution-Building Around the Pacific Rim', *Pacific Affairs* 70 (Summer), 203–18.

Garran, R. (1998) *Tigers Tamed: The End of the Asian Miracle* (St Leonards: Allen and Unwin).

Gereffi, G. and D.L. Wyman (eds) (1990) *Manufacturing Miracles: Paths to Industrialization in Latin America and East Asia* (Princeton, NJ: Princeton University Press).

Gerschenkron, A. (1962) *Economic Backwardness in Historical Perspective* (Cambridge: Harvard University Press).

Gills, B. (1993) 'The Hegemonic Transition in East Asia: A Historical Perspective', in S.Gill (ed.,) *Gramsci, Historical Materialism and International Relations* (Cambridge: Cambridge University Press), 186–212.

Gills, B.K. (2000) 'The Crisis of Postwar East Asian Capitalism: American Power, Democracy and the Vicissitudes of Globalization', *Review of International Studies* 26 (3), July, 381–403.

Girling, J.L.S. (1981) *Thailand: Society and Politics* (Ithaca: Cornell University Press).

Goh, C.T. (2003) 'Challenges for Asia', Speech given at the Research Institute for Economy, Trade and Industry, Japan, 28 March.

Gold, T.B. (1986) *State and Society in the Taiwan Miracle* (New York: Sharpe).

Gold, T.B. (1991) 'Taiwan: In Search of Identity', in S.M. Goldstein (ed.), *Mini Dragons: Fragile Economic Miracle in the Pacific* (Boulder: Westview Press), 22–63.

Gomez, E.T. and H.H.M. Hsiao (eds) (2001) *Chinese Business in South-East Asia: Contesting Cultural Explanations: Researching Entrepreneurship* (Surrey: Curzon).

Gomez, E.T. and K.S. Jomo (1997) *Malaysia's Political Economy: Politics, Patronage and Profits* (Cambridge: Cambridge University Press).

Goodstadt L. (1972) 'Hong Kong II: Economy Faces a Period of Major Adjustment', *The Financial Times*, 7 February 1972.

Gourevitch, P. (1978) 'The Second Image Reversed: The International Sources of Domestic Politics' *International Organization* 32 (4), 881–911.

Great Britain (1960) *Hong Kong* (London: Central Office of Information, Reference Division).

Greenspan, A. (1998) 'The Current Asian Crisis and the Dynamics of International Finance', Testimony of Chairman Alan Greenspan before the Committee on Banking and Financial Services, 30 January, US House of Representatives, *Federal Reserve Bulletin* 84 (No.3).

Grimes, W.W. (2001) *Unmaking the Japanese Miracle: Macroeconomic Politics, 1985–2000* (Ithaca: Cornell University Press).

Haggard, S. (1990) *Pathways from the Periphery: The Politics of Growth in the Newly Industrializing Countries* (Ithaca: Cornell University Press).

Haggard, S. (1994) 'Business, Politics and Policy in Northeast and Southeast Asia', in A. MacIntyre (ed.), *Business and Government in Industrialising Asia* (Ithaca: Cornell University Press), 268–301.

Haggard, S. (2004) 'On *Governing the Market*', *Issues and Studies* 40 (No.1, March), 14–45.

Haggard, S. and C.-I. Moon (1983) 'The South Korean State in the International Economy: Liberal, Dependent or Mercantile?' in J.G. Ruggie (ed.), *The Antinomies of Interdependence: National Welfare and the International Division of Labor* (New York: Columbia University Press), 131–89.

Haggard, S., D. Kang and C.-I. Moon (1997) 'Japanese Colonialism and Korean Development: A Critique' *World Development* 25 (6), 867–81.

Haggard, S. and E. Kim (1997) 'The Sources of East Asia's Economic Growth', *Access Asia Review* 1 (1) (Summer), 31–63.

Haggard, S. and A. MacIntyre (1998) 'The Political Economy of the Asian Economic Crisis', *Review of International Political Economy* 5 (3), 381–92.

Hall, P. (1986) *Governing the Economy: The Politics of State Intervention in Britain and France* (New York: Oxford University Press).

Hall, P. (1989) 'Conclusion: The Politics of Keynesian Ideas', in P. Hall (ed.), *The Political Power of Economic Ideas: Keynesianism Across Nations* (Princeton, NJ: Princeton University Press), 360–91.

Hall, P. and R. Taylor (1996) 'Political Science and the Three New Insitutionalisms', *Political Studies* 44 (5) 935–57.

Halliday, F. (1987) 'State and Society in International Relations: A Second Agenda', *Millennium* 16 (2), 215–29.

Hamilton, C. (1987) 'Can the Rest of Asia Emulate the NICs?', *Third World Quarterly* 9 (4): 1225–56.

Hamilton, G.G. (1991) 'The Organizational Foundations of Western and Chinese Commerce: A Historical and Comparative Analysis', in G.G. Hamilton (ed.), *Business Networks and Economic Development in East and Southeast Asia* (Hong Kong: Centre of Asian Studies, University of Hong Kong), 48–65.

Hamilton, G. (1999) 'Asian Business Networks in Transition: Or, What Alan Greenspan Does Not Know About the Asian Business Crisis', in T.J. Pempel (ed.), *The Politics of the Asian Economic Crisis* (Ithaca: Cornell University Press), 45–61.

Hamilton-Hart, N. (2002) *Asian States, Asian Bankers: Central Banking in Southeast Asia* (Ithaca: Cornell University Press).

Han, S.-J. (1978) 'The Republic of Korea and the United States: The Changing Alliance', in S.-J. Kim and C.-W. Kang (eds), *Korea: A Nation in Transition* (Seoul: Research Centre for Peace and Unification), 56–82.

Harianto, F. (1993) *Oriental Capitalism* (Toronto: Centre for International Studies, University of Toronto).

Harlen, C. M. (1999) 'A Reappraisal of Classical Economic Nationalism and Economic Liberalism', *International Studies Quarterly* 43: 733–44.

Hatch, W. and K. Yamamura (1996) *Asia in Japan's Embrace: Building a Regional Production Alliance* (Cambridge: Cambridge University Press).

Hatzfeldt, H. (1969) *Economic Situation in Southeast Asia* (Bangkok: Ford Foundation, November).

Havens, T.R.H. (1987) *Fire Across the Sea: The Vietnam War and Japan 1965–1975* (Princeton, NJ: Princeton University Press).

Hawes, G. (1987) *The Philippine State and the Marcos Regime: The Politics of Export* (Ithaca: Cornell University Press).

Hay, C. (2002) *Political Analysis: A Critical Introduction* (Basingstoke: Palgrave).

Hefner, R.W. (1998) *Market Cultures: Society and Values in the New Asian Capitalisms* (Boulder: Westview Press).

Hein, L.E. (1990) *Fuelling Growth: The Energy Revolution and Economic Policy in Postwar Japan* (Cambridge, Mass.: Harvard University Press).

Hein, L.E. (1993) 'Growth Versus Success: Japan's Economic Policy in Historical Perspective', in A. Gordon (ed.), *Postwar Japan as History* (Berkeley: University of California Press), 99–122.

Helleiner, E. (1994) *States and the Reemergence of Global Finance* (Ithaca: Cornell University Press).

Hersh, J. (1993) *The USA and the Rise of East Asia Since 1945* (Basingstoke: Macmillan).

Hewison, K. (1989) *Bankers and Bureaucrats: Capital and the Role of the State in Thailand* (New Haven, Conn.: Yale Center for International and Area Studies).

Hewison, K. (1997) 'Thailand: Capitalist Development and the State', in G. Rodan, K. Hewison and R. Robison (eds), *The Political Economy of South-East Asia: An Introduction* (Melbourne: Oxford University Press), 93–120.

Hewison, K. (2001) 'Thailand's Capitalism: Development through Boom and Bust', in G. Rodan, K. Hewison and R. Robison (eds), *The Political Economy of South-East Asia: Conflicts, Crisis, and Change*, 2nd edn (Melbourne: Oxford University Press), 71–103.

Hicks, G. (1996) 'The "Comfort Women"', in P.Duus, R.H. Myers and M.R. Peattie (eds), *The Japanese Wartime Empire, 1931–1945* (Princeton, NJ: Princeton University Press), 305–23.

Hicks, G.L. and S.G. Redding (1983) *Industrial East Asia and the Post-Confucian Hypothesis: A Challenge to Economics* (Hong Kong: University of Hong Kong Centre of Asian Studies).

Higgott, R.A. (1983) *Political Development Theory* (London: Croom Helm).

Higgott, R. (1998) 'The Asian Economic Crisis: A Study in the Politics of Resentment', *New Political Economy* 3 (November), 333–56.

Higgott, R. and R. Stubbs (1995) 'Competing Conceptions of Economic Regionalism: APEC versus EAEC in the Asia-Pacific', *Review of International Political Economy* 2 (3), Summer, 516–35.

Ho, S.P.S. (1978) *Economic Development of Taiwan, 1860–1970* (New Haven, Conn.: Yale University Press).

Ho, S.P.S. (1987) 'Economics, Economic Bureaucratic Bureaucracy, and Taiwan's Economic Development', *Pacific Affairs* 60 (2), Summer, 226–47.

Hobson, J.M. (2000) *The State and International Relations* (Cambridge: Cambridge University Press).

Hofheinz, R. Jr, and K.E. Calder (1982) *The Eastasia Edge* (New York: Basic Books).

Holloway, N. (1991) 'The New NICs', *Far Eastern Economic Review*, 28 February: 72.

Horowitz, D. (1965) *From Yalta to Vietnam: American Foreign Policy in the Cold War* (Harmondsworth: Penguin).

Hsiao, F.S.T. and M.-C. W. Hsiao (2003) ' "Miracle Growth" in the Twentieth Century? International Comparisons of East Asian Development', *World Development* 31 (2), 227–57.

Huff, W.G. (1994) *The Economic Growth of Singapore: Trade and Development in the Twentieth Century* (Cambridge: Cambridge University Press).

Hughes, C. (2005) 'Japan, East Asian Regionalism and Selective Resistance to Globalisation: Regional Divisions of Labour and Financial Cooperation', in R. Stubbs and G.R.D. Underhill (eds), *Political Economy and the Changing Global Order*, 3rd edn (Toronto: Oxford University Press).

Hughes, H. (1980) 'Achievements and Objectives of Industrialization', in J. Cody, H. Hughes and D. Wall (eds), *Policies for Industrial Progress in Developing Countries* (New York: Oxford University Press).

Hui, P.-K. (1999) 'Comprador Politics and Middleman Capitalism', in T.-W. Ngo (ed.), *Hong Kong's History: State and Society Under Colonial Rule* (London: Routledge), 30–45.

Humphrey, J.D. (1971) 'Population Resettlement in Malaya', Ph.D dissertation, Northwestern University.

Hungchangsith, B. (1974) 'Economic Impact of the US Military Presence in Thailand 1960–972', PhD, Graduate Faculty of Economic, Claremont Graduate School.

Huntington, S.H. (1991) *The Third Wave: Democratization in the Late Twentieth Century* (Norman, Okla.: Oklahoma Press).

Hutchcroft, P.D. (1998) *Booty Capitalism: The Politics of Banking in the Philippines* (Ithaca: Cornell University Press).

Ike, N. (1963) 'Japan', in G.M. Kahin (ed.), *Major Governments of Asia*, 2nd edn (Ithaca: Cornell University Press), 153–265.

Ikenberry, G.J. (1988) 'Conclusion: An Institutional Approach to American Foreign Economic Policy', in G.J. Ikenberry, D.A. Lake and M. Mastanduno (eds), *The State and American Foreign Economic Policy* (Ithaca: Cornell University Press), 219–43.

IMF (various years) *Direction of Trade, Yearbook* (Washington: International Monetary Fund).

IMF (1971) *Direction of Trade: Annual 1966–70* (Washington: International Monetary Fund).

IMF (1978) *Direction of Trade: Annual 1971–77* (Washington: International Monetary Fund).

Inada, J. (1989) 'Japan's Aid Policy: Economic, Political or Strategic?', paper presented to the International Studies Association Convention, 30 March, London.

International Bank for Reconstruction and Development (1971) *World Tables,* Economic Program Department, Socio-Economic Data Division (Washington: IBRD).

International Development Study Group (1989) 'Shortcomings of the Foreign Aid Program', *Economic Eye* 10 (Spring), 16–19.

IMF (1997) *International Financial Statistics* (Washington: International Monetary Fund, May).

IMF (2003) *Foreign Direct Investment Trends and Statistics* (Washington: International Monetary Fund, Statistics Department, October 28).

Islam, I. (1994) 'Between the State and the Market: The Case for Eclectic Neoclassical Political Economy', in Andrew MacIntrye, *Business and Government in Industrialising Asia* (Ithaca: Cornell University Press), 91–112.

Jacobs, N. (1985) *The Korean Road to Modernization and Development* (Urbana: University of Illinois Press).

Jacoby, N.H. (1966) *U.S. Aid to Taiwan: A Study of Foreign Aid, Self Help, and Development* (New York: Frederick A. Praeger).

Jansen, K. (1991) 'Thailand: The Next NIC?', *Journal of Contemporary Asia* 21 (No.1), 13–30.

Japanese Government (1993) *Annual Report of Japanese ODA* (Tokyo: Ministry of Foreign Affairs).

Jayakumar, S. (1996) *The Southeast Asian Drama: Evolution and Future Challenges*, Inaugural Distinguished Lecture on Southeast Asia (Washington, DC: Georgetown University, 22 April).

Jessop, B. (1982) *The Capitalist State: Marxist Theories and Methods* (New York: New York University Press).

Jesudason, J.V. (1989) *Ethnicity and the Economy: The State, Chinese Business, and Multinationals in Malaysia* (Singapore: Oxford University Press).

Johnson, C. (1982) *MITI and the Japanese Miracle: The Growth of Industrial Policy 1925–1975* (Stanford: Stanford University Press).

Johnson, C. (1987) 'Political Institutions and Economic Performance: The Government–Business Relationship in Japan, South Korea and Taiwan', in F.C. Deyo (ed.), *The Political Economy of New Asian Industrialism* (Ithaca: Cornell University Press).

Jomo K.S. (1987) 'Economic Crisis and Policy Response in Malaysia', in R. Robison, K. Hewison and R. Higgott (eds), *Southeast Asia in the 1980s: The Politics of Economic Crisis* (Sydney: Allen and Unwin), 113–48.

Jomo K.S. (1997) *Southeast Asia's Misunderstood Miracle: Industrial Policy and Economic Development in Thailand, Malaysia and Indonesia* (Boulder: Westview Press).

Jomo K.S. (1998a) 'Introduction: Financial Governance, Liberalisation and Crises in East Asia', in K.S. Jomo (ed.), *Tigers in Trouble: Financial Governance, Liberalisation and Crises in East Asia* (London: Zed Press), 1–32.

Jomo K.S. (1998b) 'Malaysia: From Miracle to Debacle' in K.S. Jomo (ed.), *Tigers in Trouble: Financial Governance, Liberalisation and Crises in East Asia* (London: Zed Press), 181–98.

Jomo K.S. (2001) 'Rethinking the Role of Government Policy in Southeast Asia', in J.E. Stiglitz and S. Yusuf (eds), *Rethinking The East Asian Miracle* (Oxford: Oxford University Press), 461–508.

Kahn, H. (1970) *The Emerging Japanese Super State* (Englewood Cliffs, NJ: Prentice-Hall).

Kanapathy, V. (2001) 'Industrial Restructuring in Malaysia: Policy Shifts and the Promotion of New Sources of Growth', in S. Masuyama, D. Vandenbrink and S.Y. Chia (eds), *Industrial Restructuring in East Asia: Towards the 21st Century* (Tokyo: Namura Research Institute), 139–68.

Kang, D.C. (2002) *Crony Capitalism: Corruption and Development in South Korea and the Philippines* (Cambridge: Cambridge University Press).

Karl, T.L. (1997) *The Paradox of the Plenty: Oil Booms and the Petro-States* (Berkeley: University of California Press).

Katzenstein, P.J. (1996) *Cultural Norms and National Security: Police and Military in Postwar Japan* (Ithaca: Cornell University Press).

Kerr, G. (1965) *Formosa Betrayed* (Boston, MA: Houghton-Mifflin).

Kim, S.J. (1970) 'South Korea's Involvement in Vietnam and Its Economic and Political Impact', *Asian Survey* 10: 519–32.

Kim, H.-K. (1973) 'The Japanese Colonial Administration in Korea – An Opinion', in A.H. Nahm (ed.), *Korean Under Japanese Colonial Rule: Studies in the Policy and Techniques of Japanese Colonialism*, Korea Studies Series 2 (Kalamazoo, MI: Center for Korean Studies, Western Michigan University), 44–53.

Kim, J.A. (1976) *Divided Korea: The Politics of Development, 1945–1972* (Cambridge, Mass.: East Asian Research Center, Harvard University).

Kim, J.-I. and L.J. Lau (1994) 'The Sources of Economic Growth of the East Asian Newly Industrializing Countries', *Journal of the Japanese and International Economies* 8 (No.3), 235–71.

Kim, H.-D. (1990) *Korea and the United States: The Evolving Transpacific Alliance in the 1960s* (Seoul: Research Center for Peace and Unification of Korea).

Kim, W.B. (1993) 'China and the Asian NIEs: Emerging Symbiotic Relations', Paper prepared for the Conference on China and the Asian NIEs: The Emerging Pattern of Investment, May, Shanghai.

Kim, W.B. (1995) 'Patterns of Industrial Restructuring', in G.L. Clark and W.B. Kim (eds), *Asian NIEs and the Global Economy: Industrial Restructuring and Corporate Strategy in the 1990s* (Balitimore: Johns Hopkins University Press), 219–51.

King, D.C. (1995) 'South Korean and Taiwanese Development and the New Institutional Economics', *International Organization* 49 (Summer), 555–87.

Kingsbury, D. (2001) *South-East Asia: A Political Profile* (Melbourne: Oxford University Press).

Knack, S. and P. Keefer (1995) 'Institutions and Economic Performance: Cross-Country Tests Using Alternative Institutional Measures', *Economics and Politics* 7 (3), 207–27.

Kobayashi, H. (1996) 'The Postwar Economic Legacy of Japan's Wartime Empire', in P.Duus, R.H. Myers and M.R. Peattie (eds), *The Japanese Wartime Empire, 1931–1945* (Princeton, N.J.: Princeton University Press) 324–34.

Koh, C.H. (1970) *The Impact of the War in Vietnam on the Economy of Singapore (1965–1969)* (Singapore: Economics Section, Economic Development Division, Ministry of Finance).

Kohama, H. (2003) 'Japan's Development Cooperation in East Asia: A Historical Overview of Japan's ODA and Its Impact', in H. Kohama (ed.), *External Factors for Asian Development* (Singapore: Institute of Southeast Asian Studies), 8–46.

Kohli, A. (1994) 'Where do High Growth Political Economies Come From? The Japanese Lineage of Korea's "Developmental State"', *World Development* 22 (9), 1269–93.

Kohli, A. (1997) 'Japanese Colonialism and Korean Development: A Reply', *World Development* 25 (6), 883–8.

Koo, H. (1984) 'The Political Economy of Income Distribution in South Korea: The Impact of the State's Industrial Policy', *World Development* 12 (10), 1029–37.

Kotch, J. (1983) 'The Origins of the American Security Commitment to Korea', in B. Cumings (ed.), *Child of Conflict: The Korean-American Relationship, 1943–1957* (Seattle: University of Washington Press), 239–59.

Kraitzer, B. (1972) 'Doubts Over Electronics', *The Financial Times*, 7 February (Hong Kong Supplement).

Krasner, S.D. (1988) 'Sovereignty: An Institutional Perspective', *Comparative Political Studies*, 21 (1), 66–94.

Krause, L.B. (1988) 'Hong Kong and Singapore: Twins or Kissing Cousins?', *Economic Development and Cultural Change* 36 (3), April Supplement, S45–S66.

Kristof, N.D. (1998) 'Crisis Pushing Asian Capitalism Closer to US-Style Free Market', *New York Times*, 17 January.

Krueger, A.O. (1978) *Foreign Trade Regimes and Economic Development: Liberalization Attempts and Consequences* (Cambridge, MA: Ballinger for the National Bureau of Economic Research).

Krugman, P. (1994) 'The Myth of Asia's Miracle', *Foreign Affairs* 73 (6), November/December, 62–78.

Kugler, J. and M. Arbetman (1989) 'Exploring the "Phoenix Factor" with the Collective Goods Perspective', *Journal of Conflict Resolution* 33 (1), March, 84–112.

Kuznets, P.W. (1980) 'The Korean Economy: A Contemporary Case of Accelerated Growth', in D.C. Cole, Y. Lim and P.W. Kuznets (eds), *The Korean Economy – Issues of Development*, Korea Research Monograph No.1 (Berkeley: Institute of East Asian Studies, University of California), 59–80.

Kwon, J. (1994) 'The East Asia Challenge to Neoclassical Orthodoxy', *World Development* 22 (4), 635–44.

Kwon, T.-S. (2003) 'The IMF Must Learn From Its Mistakes', *Financial Times*, 14 August, 13.

Lall, S. (1994) '*The East Asian Miracle*: Does the Bell Toll for Industrial Strategy?', *World Development* 22 (4), 645–54.

Lau, A. (1998) *A Moment of Anguish: Singapore in Malaysia and the Politics of Disengagement* (Singapore: Times Academic Press).

Lau S.-K. (1983) *Society and Politics in Hong Kong* (Hong Kong: The Chinese University Press).

Lee K.Y. (1998) *The Singapore Story: Memoirs of Lee Kuan Yew* (Singapore: Prentice Hall).

Lee, J. (1999) 'East Asian NIEs' Model of Development: Miracle, Crisis, and Beyond', *The Pacific Review* 12 (2), 141–62.

Lee, Y.-H (2000) 'The Failure of the Weak State in Economic Liberalization: Liberalization , Democratization and the Financial Crisis in South Korea', *The Pacific Review* 13 (1), 115–31.

Lee, Y.-H. and H.-R. Kim (2000) 'The Dilemma of Market Liberalization: The Financial Crisis and the Transformation of Capitalism', in R. Robison, M. Beeson, K. Jayasuria and H.-R. Kim (eds), *Politics and Markets in the Wake of the Asian Crisis* (London: Routledge), 116–29.

Leifer, M. (2000) *Singapore's Foreign Policy: Coping with Vulnerability* (London: Routledge).

Levin, N.D.and R.L. Sneider (1983) 'Korea in Postwar Security Policy', in G.L. Curtis and S.-J. Han (eds), *The US South Korean Alliance: Evolving Pattens in Security Relations* (Lexington: Lexington Books), 31–64.

Li, K.-W. (2002) *Capitalist Development and Economism in East Asia: The Rise of Hong Kong, Singapore, Taiwan, and South Korea* (London: Routledge).

Liang, K.-S. and T.-H. Lee (1975) 'Taiwan', in S. Ichimura (ed.), *The Economic Development of East and Southeast Asia* (Honolulu: University Press of Hawaii), 269–346.

Lim C.Y. and Ow C.H. (1971) 'The Singapore Economy and the Vietnam War', in You P.S. and Lim C.Y., *In the Singapore Economy* (Singapore: Eastern Universities Press).

Lim H.S. (2003) *Japan's Role in Asia: Mutual Development or Ruthless Competition*, 4th edn (Singapore: Eastern Universities Press).

Lim, L.Y.C. (1983) 'Singapore's Economy: The Myth of the Free Market Economy', *Asian Survey* 23 (6), 752–64.

Lin, T.-B. and V.Mok (1985) 'Trade, Foreign Investment and Development in Hong Kong', in W. Galenson, *Foreign Trade and Investment* (Wisconsin: University of Wisconsin Press), 219–56.

Lindblad, J.T. (1998) *Foreign Investment in Southeast Asia in the Twentieth Century* (Basingstoke: Macmillan).

Littauer, R. and N. Uphoff (eds), (1972) *The Air War in Indochina*, revised edn (Boston, MA: Beacon Press).

Little, I.M.D. (1979) 'An Economic Reconnaissance', in W. Galenson, *Economic Growth and Structural Change Taiwan: The Post War Experience of the Republic of China* (Ithaca: Cornell University Press), 449–65.

Little, I.M.D. (1982) *Economic Development: Theory, Policy and International Relations* (New York: Basic Books).

Little, I.M.D., T. Scitovsky and M. Scott (1970) *Industry and Trade in Some Developing Countries: A Comparative Study* (Oxford: Oxford University Press).

Liu, S. (1997) 'Hong Kong: A Survey of its Political and Economic Development Over the Past 150 Years', *China Quarterly* 151 (September), 583–92.

Loh, S.H. (1970–1) 'The Impact of the Vietnam War on the Economy of Singapore', An Academic Exercise Presented to the Department of Economics, University of Singapore.

Loriaux, M. (1997) 'The End of Credit Activism in Interventionist States', in M. Loriaux *et al.*, *Capital Ungoverned: Liberalizing Finance in Interventionist States* (Ithaca: Cornell University Press), 1–16.

Low, L. (2001) 'The Role of the Government in Singapore's Industrialization', in K.S. Jomo (ed.), *Southeast Asia's Industrialization: Industrial Policy, Capabilities and Sustainability* (Basingstoke: Palgrave), 113–28.

Lowe, P. (1997) *The Origins of the Korean War*, 2nd edn (London: Longman).

Lucas, R.E.B. (1993) 'On the Determinants of Direct Foreign Investment: Evidence from East and Southeast Asia', *World Development* 21 (3), 391–406.

Luk, B.H.-K. (2003) 'Hong Kong's Post-1997 Transition in Perspective', *Pacific Affairs* 76 (Summer), 257–63.

Lyons, G.M. (1961) *Military Policy and Economic Aid: The Korean Case, 1950–1953* (Columbus: The Ohio State University Press).

Ma, K. (2001) 'Taiwan as the Asia-Pacific Regional Operations Centre: Its Significance and Prospects', in S. Masuyama, D. Vandenbrink and S.Y. Chia (eds), *Industrial Restructuring in East Asia: Towards the 21st Century* (Tokyo: Namura Research Institute), 239–55.

McBeth, J. (1989) 'The Boss System: Manila's Disarray Leaves Countryside Under Local Barons', *Far Eastern Economic Review*, 14 September.

Macdonald, D.S. (1988) *The Koreans: Contemporary Politics and Society* (Boulder: Westview Press).

McDonald, T.J. (ed.) (1996) *The Historic Turn in the Human Sciences* (Ann Arbor: University of Michigan Press).

McGurn, W. (1996) 'Diminishing Returns', *Far Eastern Economic Review* (June 13), 62–6.

McLeod, R. and R. Garnaut (eds) (1998) *East Asia in Crisis: From Being a Miracle to Needing One?* (London: Routledge).

MacIntyre, A. (1994a) 'Business, Government and Development: Northeast and Southeast Asian Comparisons', in A. MacIntyre (ed.), *Business and Government in Industrialising Asia* (Ithaca: Cornell University Press), 1–28.

MacIntyre, A. (1994b) 'Power, Prosperity and Patrimonialism: Business and Government in Indonesia', in A. MacIntyre (ed.), *Business and Government in Industrialising Asia* (Ithaca: Cornell University Press), 244–67.

MacIntyre, A. (2001) 'Institutions and Investors: The Politics of the Economic Crisis in Southeast Asia', *International Organization* 55 (Winter), 81–122.

Maddison, A. (2003) *The World Economy: Historical Statistics* (Paris: Development Centre, Organisation for Economic Co-operation and Development).

Mahathir M. and S. Ishihara (1995) *The Voice of Asia: Two Leaders Discuss the Coming Century* (Tokyo: Kodansha International).

Mahbubani, K. (1995) 'The Pacific Way', *Foreign Affairs* 74 (January/February), 100–12.

Malaya, Federation of (1956) *Rubber Statistics Handbook* (Kuala Lumpur: Government Printer).

Malaysia (1979) *Mid-Term Review of the Third Malaysia Plan 1976–80* (Kuala Lumpur: Government of Malaysia).

March, J.G and J.P. Olsen (1989) *Rediscovering Institutions: The Original Basis of Politics* (New York: The Free Press).

Masuyama, S. and D. Vandenbrink (2001) 'Industrial Restructuring in East Asian Economies for the Twenty-First Century', in S. Masuyama, D. Vandenbrink and S.Y. Chia (eds), *Industrial Restructuring in East Asia: Towards the 21st Century* (Tokyo: Namura Research Institute), 3–54.

Mathias, R. (1999) 'Women and the War in Japan', in E. Pauer (ed.), *Japan's War Economy* (London: Routledge), 65–84.

Mauzy, D. (1983) *Barisan Nasional: Coalition Government in Malaysia* (Kuala Lumpur: Maricans).

Mauzy, D. (2001) 'Democracy, Asian Values and the Question of Governance', in A. Acharya, B.M. Frolic and R. Stubbs (eds), *Democracy, Human*

Rights, and Civil Society in South East Asia (Toronto: Joint Centre for Asia Pacific Studies, York University–University of Toronto), 107–22.

Mays, M. and M. Preiss (2003) 'The Asian Bond Market Initiative', FinanceAsia.com, 7 November, www.financeasia.com/ (10/11/03).

Means, G.P. (1976) *Malaysian Politics* (London: Hodder and Stoughton).

Mehmet, O. (1986) *Development in Malaysia: Poverty, Wealth and Trusteeship* (London: Croom Helm).

Merrill, J. (1983) 'Internal Warfare in Korea, 1948–1950: The Local Setting of the Korean War', in B. Cumings (ed.), *Child of Conflict: The Korean–American Relationship, 1943–1957* (Seattle: University of Washington Press), 133–62.

Migdal, J.S. (1988) *Strong Societies and Weak States: State–Society Relations and State Capabilities in the Third World* (Princeton, NJ: Princeton University Press).

Migdal, J.S. (2001) *State in Society: Studying How State and Societies Transform and Constitute One Another* (Cambridge: Cambridge University Press).

Miller, A.C. (1968) 'Hong Kong Captures a Boom Market', *The Observer Foreign News Service*, 2 July.

Milliband, R. (1969) *The State in Capitalist Society: An Analysis of the Western System of Power* (London: Weidenfeld and Nicolson).

Mills, C.W. (1956) *The Power Elite* (New York: Oxford University Press).

Milne, R.S. and D.K. Mauzy (1978) *Politics and Government in Malaysia* (Vancouver: University of British Columbia Press).

Milne, R.S. and D.K. Mauzy (1990) *Singapore: The Legacy of Lee Kuan Yew* (Boulder: Westview).

Milne, R.S. and D.K. Mauzy (1999) *Malaysian Politics Under Mahathir* (London: Routledge).

Milner, A. (2003) 'Asia-Pacific Perceptions of the Financial Crisis: Lessons and Affections', *Contemporary Southeast Asia* 25 (August), 284–305.

Miners, N.J. (1975) *The Government and Politics of Hong Kong* (Hong Kong: Oxford University Press).

Mitchell, B.R. (1982) *International Historical Statistics: Africa and Asia* (London: Macmillan).

Montes, M.F. (1998) *The Currency Crisis in Southeast Asia: Updates Edition* (Singapore: Institute of Southeast Asian Studies).

Montes, M.F. and M.A. Abdusalamov (1998) 'Indonesia: Reaping the Market', in K.S. Jomo (ed.), *Tigers in Trouble: Financial Governance, Liberalisation and Crisis in East Asia* (London: Zed Books), 162–80.

Morishima, M. (1982) *Why Has Japan 'Succeeded'?: Western Technology and the Japanese Ethos* (Cambridge: Cambridge University Press).

Morris-Suzuki, T. (1989) *A History of Japanese Economic Thought* (London: Routledge).

Muscat, R.J. (1990) *Thailand and the United States: Development, Security, and Foreign Aid* (New York: Columbia University Press).

Muscat, R.J. (1994) *The Fifth Tiger: A Study of Thai Development Policy* (Armonk: M.E. Sharpe/United Nations University Press).

Nakamura, T. (1981) *The Postwar Japanese Economy: Its Development and Structure* (Tokyo: Tokyo University Press).

Naya, S. (1971) 'The Vietnam War and Some Aspects of Its Economic Impact on Asian Countries', *The Developing Economies* 9 (1) (March), 31–57.

Nelson, R.R. and H. Pack (1999) 'The Asian Growth Miracle and Modern Growth Theory', *Economic Journal* 109 (July), 416–36.

Nesadurai, H.E.S. (2000) 'In Defence of National Economic Autonomy? Malaysia's Response to the Financial Crisis', *The Pacific Review* 13 (1), 73–114.

Nordlinger, E.A. (1981) *On the Autonomy of the Democratic State* (Cambridge, Mass.: Harvard University Press, 1981).

North, D.C. (1990) *Institutions, Institutional Change and Economic Performance* (New York: Cambridge University Press).

Nuechterlein, D.E. (1967) 'Thailand: Another Vietnam?', *Asian Survey* 7 (February), 126–30.

OECD (1979) *The Impact of Newly Industrializing Countries on Production and Trade in Manufactures* (Paris: Organisation for Economic Cooperation and Development).

OECD (various dates) *International Direct Investment Statistics Yearbook* (Paris: Organisation for Economic Cooperation and Development).

Onis, Z. (1991) 'The Logic of the Developmental State', *Comparative Politics* 24 (1), October, 109–26.

Ono, H. (2001) 'Restructuring Strategy of Japan's Services Sector in the Twenty-First Century', in S. Masuyama, D. Vandenbrink and S.Y. Chia (eds), *Industrial Restructuring in East Asia: Towards the 21st Century* (Tokyo: Namura Research Institute), 327–52.

Organski, A.F.K. and J. Kugler (1977) 'The Costs of Major Wars: The Phoenix Factor', *American Political Science Review* 71 (4), 1347–66.

Organski, A.F.K. and J. Kugler (1980) *The War Ledger* (Chicago: University of Chicago Press).

Orr, R.M. Jr (1987) 'The Rising Sun: Japan's Foreign Aid to ASEAN, the Pacific Basin and the Republic of Korea', *Journal of International Affairs* 41 (Summer/Fall), 39–62.

Orr, R.M. Jr (1990) *The Emergence of Japan's Foreign Aid Power* (New York: Columbia University Press).

Orrù, M. (1991) 'Practical and Theoretical Aspects of Japanese Business Networks', in G.G. Hamilton (ed.), *Business Networks and Economic Development in East and Southeast Asia* (Hong Kong: Centre of Asian Studies, University of Hong Kong), 244–71.

Orrù, M. (1997) 'The Institutional Analysis of Capitalist Economies', in M Orrù, N.W. Biggart, and G.G. Hamilton (eds), *The Economic Organization of East Asian Capitalism* (Thousand Oaks: Sage), 297–310.

Orrù, M., N.W. Biggart and G.G. Hamilton (1991) 'Organizational Isomorphism in East Asia', in W.W. Powell and P.J. DiMaggio (eds), *The New Institutionalism in Organizational Analysis* (Chicago: University of Chicago Press), 361–89.

Ortis, C. (1999) 'The Asian Economic Crisis: The Changing Nature of the Relationship Between Domestic Institutions and the International System', MA Thesis, Department of Political Science, McMaster University.

Packer, F. (1994) 'The Role of Long-term Credit Banks Within the Main Bank System', in M. Aoki and H. Patrick (eds), *The Main Bank System: Its Relevance for Developing and Transforming Economies* (Oxford: Oxford University Press), 142–87.

Pang, E.-S. (2000) 'The Financial Crisis of 1997–98 and the End of the Asian Developmental State', *Contemporary Southeast Asia* 22 (3), 570–93.

Pasuk, P. (1987) *Decision-Making on Overseas Direct Investment by Japanese Small and Medium Industries* (Bangkok: Economics Research Unit, Chulalongkorn University).

Pasuk, P. (1990) *The New Wave of Japanese Investment in ASEAN* (Singapore: Institute of Southeast Asian Studies).

Pasuk, P. and C. Baker (1995) *Thailand: Economy and Politics* (Kuala Lumpur: Oxford University Press).

Pasuk, P. and C. Baker (1998) *Thailand's Boom and Bust* (Chiang Mai: Silkworm Books).

Pasuk, P and C. Baker (2004) *Thaksin: The Business of Politics in Thailand* (Chiang Mai: Silkworm Books).

Patrick, H. and H. Rosovsky (1976) *Asia's New Giant: How the Japanese Economy Works* (Washington: Brookings Institute).

Pempel, T.J. (1998) *Regime Shift: Comparative Dynamics of the Japanese Political Economy* (Ithaca: Cornell University Press).

Pempel, T.J. (1999) 'The Developmental Regime in a Changing World Order', in M. Woo-Cumings (ed.), *The Developmental State* (Ithaca: Cornell University Press), 137–81.

Petri, P. (1993) 'The East Asian Trading Bloc: An Analytical History', in J. Frankel and M. Kahler (eds), *Regionalism and Rivalry: Japan and the US in Pacific Asia* (Chicago: University of Chicago Press), 21–48.

Pierson, P. (2000a) 'Increasing Returns, Path Dependence, and the Study of Politics', *American Political Science Review* 94 (June), 251–67.

Pierson, P. (2000b) 'Not just what, but When: Timing and Sequence in Political Processes', *Studies in American Political Development* 14: 72–92.

Polanyi, K. (1944) *The Great Transformation* (Boston, MA: Beacon Press).

Porter, B.D. (1994) *War and the Rise of the State: The Military Foundations of Modern Politics* (New York: The Free Press).

Powell, W.W. and P.J. DiMaggio (eds) (1991) *The New Institutionalism in Organizational Analysis* (Chicago: Chicago University Press).

Pye, L. (1985) *Asian Power and Politics: The Cultural Dimensions of Authority* (Cambridge, MA: Harvard University Press).

Ramsey, J.A. (1976) 'Modernization and Centralization in Northern Thailand, 1875–1910', *Journal of Southeast Asian Studies* 7 (March), 16–32.

Rao, B. (2001) *East Asian Economies: The Miracle, a Crisis and the Future* (Singapore: McGraw-Hill).

Ravenhill, J. (2000) 'APEC Adrift: Implications for Economic Regionalism in Asia and the Pacific', *The Pacific Review* 13 (2), 319–33.

Redding, S.G. (1990) *The Spirit of Chinese Capitalism* (New York: de Gruyter).

Redding, S.G. (1991) 'Weak Organizations and Strong Linkages: Managerial Ideology and Chinese Family Business Networks', in G.G. Hamilton (ed.), *Business Networks and Economic Development in East and Southeast Asia*

(Hong Kong: Centre of Asian Studies, University of Hong Kong), 30–47.

Rees, D. (1964) *The Limited War* (New York: St Martin's Press).

Reischauer, E.O. and A.M. Craig, (1978) *Japan: Tradition and Transformation* (Boston, MA: Houghton Mifflin).

Republic of China (various years) *Key Statistics*, Industrial Development and Investment Center, MOEA, http://investintaiwan.nat.gov.tw/en/env/ stats/gdp_growth.html last accessed 16 March 2005.

Rich, P. and R. Stubbs, (1997) 'Introduction', in P. Rich and R. Stubbs (eds.), *The Counter-insurgent State* (London: Macmillan), 1–25.

Riedel, J. (1988) 'Economic Development in East Asia: Doing What Comes Naturally?', in Helen Hughes (ed.), *Achieving Industrialization in East Asia* (Cambridge: Cambridge University Press), 1–38.

Robertson, J.L. (2005) 'Capitalizing on Crisis? U.S. Power in the Aftermath of the Asian Financial Crisis', PhD thesis, Department of Politics and International Studies, Warwick University.

Robison, R. (1986) *Indonesia: The Rise of Capital* (North Sydney: Allen and Unwin).

Robison, R. (2001) 'Indonesia: Crisis, Oligarchy and Reform', in G. Rodan, K. Hewison and R. Robison, *The Political Economy of South-East Asia: Conflicts, Crises and Change* (Melbourne: Oxford University Press), 104–37.

Robison, R. and A. Rosser (2000) 'Surviving the Meltdown: Liberal Reform and Political Oligarchy in Indonesia', in R. Robison, M. Beeson, K. Jayasuria and H.-R. Kim (eds), *Politics and Markets in the Wake of the Asian Crisis* (London: Routledge), 171–91.

Rodan, G. (1989) *The Political Economy of Singapore's Industrialization: National State and International Capital* (Basingstoke: Macmillan).

Rodan, G. (2001) 'Singapore: Globalisation and the Politics of Economic Restructuring', in G. Rodan, K. Hewison and R. Robison (eds), *The Political Economy of South-East Asia: Conflicts, Crises, and Change* (Melbourne: Oxford University Press), 138–77.

Rodrik, D. (1998) 'TFPG Controversies, Institutions and Economic Performance in East Asia', in Y. Hayami and M. Aoki (eds), *The Institutional Foundations of East Asian Economic Development: Proceedings of the IEA Conference Held in Tokyo, Japan* (Basingstoke: Macmillan), 79–105.

Rudner, M. (1989) 'Japanese Official Development Assistance to Southeast Asia', *Modern Asian Studies* 23 (1), 73–116.

Rueschemeyer, D. and P.B. Evans (1985) 'The State and Economic Transformation: Toward an Analysis of the Conditions Underlying Effective Intervention', in P.B. Evans, D. Rueschemeyer and T. Skocpol (eds), *Bringing the State Back in* (Cambridge: Cambridge University Press), 44–77.

Russett, B.M. (1966) 'The Asia Rimland as a "Region" for Containing China', *Southeast Asia Development Advisory Group, Paper 3* (New York: The Asia Society, 19 December).

Sakakibara, E. (2001) 'Interview With Eisuke Sakakibara', PBS: Commanding Heights, 15 May, www.pbs.org/wgbh/commandingheights

Samuels, R.J. (1994) *'Rich Nations Strong Army': National Security and the Technological Transformation of Japan* (Ithaca: Cornell University Press).

Scalapino, R.A. (1980) 'Foward', in D.C. Cole, Y. Lim and P.W. Kuznets (eds), *The Korean Economy – Issues of Development*, Korea Research Monograph No. 1 (Berkeley: Institute of East Asian Studies, University of California), i–iv.

Schaller, M. (1997) *Altered States: The United States and Japan Since the Occupation* (New York: Oxford University Press).

Scharpf, F. (1999) *Governing in Europe: Effective and Democratic* (Oxford: Oxford University Press).

Schiffer, J. (1983) *Anatomy of a Laissez-Faire Government: The Hong Kong Growth Model Reconsidered* (Hong Kong: Centre for Urban Studies, University of Hong Kong).

Schive, C. (1990) 'The Next Stage of Industrialization in Taiwan and South Korea', in G. Gereffi and D.L. Wyman (eds), *Manufacturing Miracles: Paths of Industrialization in Latin America and East Asia* (Princeton, NJ: Princeton University Press), 267–91.

Scott, M.F. (1979) 'Foreign Trade', in W. Galenson (ed.), *Economic Growth and Structural Change in Taiwan: The Postwar Experience of the Republic of China* (Ithaca: Cornell University Press), 308–83.

Seah C.M. (1987) 'The Civil Service', in J.S.T. Quah, Chan H.C. and Seah C.M. (eds), *Government and Politics of Singapore* (Singapore: Oxford University Press), 92–119.

Senkuttuvan, A. (1972) 'British Withdrawal: Meeting an Economic Challenge', *Far Eastern Economic Review*, 5 August, Singapore Focus, 4–5.

Sewell, W.H. Jr (1996) 'Three Temporalities: Towards an Eventful Sociology', in T.J. McDonald (ed.), *The Historic Turn in the Human Sciences* (Ann Arbor: University of Michigan Press).

Shin, W. (1994) 'Geopolitical Determinants of Political Economy: The Cold War and South Korean Political Economy', *Asian Perspective* 18 (2) Fall/Winter, 119–40.

Shinohara, M. (1976) 'MITI's Industrial Policy and Japanese Industrial Organization – A Retrospective Evaluation', *Developing Economies* 14 (4), December, 366–80.

Short, A. (1975) *The Communist Insurrection in Malaya 1948–1960* (London: Frederick Muller).

Skocpol, T. (1979) *States & Social Revolutions* (Cambridge: Cambridge University Press).

Skocpol, T. (1985) 'Bringing the State Back In: Strategies of Analysis in Current Research', in P.B. Evans, D. Rueschemeyer and T. Skocpol (eds), *Bringing the State Back in* (Cambridge: Cambridge University Press), 3–37.

Slimming, J. (1969) *Death of a Democracy* (London: John Murray).

Smith, H. (1998) 'Korea', in R.H. McLeod and R. Garnaut (eds), *East Asia in Crisis from Being a Miracle to Needing One?* (London: Routledge), 66–84.

Snow, P. (2003) *The Fall of Hong Kong: Britain, China and the Japanese Occupation* (New Haven, CT: Yale University Press).

So, A.Y. and S.W.K. Chiu (1995) *East Asia in the World Economy* (Thousand Oaks: Sage).

Soesastro, H. (2000) 'The Indonesian Economy Under Abdurrahman Wahid', in Daljit Singh (ed.), *Southeast Asian Affairs 2000* (Singapore: Institute of Southeast Asian Studies), 134–44.

Soh, C.S. (1996) 'Korean "Comfort Women": Movement for Redress', *Asian Survey* 36 (12), 1227–40.

Solingen, E. (2004) 'Southeast Asia in a New Era: Domestic Coalitions from Crisis to Recovery', *Asian Survey* 44 (March/April), 189–212.

Song, B.-N. (1990) *The Rise of the Korean Economy* (Oxford: Oxford University Press).

Stein, A.A. and B.M. Russett (1980) 'Evaluating War: Outcomes and Consequences', in T. Gurr (ed.), *The Handbook of Political Conflict* (New York: Free Press): 399–422.

Steinmo, S., K. Thelen and F. Longstreth (eds) (1992) *Structuring Politics: Historical Institutionalism in Comparative Analysis* (New York: Cambridge University Press).

Stevens, R.W. (1976) *Vain Hopes, Grim Realities: The Economic Consequences of the Vietnam War* (New York: New Viewpoints).

Stiglitz, J.E. (2001) 'From Miracle to Crisis to Recovery: Lessons from Four Decades of East Asian Experience', in J.E. Stiglitz and Shahid Yusuf (eds), *Rethinking the East Asian Miracle* (Oxford: Oxford University Press), 509–26.

Stiglitz, J. (2002) *Globalization and Its Discontents* (London: Allen Lane).

Stockwin, H. (1975) 'Asia and the Backlash of Vietnam', *Far Eastern Economic Review* (25 April), 53–6.

Strange, S. (1998) *Mad Money: When Markets Outgrow Governments* (Ann Arbor: University of Michigan).

Stubbs, R. (1974) *Counter-Insurgency and the Economic Factor: The Impact of the Korean War Prices Boom on the Malayan Emergency*, Occasional Paper No. 19 (Singapore: Institute of Southeast Asian Studies).

Stubbs, R. (1989a) 'Geopolitics and the Political Economy of Southeast Asia', *International Journal* 44 (3), Summer, 517–40.

Stubbs, R. (1989b) *Hearts and Minds in Guerrilla Warfare: The Malayan Emergency 1948–1960* (Singapore: Oxford University Press), republished (Singapore: Eastern Universities Press, 2004).

Stubbs, R. (1992) 'US–Japanese Trade Relations: The ASEAN Dimension', *The Pacific Review* 5 (1), 60–7.

Stubbs, R. (1997) 'The Malayan Emergency and the Development of the Malaysian State', in P.B. Rich and R. Stubbs (eds), *The Counter-Insurgent State: Guerrilla Warfare and Sate Building in the Twentieth Century* (Basingstoke: Macmillan), 50–71.

Stubbs, R. (1998) 'Asia-Pacific Regionalism Versus Globalization: Competing Forms of Capitalism', in W.D. Coleman and G.R.D. Underhill (eds), *Regionalism and Global Economic Integration: Europe, Asia and the Americas* (London: Routledge), 68–80.

Stubbs, R. (2000) 'Signing on to Liberalization: AFTA and the Politics of Regional Economic Cooperation', *The Pacific Review* 13 (2), 297–318.

Stubbs, R. (2001) 'Performance Legitimacy and "Soft Authoritarianism"', in A. Acharya, B.M. Frolic and R. Stubbs, *Democracy, Human Rights, and*

Civil Society in South East Asia (Toronto: Joint Centre for Asia Pacific Studies), 37–54.

Stubbs, R. (2002) 'ASEAN Plus Three: Emerging East Asian Regionalism?', *Asian Survey* 42 (May/June), 440–55.

Suehiro, A. (1985) *Capital Accumulation and Industrial Development in Thailand* (Bangkok: Social Research Institute, Chulalongkorn University).

Surachat, B. (1988) *United States Foreign Policy and Thai Military Rule 1947–1977* (Bangkok: Editions Duang Kamol).

Tai, H.C. (1989) 'The Oriental Alternative: A Hypothesis on East Asian Culture and Economy', *Issues and Studies* 25 (3), March, 10–36.

Taiwan Government (various dates) *Taiwan Statistical Data Book* (Taipei).

Tan, G. (1992) *The Newly Industrializing Countries of Asia* (Singapore: Times Academic Press).

Tang, T.H.J (1999) 'Hong Kong', in I. Marsh, J. Blondel and T. Inoguchi, (eds), *Democracy, Governance, and Economic Performance: East and Southeast Asia* (Tokyo: United Nations University Press), 305–30.

Tay, S. (2001) 'ASEAN Plus Three: Challenges and Cautions About a New Regionalism', paper presented at the 15th Asia-Pacific Roundtable, Kuala Lumpur, June.

Taylor, M. and M. Ward (1994) 'Industrial Transformation since 1970: The Context and the Means', in H. Brookfield (ed.), *Transformation and Industrialization in Peninsular Malaysia* (Kuala Lumpur: Oxford University Press), 95–121.

Thelen, K. (1999) 'Historical Institutionalism in Comparative Politics', *Annual Review of Political Science* 2: 369–404.

Thelen, K. and S. Steinmo (1992) 'Historical Institutionalism in Comparative Politics', in S. Steinmo, K. Thelen and F. Longstreth (eds), *Structuring Politics: Historical Institutionalism in Comparative Analysis* (New York: Cambridge University Press).

Thitinan, P. (2003) 'Thailand: Democratic Authoritarianism', D. Singh and K.W. Chin (eds), *Southeast Asian Affairs 2003* (Singapore: Institute of Southeast Asia Studies), 277–90.

Thompson, W.S. (1975) *Unequal Partners: Philippine and Thai Relations with the United States 1965–75* (Lexington, MA: Lexington Books).

Thurbon, E. (2003) 'Ideational Inconsistency and Institutional Incapacity: Why Financial Liberalisation in South Korea Went Horribly Wrong', *New Political Economy* 8 (2), 341–62.

Thurow, L. (1992) *Head to Head: The Coming Economic Battle Among Japan, Europe and America* (New York: William Morrow and Co.).

Tiglao, R. (1994) 'Paralysed by Politics', *Far Eastern Economic Review* (12 May), 45–6.

Tilly, C. (ed.) (1975) *The Formation of National States in Western Europe* (Princeton, NJ: Princeton University Press).

Tilly, C. (1985) 'War Making and State Making as Organized Crime', in P. Evans, D. Rueschemeyer and T. Skocpol (eds), *Bringing the State Back In* (Cambridge: Cambridge University Press), 169–91.

Tilly, C. (1992) *Coercion, Capital, and European States, AD 990–1992* (Cambridge, MA: Blackwell).

Truong, T.-D. (1990) *Sex, Money and Morality: Prostitution and Tourism in Southeast Asia* (London: Zed Books).

Tsuru, S. (1993) *Japan's Capitalism: Creative Defeat and Beyond* (Cambridge: Cambridge University Press).

Tu, W.-M. (ed.) (1996) *Confucian Traditions in East Asian Modernity: Moral Education and Economic Culture in Japan and the Four Mini-Dragons* (Cambridge, MA: Harvard University Press).

Turnbull, C.M. (1989) *A History of Malaysia, Singapore and Brunei* (Sydney: Allen & Unwin). Oreign Relations, United inety-first Congress, First Session, Part 3, November.

UN (1970) *Foreign Trade Statistics of Asia and the Pacific* (New York: United Nations).

Underhill, G.R.D. (1998) *Industrial Crisis and the Open Economy* (London: Macmillan).

US Senate (1969) *United States Security Agreements and Commitments Abroad*, Hearings Before the Subcommittee on United States Security Agreements and Commitments Abroad of the Committee on Foreign Relations, United States Senate, Ninety-first Congress, First Session, Part 3, November.

US Senate (1969/70) *United States Security Agreements and Commitments Abroad: Republic of China*, Hearings Before the Subcommittee on United States Security Agreements and Commitments Abroad of the Committee on Foreign Relations, United States Senate, Ninety-first Congress, Second Session, Part 4, November, May).

US Senate (1971) *Impact of the Vietnam War*, Prepared for the Committee on Foreign Relations by the Foreign Affairs Division, Congressional Research Services, Library of Congress, Ninety-second Congress, First Session (Washington: US Government Printing Office, 30 June).

Vernon, R. (1971) *Sovereignty at Bay* (New York: Basic Books).

Viksnins, G.J. (1973) 'United States Military Spending and the Economy of Thailand, 1967–1972', *Asian Survey* 13: 441–57.

Vogel, E.F. (1991) *The Four Little Dragons: The Spread of Industrialization in East Asia* (Cambridge, MA: Harvard University Press).

Wade, R. (1990) *Governing the Market: Economic Theory and the Role of Government in East Asian Industrialization* (Princeton, NJ: Princeton University Press); reprinted with a new 'Introduction' 2004.

Wade, R. (1992) 'East Asia's Economic Success', *World Politics* 44 (January), 270–320.

Wade, R. (2004) 'The Reprinting of *Governing the Market*: A Dinner Table Conversation', *Issues and Studies* (No. 1, March), 103–34.

Wallerstein, I. (1995) *After Liberalism* (New York: The New Press).

Wallerstein, I. (1997) 'The Rise of East Asia, or The World-System in the Twenty-First Century', Keynote address at the Symposium on 'Perspective of the Capitalist World-System in the Beginning of the Twenty-First Century', Institute of International Studies, Meiji Gakuin University, 23–24 January 1997, http://fbc.binghamton.edu/iwrise.htm.(23/3/05).

Weber, M. (1968) *The Religion of China: Confucianism and Taoism*, trans. and ed. H.H. Gerth (New York: Free Press).

Webber, M. (1995) 'Changing Places in East Asia', in G.L. Clark and W.B. Kim (eds), *Asian NIEs and the Global Economy: Industrial Restructuring and Corporate Strategy in the 1990s* (Baltimore: Johns Hopkins University Press), 22–51.

Weintraub, P. (1978) 'The South: Despite Withdrawal, the US Commitment is Solid', *Far Eastern Economic Review*, 26 May, 37–40.

Weiss, L. (1998) *The Myth of the Powerless State: Governing the Economy in a Global Era* (Cambridge: Polity Press).

Weiss, L. (2000) 'Developmental States in Transition: Adapting, Dismantling, Innovating, Not 'Normalizing', *The Pacific Review* 13 (1), 21–56.

Weiss, L. (2003) 'Guiding Globalization in East Asia: New Roles for Old Developmental States', in L. Weiss (ed.), *States in the Global Economy: Bringing Domestic Institutions Back In* (Cambridge: Cambridge University Press), 245–70.

Whang, I.-J. (1987) 'The Role of Government in Economic Development: The Korean Experience,' *Asian Development Review* 5 (2), 70–87.

Wheeler, H.G. (1975) 'Effects of War on Industrial Growth', *Society* 12: 48–52.

Wheeler, H.G. (1980) 'Postwar Industrial Growth', in J.D. Singer (ed.), *The Correlates of War, II: Testing Some Realpolitik Models* (New York: Free Press), 258–84.

White, G. (1988) 'State and Market in China's Socialist Industrialisation', in G. White (ed.), *Developmental States in East Asia* (Basingstoke: Macmillan), 153–92.

White, G. (1993) *Riding the Tiger: The Politics of Economic Reform in Post-Mao China* (Stanford: Stanford University Press).

Wolferen, K.V. (1989) *The Enigma of Japanese Power: People and Politics in a Stateless Nation* (London: Macmillan).

Wong, J. (2003) 'Deepening Democracy in Taiwan', *Pacific Affairs* 76 (Summer), 235–56.

Wong, S.-L. (1988) *Emigrant Entrepreneurs: Shanghai Industrialists in Hong Kong* (Hong Kong: Oxford University Press).

Woo, C. (2001) 'Industrial Upgrading in Korea: Process, Prospects and Policies', in S. Masuyama, D. Vandenbrink and S.Y. Chia (eds), *Industrial Restructuring in East Asia: Towards the 21st Century* (Tokyo: Namura Research Institute), 256–306.

Woo, J.-E. (1991) *Race to the Swift: State and Finance in Korean Industrialization* (New York: Columbia University Press).

Woo, W.T. (2000) 'The Asian Financial Crisis: Hindsight, Insight, Foresight', *ASEAN Economic Bulletin* 17 (August), 113–19.

Woo-Cumings, M.J.-E. (1998) 'National Security and the Rise of the Developmental State in South Korea and Taiwan', in H.S. Rowen (ed.), *Behind East Asian Growth: The Political and Social Foundations of Prosperity* (London: Routledge, 1998), 319–37.

Woo-Cumings, M. (ed.) (1999) *The Developmental State* (Ithaca: Cornell University Press).

World Bank (1993) *The East Asian Miracle: Economic Growth and Public Policy*, Policy Research Report (Washington: The World Bank).

World Bank (various years) *World Development Report* (Washington, World Bank).

Yager, J.A. (1988) *Transforming Agriculture in Taiwan: The Experience of the Joint Commission on Rural Reconstruction* (Ithaca: Cornell University Press).

Yoshihara, K. (1978) *Japanese Investment in Southeast Asia* (Honolulu: The University Press of Hawaii).

Yoshihara K. (1994) *Japanese Economic Development*, 3rd edn (Kuala Lumpur: Oxford University Press).

Young, A. (1994) 'Lessons from the East Asian NICs: A Contrarian View', *European Economic Review* 38 (3–4), 964–73.

Youngson, A.J. (1982) *Hong Kong: Economic Growth and Policy* (Hong Kong: Oxford University Press).

Zakaria, F. (1994) 'Culture Is Destiny: A Conversation with Lee Kuan Yew', *Foreign Affairs* 73 (March/April), 109–27.

Zakaria, H.A. (1977) 'The Police and Political Development in Malaysia: Change, Continuity and Institution Building of a "Coercive" Apparatus in a Developing Ethnically Divided Society', PhD dissertation, Massachusetts Institute of Technology.

Zhang, X. (2002) 'Domestic Institutions, Liberalization Patterns, and Uneven Crises in Korea and Taiwan', *The Pacific Review* 15 (3), 409–42.

Zhu, T. (2002) 'Developmental States and Threat Perception in Northeast Asia', *Conflict, Security and Development* 2 (1), 5–29.

Zhu, T. (2003) 'Building Insitutional Capacity for China's New Economic Opening', in L. Weiss (ed.), *States in the Global Economy: Bringing Domestic Institutions Back In* (Cambridge: Cambridge University Press), 142–60.

Zysman, J. (1996) 'The Myth of the "Global Economy": Enduring National Foundations and Emerging Regional Realities', *New Political Economy* 1 (July), 157–84.

Index